CROMWELL'S GENERALS

By the same author

FINANCIAL AND COMMERCIAL POLICY UNDER THE CROMWELLIAN PROTECTORATE

OLIVER CROMWELL: THE CONSERVATIVE DICTATOR

MARLBOROUGH

LOUIS XIV AND THE GREATNESS OF FRANCE

JOHN WILDMAN

MR. PRESIDENT

CROMWELL'S GENERALS

by

MAURICE ASHLEY

NEW YORK
ST MARTIN'S PRESS INC
1955

Library of Congress Catalog Card Number 55-9052

PRINTED IN GREAT BRITAIN

CONTENTS

ILLUSTRATIONS

FOREWORD

This book is a study in the characters of Oliver Cromwell's Generals and their relations with each other and with the Lord Protector. Although separate biographies have been written of some of the Generals, I believe they are here brought together for the first time in one volume. The book does not pretend to cover the political or military history of the Protectorate, but I venture to offer a fresh account of the battles of Dunbar and Worcester, based on a re-examination of the sources and of the ground.

I have given short bibliographies at the end of each chapter, but I should like to acknowledge my debt to two books: Sir Charles Firth and Godfrey Davies, *The Regimental History of Cromwell's Army* (1940) and W. C. Abbott, *Writings and Speeches of Oliver Cromwell* (1947). These two works of reference have eased the task of the historian of the seventeenth century since Gardiner and Firth published their pioneer histories of the Interregnum at the beginning of the present century. I am indebted to Brigadier C. J. Molony for reading my first three chapters, to the Reverend J. R. Powell for reading chapter VII, to Mr. E. S. de Beer and Mr. Ian Watts for reading the whole before publication, and to Mr. H. H. Mitchell for conducting me round Worcester.

Spelling in quotations has usually been modernized. I have also taken the more popular version of proper names, for example Monk instead of Monck, Montagu instead of Mountague, Desborough instead of Disbrowe, though I am aware that pedantry demands the latter variants. My readers should also notice the confusing fact that the rank of Major-General was sometimes superior to that of Lieutenant-General: for example, Lieutenant-General Monk was junior to Major-General Deane and Lieutenant-General Ludlow served under Major-General Ireton. A note on the appointment, powers and pay of Cromwell's Generals appears at the end of the book.

Although I hope that the book will hold some interest for the specialist historian, it is intended for the general reader; for the courage and faith, the ambitions and jealousies, the crises and tragedies in the lives of these soldiers 300 years ago form a part of the story of men of character in all places and at all times.

I dedicate *Cromwell's Generals* to the Right Honourable Isaac Foot, P.C., and my other friends in the Cromwell Association.

MAURICE ASHLEY

London, October 1953

CROMWELL'S GENERALS

CHAPTER I

THE DELEGATION TO LORD FAIRFAX: MIDSUMMER, 1650

WHEN the summer of 1650 came the Free Commonwealth of England was in peril. Surrounded by enemies, it appeared to have been born only at once to die. Prince Rupert of the Palatinate, defeated on land, was at sea, menacing the trade routes; Royalist agents were scouring the Continent for succour; Ireland was not yet subdued; and for a fourth time in less than a dozen years the villagers of Yorkshire and Lancashire expected to hear the thud of hordes of Scots moving down from the Lowlands, soldiers of the Kirk on duty bound.

In 1639 a Scottish army had helped to shake King Charles I on his throne and in 1644 to tumble him from it; four years later another Scottish force, though unblessed by the Calvinist ministers, had marched south intending to restore the King to Whitehall Palace, only to be pierced, crushed and driven out in a campaign superbly directed by Lieutenant-General Oliver Cromwell. In each case the Scots had struck to safeguard the Presbyterian religion in their own land and to impose it on that of their neighbours. Now they were preparing to try again in the name of the nineteen-year-old king, Charles II, whom they had recognized as heir to the throne of his martyred father. By the Treaty of Heligoland, signed on June 11th, as he sailed from Holland to Scotland, Charles II had undertaken to fasten Presbyterianism on both his kingdoms, if the Scots should win them back for him from the rebels south of the border.

But long before that the English Council of State, the forty-four statesmen who governed in London in place of the monarchy, were aware of what was brewing. As early as January 2nd, alarmed by reports of confabulations between King Charles II and Scottish Commissioners at The Hague, the House of Commons, which now called itself the Parliament of

England, had passed an Act requiring every man in the country to take an oath to be faithful to the Commonwealth, without King or House of Lords, on penalty of outlawry; and six days afterwards it had summoned Oliver Cromwell home from Ireland, though he had not yet subjected that country by fire and sword to her new masters. The scare then sweeping Westminster had passed away— and Cromwell in fact did not leave Ireland until late in May— but on April 9th Parliament had ordered the Council of State to exercise every precaution against invasion from abroad or risings at home. It was clear that the first English republic must now do battle or succumb to its enemies. But who was to command the soldiers of the Commonwealth?

The Commander-in-Chief of the Parliamentary forces, who had held his post almost without challenge or criticism ever since the New Model Army had been raised in 1644, was Thomas, Lord Fairfax, scion of an old Scottish family, which, like many other country gentlemen, including the Cromwells, had waxed in landed wealth after the Reformation and were now realizing their claims to be the 'natural rulers' of their country. Though he had a dark and melancholy look about him, General Fairfax was, by universal witness, a 'sweet-tempered' man, taking after his father, Ferdinando, a meek Yorkshireman— if such there be— rather than after his grandfather, an irascible squire who survived to the age of eighty and considered soldiering the only career fit for a youngster. Well liked and trusted on all sides, Thomas Fairfax did not put a foot wrong in carrying out his duties as a commander. On the other hand, he was not much of a politician, or, to be more precise, his politics were inoffensive. Indeed he had been chosen general because he was deemed to be the most capable officer available who was not a member of either House at a time when Parliament had introduced a self-denying ordinance on all its members forbidding them to hold commissions.

While he was in his early twenties, Thomas Fairfax, serving under his father, had won distinction in the campaign to sustain the Parliamentary cause in his native county, after having enjoyed a little military apprenticeship as a volunteer in the Low Countries and a little more as a captain of a troop of dragoons (or mounted infantry) known as the Yorkshire Redcaps when King Charles I had ridden towards Berwick in an attempt to thrust a prayer book on to the pews of his Scottish subjects. Fairfax had fought side by side with Cromwell at the hamlet of Winceby in Lincolnshire where these two colonels of horse had learned to respect each other's prowess. At the battle of Marston Moor they had again fought together but on opposite wings. In that contest Fairfax gave an example of the irreproachable personal courage that lit his service in the army. Though unhorsed and wounded by a cut of the sabre, which left a scar he had to carry on his face all his life, though his men were beaten and his higher commanders deserted the field, he did not himself for a moment contemplate flight. On the contrary, he tore from his hat the white handkerchief which distinguished the Parliamentary troops from the Cavaliers, and rode right through the enemy to the other wing. There he joined Cromwell who, with the Scot, David Leslie, had broken Prince Rupert's charge and with them brought back the help that was to transform defeat into victory.

At the battle of Naseby, where Fairfax himself was in command, he led the advance of his cavalry on the right wing, returned, having lost his helmet, to rally the infantry in the centre, and, after he and his lifeguard had routed the enemy's foot, linked with Cromwell's Ironsides in reducing the last Royalist core of resistance furnished by Sir George Lisle's gallant Bluecoats, slaying an ensign with his own hand and seizing his colours. At the battle of Langport in July 1645, which he had brought on by an advance so swift as to surprise his enemy, Fairfax extinguished Royalist hopes in the south-west, and in the autumn he had negotiated with Prince Rupert the surrender of Bristol after he had prepared to take the city by storm. Next year by occupying Oxford he closed the first civil war. In the second civil war, though suffering from gout, he rode with his foot wrapped in bandages to attack Maidstone and to besiege Colchester. While Cromwell was winning the battle of Preston, Fairfax broke the Royalist insurrection in the south-east.

Fairfax belonged to the class of cultured soldier, in line with the Wolfes and Wavells of our history. During the siege of

York he took pains to preserve the Minster, the bells and porch of St. Nicholas, and other monuments and muniments. When the Royalist garrison of Oxford marched out in June 1646, he at once posted guards to protect the Bodleian Library from harm. Like the Marquis of Montrose he wrote indifferent poetry in his leisure hours and after he retired from active service he translated the Psalms and pottered with literature and roses. In all this he was not unique. Indeed many of the officers in the English civil wars dabbled in flowers and verse; and it is one of the blessings that Cromwell conferred on posterity that he left no poetry behind him for his biographers dutifully to print in their appendices. But Fairfax was no dilettante. A soldier of capacity, he proved himself an administrator and negotiator of the first water on many occasions. Contemporaries who said, and historians who have repeated, that he was a cipher while Cromwell was the figure in the New Model Army, ignored his record. His soldiers loved him and called him 'Black Tom' and his fellow countrymen — on both sides — regarded him as a man of honour who tempered discipline with clemency. His son-in-law was to write of him:

> Both sexes' virtues were in him combined,
> He had the fierceness of the manliest mind,
> But all the meekness too of womankind.
>
> He never knew what envy was nor hate,
> His soul was filled with worth and honesty
> And with another thing quite out of date,
> Called modesty. . . .

That was why everyone in 1650 wanted to retain his services, if they could.

The difficulty was that Fairfax was no republican. Whatever after-generations may have believed, the men who waged the first civil war did not think they were fighting against the King, but only against the counsellors who had advised him to transgress the law. Above the sovereign, their chief officer, they perceived not the divine power but the majesty of the ancient laws which the King by his coronation oath had sworn to defend. Below him sat his accredited law makers in the Lords and Commons. Thus a monarch who ignored his oath

THOMAS, THIRD LORD FAIRFAX OF CAMERON

and failed to follow the advice of his Parliament was being wickedly led astray. And men like Fairfax did not fight *against* their King, but *for* the King — *and* Parliament.

In Yorkshire while the inhabitants of the clothing towns in the West Riding, in Leeds, Wakefield and Bradford, where puritanism prevailed, were strong for Parliament and vigorously repulsed raids by Royalists from the East and North Ridings, the gentry were divided often according to temperament and habit of mind rather than by deep attachment to constitutional principles. During the sixteen-twenties there had been two political sections in the county, one led by Sir John Savile of Howley, the other by Sir Thomas Wentworth of Wentworth Woodhouse, the Saviles standing for the King, Wentworth (at that time) for the King's critics in Parliament. Fairfax's grandfather had been the friend and colleague of Wentworth. But several of Fairfax's intimates had belonged to the other side. His old friend Sir Henry Slingsby, for example, was one of the most faithful of the Yorkshire Royalists. Like Fairfax, Slingsby was beyond fear and at the battle of Marston Moor when his regiment was ordered to garrison York, he himself disdained to stay behind, but hurried to the front to risk his life for his King. Fairfax's cousin, John Bellasis, was Royalist Governor of York. Many of Fairfax's other friends, relations and neighbours took the field against him and, on the whole, the atmosphere around his home at Nunappleton, a few miles south of York, smelt Cavalier. A factor in turning the Fairfaxes the other way had been that Ferdinando Fairfax had taken part in the Long Parliament and had been among those Lords who had presented the Grand Remonstrance to the King in 1641. Some of the Yorkshire landlords had been annoyed by the expenses to which they had been put in serving in the King's army against the Scots and in billeting his men. When Sir Thomas Fairfax had submitted a petition to the King on Heyworth Moor in May 1642, protesting over the treatment of Parliament, he had been nearly trodden under foot by Charles I's horse — an incident calculated to provoke the most sweet-tempered of knights.

Nevertheless so closely bound up were all these Yorkshire gentry with one another — the Fairfaxes, Bellasises, Mauleverers,

Slingsbys, Saviles and the like — that the Yorkshire Parliamentarians and Royalists actually concluded a treaty of neutrality with each other in September 1642, in the hope that they could keep the civil war out of their county. However, the agreement was repudiated by Parliament and the first Parliamentary Commander-in-Chief, the Earl of Essex, made Ferdinando Fairfax responsible for all the forces raised in the northern counties. But when later the Queen, who had been to the Netherlands to seek help for her husband, landed at Bridlington, Lord Fairfax thought it in no way incongruous to offer her his personal escort, for he did not conceive himself to be in the least the enemy of the Royal Family; his duty was only to compel the courtiers to recognize the error of their ways. Nor did the King express any dislike of the younger Fairfax. When in February 1647 Thomas Fairfax rode with him into Nottingham, they had an agreeable conversation, Fairfax kissed his hand, and Charles I dubbed him 'a man of honour'. Thus up to this point everything had been smooth and gentlemanly like a good game of cricket. The best side had won and now they would all sit down to supper together on the understanding that there should be no return match.

But the second civil war in 1648 exacerbated feelings in the Parliamentary army against the Royalists. They had ceased to play the game. After the surrender of Colchester even Fairfax departed from his usual path of mercy and ordered two of the defenders, Sir Charles Lucas and Sir George Lisle (whose regiment had fought so bravely at Naseby) to be shot so as to satisfy military justice and avenge innocent blood. But Fairfax, unlike Cromwell, could not see that if it was just to punish with death any of the King's servants for reviving the war, it was also right to kill the King. That Fairfax believed that Charles I should be punished by deposition or banishment is clear, since he voluntarily took his place among the commissioners who gathered in January 1649 to sit in judgment on Charles I. Yet when he realized that the monarch was on trial for his life, he withdrew from any further part in the proceedings.

Fairfax had married a daughter of Lord Vere of Tilbury under whom he served as a volunteer in the Low Countries.

Anne Vere was a woman of character, who, brought up among the Dutch, had imbibed the Calvinist faith, and it was commonly said that she influenced her husband towards Presbyterianism and against the Republic set up by the Independents. But it was not as simple as that. Indeed there is contemporary evidence that Fairfax himself preferred Independency. But he had not foreseen when he grasped his sword that he was binding himself to the wheel of revolution. He hoped that the King would appreciate that he was beaten and concede the demands of Parliament. Moreover he found that the New Model Army, which he had helped to forge out of the Independent soldiery, was itself becoming a political party provoked to indignation against the Long Parliament not only by the way in which the majority in it favoured an all-embracing Presbyterianism against their own separate gathered congregations but also by the failure of the Commons to meet its pay and arrears. In his *Short Memorial*, which he wrote to justify himself after the monarchy had been restored, Fairfax went so far as to claim that after June 1647 he never consented to anything the army did, an extraordinary assertion for a Commander-in-Chief. No doubt he tried to separate political questions from military affairs. It was impossible. He was in fact carried forward by the torrent that engulfed the old constitution. Perhaps by keeping his command he aspired to reconcile the army with Parliament and to save the King. At any rate as the landmarks toppled over he still stayed at his post, affable but surprised. If it is true that during the King's trial his wife cried out from the public galleries 'Oliver Cromwell is a traitor!' her words can hardly have represented the inner thoughts of her husband, otherwise the two men could scarcely have continued to sit in intimate counsel together or ridden post-haste from London to Oxford to suppress the mutiny in the army that occurred after the King's execution.

Fairfax never hid his mind. He always thought that his first duty was to maintain order. He saw himself as the servant of King-and-Parliament and when Charles I was executed, he accepted, if he did not welcome, the Commonwealth as an instrument of discipline and peace. He became a member of the Council of State and chairman of its military affairs committee. But he refused to take any oath that would imply his consent to the King's death or even his approval of the new form of government without a King or House of Lords. He swore that he would be 'faithful in performance of the trust committed to him'; but as for the past — well, it was all very unfortunate; he had obeyed superior orders. If his uncle, Sir William Constable, had elected to sign the King's death warrant, that was his own concern; if his second in command had considered it right to execute exemplary justice on the makers of the second civil war and then to lead an army to Ireland to prevent Charles II from establishing a base there, Fairfax acquiesced. As for himself, he remained in London, nursing his scars and his gout, and longed to go home to Yorkshire, to grow roses, and make friends again with all his neighbours.

Thus it was proof of the esteem in which Thomas Fairfax was held by his colleagues in the Council of State during those midsummer days of 1650 that they were ready to yield every concession to keep so reluctant a republican, so open a monarchist at the head of their army. As lately as February the Council had condoned his refusal to take a new oath to be faithful to the Commonwealth and so well known was the lukewarm quality of his loyalty that King Charles II had contemplated conferring on him the Earldom of Essex as a bribe for changing sides, the very same Earldom that King Charles I had dangled before Oliver Cromwell on the eve of the second Civil War. But on one question the majority of the Council of State were resolute: they were determined that this time the soldiers of the Commonwealth should be dispatched into Scotland to anticipate another invasion of the north of England rather than that once again they should wait to be attacked and engage in a defensive war.

The command of the invasion force was offered to Fairfax on June 20th, 1650, and he took a couple of days to make up his mind, during which it was thought, naturally enough, that he consulted his wife. Since she was hotly Presbyterian, the weight of her influence was thrown — and judging by her behaviour at the King's trial, she was a lady of force — against an assault on the home ground of her religion. Fairfax maintained that there was no certainty that the Scots intended to invade England and that it would be a breach of the Solemn League and Covenant, concluded between the representatives of England and Scotland in 1643, for them to launch an attack on their neighbour and ally. Oliver Cromwell now came forward with a compromise: he suggested that, following the precedent established in the case of the Irish war, General Fairfax should retain the command of the English armies as a whole, while he himself as his Lieutenant-General with picked regiments should direct the campaign against the Scots — for, he professed, 'that he would rather choose to serve under him in his post than to command the greatest army in Europe'. But the Council of State was of the opinion that concessions enough had been given to Fairfax and rejected that plan; instead both private and public efforts were exerted to argue Fairfax into changing his mind. On June 24th, at Cromwell's instigation, a sub-committee of five, appointed by the Council of State, interviewed the General in a room in Whitehall. The sub-committee was composed of two judges, Bulstrode Whitelocke and Oliver St. John, and three officers, Lieutenant-General Cromwell, Major-General John Lambert, and Major-General Thomas Harrison.

Oliver Cromwell was a month over fifty-one when he left Ireland (where he had been Lord Lieutenant as well as Commander-in-Chief) in obedience to the orders of the Council of State, and on his return he at once entered exuberantly into the conferences about the expected Scottish war. To all appearances he was on the friendliest terms with Fairfax. When he arrived back in London on June 1st he had been ceremoniously greeted by the General with attendant dignitaries from Parliament and the City, in a grand show on Hounslow Heath. Two days afterwards Cromwell had called upon Fairfax at his house in Queen Street and according to the official Commonwealth newspaper, *Mercurius Politicus*, 'there passed many remarkable expressions of mutual love and courtesy, sufficient to check the false tongues and wishes of the enemies of the nation'. That tongues — false or true — were wagging was understandable. Why indeed had Cromwell been recalled from Ireland at all before his campaign there was finished if Fairfax was thought willing and able to dispose of the threat from Scotland? Andrew Marvell, the poet who at that time was in the service of the Council of State, wrote an ode on Cromwell's return from Ireland in which he said:

> How good he is, how just,
> And fit for highest trust;
> Nor yet grown stiffer with command,
> But still in the Republic's hand. . . .

Transparently he was a candidate to take over from the disgruntled Yorkshireman.

On the other hand, Fairfax was over twelve years younger than Cromwell, and at fifty-one might a man not be resigned to being the eternal Number Two, unless God were to show that He had intended it otherwise? Moreover Cromwell was afraid — in common with the rest of the Council — that Fairfax's resignation might be fatal to the Commonwealth both through its repercussions in the army where he was so popular and on public opinion which regarded him as a bulwark of the State. Soon Cromwell was labouring 'almost all night' to overcome the General's scruples. Everyone whose account of those June days has survived agrees that they were convinced at the time that Cromwell was sincere in his endeavours to persuade Fairfax that it was his duty to go to Scotland. That ambition was there we know. Yet if Cromwell was acting, it was the finest performance in his career.

John Lambert, the second officer in the delegation to Fairfax, was a fellow Yorkshireman and indeed a protégé of the General, having been first commissioned in his dragoon regiment. His progress as a soldier had been astonishing. He became a colonel of cavalry when he was twenty-four and was a general at the age of twenty-six. Since 1647 he had held the rank of Major-General and his part in the Preston campaign had been scintillating. While the King was being tried, he had been absorbed in repressing the last Royalist resistance in Yorkshire, and it is likely enough that he agreed with Fairfax in being opposed to the execution of Charles I. On Fairfax's proposal Lambert had been generously rewarded for his services and he was soon engaged in investing money in land sold by the Commonwealth Government to meet its debts. Life stretched out temptingly before him. It was to his interest to see his friend and patron keep his command, but even more to sustain the Republic in peace and prosperity.

If Lambert was (in his age) a worldling, Thomas Harrison, who was nearly thirty-four, was an extreme puritan. And if Lambert were a Fairfaxian, Harrison was a Cromwellian. As a lifeguardsman of Lord Essex, he had fought with Cromwell on the field of Edgehill. After the battle of Marston Moor, Cromwell had dispatched him, now a major, to London to carry the report of the victory to Parliament. Here, to the annoyance of the Scots, he 'trumpeted all over the City . . . that Cromwell alone with his unspeakable valorous regiments had done all the service'. He was promoted colonel in 1647, and Cromwell's younger son, Henry, had served under him as captain of a troop. Somewhere about this time, Harrison joined the Fifth Monarchy sect which believed, in accordance with the Book of Daniel, that after four secular monarchies had ruled the earth, the Lord Himself would shortly come to reign over it: meanwhile his Saints were to take charge. Unlike Fairfax or Lambert, Harrison had been prominent and energetic in the trial and condemnation of the King. When Cromwell's men were embarking for Ireland, Fairfax had put Harrison in command of South Wales where he had launched an evangelical campaign to wipe Royalism from the mountains and convert the heretics of the west with a battery of bibles and a commando of preachers to faith in the Fifth Monarchy. He had been recalled from Wales, as Cromwell from Ireland, in the summer. Between Harrison and Cromwell existed an occult sympathy, and one may reasonably suppose that in supporting the plea to Fairfax to keep his command, Harrison was accepting the leadership of Cromwell rather than the dictates of his own heart.

In the conference with Fairfax Harrison showed that he had no doubt about the wisdom of the decision taken by the Council of State to invade Scotland. Here is an extract from Whitelocke's report.

> *General Fairfax:* If we were assured of their coming with their army into England, I confess it were prudence for us to prevent them, and [if] we are ready to advance into

Scotland before they march into England; but what warrant have we to fall upon them unless we can be assured of their purpose to fall upon us?
Harrison: I think, under favour, there cannot be greater assurance or human probability of the intentions of any state than we have of theirs to invade our country, else what means their present levies of men and money, and their quartering soldiers upon our borders? It is not long since they did the like to us, and we can hardly imagine what other design they can have to employ their forces.
Fairfax: Human probabilities are not sufficient grounds to make war upon a neighbour nation. . . .

Later Harrison went further and added: 'It is indeed, my Lord, the most righteous and the most glorious cause that ever any of this nation appeared in . . .' In that sentiment Lambert concurred and pleaded with Fairfax 'not (especially at this time) to leave your old servants and officers', as he was 'very fearful of the mischiefs which might ensue'. No one was more vehement in the delegation's attempt to persuade Fairfax to alter his decision than Cromwell, but it was becoming obvious that he himself would be compelled to take Fairfax's place. Before the delegation left the Council chamber, Colonel Edmund Ludlow, a keenly republican officer from Wiltshire, who had been appointed by a special vote to the Council of State, went up to him to say that he hoped that the Lieutenant-General would not also obstruct the service of the nation by refusing to take the command either out of modesty or out of deference to General Fairfax. Though yet further efforts were arranged to dissuade Fairfax from his refusal, the General was determined to lay down all his offices rather than acquiesce in a policy of which he disapproved. Parliament then was left with no alternative: the Act that had created Fairfax Commander-in-Chief was repealed, and Cromwell was unanimously voted the post of General and made Commander-in-Chief of all the Parliament's forces. Thenceforward John Lambert, Thomas Harrison, Edmund Ludlow and the rest became Cromwell's Generals.

Fairfax was thirty-eight when he laid down his commission on June 26th, on the same day that Parliament declared war on Scotland. To quieten opinion in England it was announced that the cause of his retirement was ill health. No public mention was made — or indeed could be made — of his scruples about invading Scotland. 'You have his heart still in the camp,' observed a popular preacher. Charles Fleetwood, on the surface no pushing fellow but a sound officer from Northamptonshire who, like Harrison, had begun his military career in Essex's lifeguard, was promoted in Cromwell's place as Lieutenant-General in the expeditionary army. Cromwell's cousin, Edward Whalley, was put second in command of the horse, under Fleetwood, as Commissary-General. Major-General Lambert accompanied Cromwell bearing the responsibility for commanding the foot and for drawing up the order of battle — virtually his Chief of Staff. Major-General Harrison was left in military charge of England during the absence of Cromwell, Fleetwood and Lambert in Scotland. To Harrison's own regiment was added a force of militia raised and placed under the direction of republican commissioners who had superseded the lords-lieutenant of Charles I. Colonel Ludlow, who was thirty-three, was invited by Cromwell to take the post of Lieutenant-General of Horse in Ireland, to fill the place left vacant by General Michael Jones, a hero of the Irish war, who had perished of fever the previous December. Henry Ireton, a 'grave, serious and religious person', Cromwell's friend, mentor and son-in-law, had been left in Ireland as the Lord Lieutenant's Deputy. Cromwell begged Ludlow to cross the sea at once so that if any mishap should befall Ireton he would have a dependable officer capable of taking over. Before he put the proposal to Ludlow, who was a gruff and fierce-tempered man more noted for his political enthusiasm than for his abilities as a soldier, Cromwell discoursed to him for one hour on the 110th Psalm. Nevertheless Ludlow took much persuading: he had just married a wife and bought some land. But the Council of State would brook no denial. Major-General Phillip Skippon, an old professional soldier much trusted in the City, was left in command of London.

Ireton, Harrison, Whalley and Ludlow had signed the King's death warrant — were 'regicides'. Fleetwood, Lambert and Skippon were not. Fairfax went home to Nunappleton to nurse his wounds, forget or shelve politics, and dispense hospitality to his neighbours round York. Parliament voted him an annuity of £4000 for his services, which he was never paid. On June 28th, 1650, Cromwell, accompanied by Lieutenant-General Fleetwood and Major-General Lambert, with four regiments of cavalry and two of foot, set forth on the Great North Road.

So Cromwell had the men he trusted where he wanted them: Henry Ireton in Ireland, Thomas Harrison in England, Charles Fleetwood, John Lambert and Edward Whalley in Scotland. Now to battle.

BIBLIOGRAPHY TO CHAPTER I

There are two lives of General Fairfax: Clements R. Markham, *A Life of the Great Lord Fairfax* (1870) and M. A. Gibb, *The Lord General: A Life of Thomas Fairfax* (1938). The Fairfax correspondence was published in four volumes in 1848 and 1849, two edited by G. W. Johnson and two by R. Bell. Some unpublished papers are in the British Museum and the Bodleian. The report of the delegation to Fairfax in 1650 is in Bulstrode Whitelocke, *Memorials of the English Affairs* (Oxford edition of 1853), III, 207-11, and there is an account by Edmund Ludlow in his *Memoirs* (ed. Firth, 1894), I, 242-4. Fairfax's *A Short Memorial*, etc. (1699) has been reprinted several times. The political background in Yorkshire is described in vol. III of Yorkshire in the *Victoria County History*.

CHAPTER II

THE DUNBAR CAMPAIGN: JULY-SEPTEMBER 1650

It took Cromwell and his Generals three-and-a-half weeks from the time they left London to collect an army and lead it into Scotland. When they rode out of the English capital they had with them only about a quarter of the forces assigned to the invasion of the Lowlands by the Council of State. The bulk of the regiments had been ordered to concentrate in the north of England. The Generals rode by way of Ware, Cambridge, Northampton, Leicester, York and Durham to Newcastle-upon-Tyne, the flourishing industrial town and seaport which, under the governorship of Sir Arthur Hazlerigg, was to be their rear base in England.

At Ware Cromwell had expected to meet Major-General Harrison who in effect was now in charge of the southern counties, as Hazlerigg was of the northern. However, Harrison failed to appear at the rendezvous; instead he sent Cromwell a letter explaining that he had been detained by the Council of State and conveying this salutary advice:

> My Lord, let waiting upon Jehovah be the greatest and most considerable business you have every day; reckon it so, more than to eat, sleep, or counsel together. Run aside sometimes from your company, and get a word with the Lord. Why should you not have three or four precious souls always standing at your elbow, with whom you might now and then turn into a corner? I have found refreshment and mercy in such a way.

Harrison then reverted to organizing the militia.

In Cambridge Cromwell saw the Vice-Chancellor of the University at the Bear inn and listened to a petition asking that he and his colleagues might be absolved from subscribing to the oath to be faithful to the Commonwealth. At Northampton the Generals were greeted by enthusiastic crowds, but Cromwell said to Lambert: 'Do not trust to that, for these very persons would shout as much if you or I were going to be hanged.' In York they were dined and 'highly caressed'. At Durham Cromwell was met by Colonel Francis Hacker of Nottinghamshire, who led a regiment of horse, and by Colonel Thomas Pride, who commanded a foot regiment. They were both tough men who had signed the King's death warrant. Pride's musketeers had 'purged' the House of Commons in December 1648; Hacker had supervised the execution of Charles I. It was to Hacker that Cromwell was later to say: 'Truly I think he that prays and preaches best will fight best.'

In the second week of July the invasion force formed up in the neighbourhood of Newcastle. Lambert's regiment of horse, which had seen much of its service in the north since it had been raised in Derbyshire and Lincolnshire in the summer of 1645, probably joined there, as did also Colonel Robert Lilburne's regiment. These two cavalry regiments had been busy maintaining order near the Scottish frontier since the end of the English civil wars, coping in particular with the cattle thieves known as 'moss troopers'. Besides Pride's regiment of foot, two other foot regiments which reinforced the army in the north were those of Colonel John Mauleverer and Colonel Charles Fairfax, both men of substance in Yorkshire, the latter an uncle of Lord Fairfax, the retired Commander-in-Chief. Another foot regiment, Colonel Daniel's, had been raised in Cheshire especially for the new war and had been ordered to Doncaster to be equipped by Major-General Lambert.

One other Yorkshire foot regiment, that of Colonel John Bright, suddenly found itself without a commander. Bright had asked Cromwell for a fortnight's leave to attend to his private affairs, and when it was refused, had resigned his commission. But the reason for his resignation was really that he was one of those Yorkshire gentlemen (like Lord Fairfax) who, though they had fought for Parliament, disapproved of the execution of Charles I. Cromwell wanted to confer the vacancy on George Monk, a supernumerary colonel of forty-three, who had accompanied him from London and to whom he had promised a regiment.

Unlike Fleetwood, Lambert and Cromwell himself, Monk

was no amateur soldier thrown up by the civil wars. Born in North Devonshire in 1608, he had opened his military career when he served as a volunteer under his kinsman, Sir Richard Greenville, on the expedition against Cadiz in 1625. By 1631 he had been promoted captain-lieutenant in Colonel George Goring's regiment and served for seven years in the Low Countries where he acquired much knowledge of the art of war. Afterwards his career had ups and downs. For two years he fought first as lieutenant-colonel and then as colonel against the Irish, but he was deprived of his regiment in 1643 for refusing to take an oath to serve against the English Parliament. However, he was later induced by the charm of King Charles I to fight on the side of the Cavaliers, only to be made prisoner by Thomas Fairfax's men at the battle of Nantwich on January 26th, 1644. He was then sent to the Tower of London, but after his release at the end of the first civil war in 1646 the Council of State decided to benefit from his experience in Ireland by appointing him as a Major-General in Ulster. Here he succeeded as a soldier, but incurred odium in Parliament as a negotiator. However, Cromwell was impressed with his personality, knowledge and defence of his own conduct. No doubt when Cromwell was Lord Lieutenant in Ireland in 1649, he learned more about what Monk had accomplished there. At any rate as soon as he returned to England and became Commander-in-Chief of all the armies of the Commonwealth he sent for this unemployed professional officer and volunteered to take him with him to Scotland.

Unfortunately the regiment that Cromwell now had in mind for George Monk to command had fought in the battle of Nantwich and the General therefore thought it wise to sound the officers and men about the proposed appointment. At Alnwick in Northumberland 'several colonels came into the head of the regiment, and told the soldiers the General was much troubled such a regiment should want a colonel; who would they have? The soldiers told them they had a good colonel, but he had left them, and they knew not whom they might have. The colonels asked, if they would have Colonel Monk? "*Colonel Monk!*" said some of them, "what! to betray us? we took him, not long since, at Nantwich, prisoner: we'll have none of him." ' Now it happened that Major-General Lambert, then in command of a regiment of dragoons, had distinguished himself at Nantwich and was popular in the army and throughout Yorkshire. So instead of Monk they were offered Lambert as their colonel, at which 'they all threw up their hats, and shouted: "*a Lambert! a Lambert!*" ' 'From that moment,' commented one of Monk's biographers, 'the two most celebrated of Cromwell's lieutenants were doomed to incessant rivalry.'

Not to be outdone, Cromwell formed for Monk a foot regiment out of five companies of the garrison at Newcastle and five of the garrison of Berwick. This foot regiment exists today under the name of the Coldstream Guards, and since the companies from Newcastle had originally formed part of a regiment which had been in the New Model Army, the Coldstream Guards are a historical link between the modern British army and the New Model. Monk was also put in charge of the ordnance and later his foot regiment was brigaded with other foot regiments so that by the time the army entered Scotland he had become, like Lambert, in fact, if not yet in rank, one of Cromwell's Generals.

The English army that crossed the frontier north of Berwick on July 22nd, 1650, consisted therefore of eight cavalry regiments, that is, the four New Model regiments of Cromwell, Fleetwood, Whalley and Twistleton, which probably came up from the south, Lambert's, Robert Lilburne's and Hacker's, which joined the concentration in the north, and Okey's dragoons. The cavalry were the cream of the expedition, men 'of good parts and learning', including among the troopers 'many physicians and students in other liberal arts that thought it a preferment'. The infantry consisted of eight foot regiments which, except for Cromwell's own and perhaps Colonel Coxe's, joined in the north. Thus the army contained a great many northerners who had reason to feel resentful against the Scots. Including the train or 'tail', which was infinitely smaller than that of a modern army, the estimated strength of Cromwell's army when it entered Scotland was 16,000 men. The navy carried the bulk of the provisions and some of the artillery ready to be landed on the east coast of Scotland. Otherwise transport and commissariat would have been inadequate. Political warfare was not neglected. The General and his Council of Officers had printed two declarations, one long and one short, justifying their advance beyond the Tweed, for distribution among the Scots. The English, they explained, were fighting against kingship and for liberty of conscience. Presbyterianism would be tolerated, but not universally imposed. Because the Scots had taken their 'grand enemy' — Charles II — 'into their bosoms' the English republicans had been compelled to defend themselves. And the Scottish attack on England in 1648 excused them for adopting the same aggressive method, as old as the hills, as new as twentieth-century dictators, of defence by invasion.

The number of men at Cromwell's disposal was fewer than he had intended. For it had been thought necessary to leave behind nearly as many soldiers as marched into Scotland to protect England against Royalist risings or incursions from the Continent. The target set by Parliament had been an expeditionary army of 25,000, and one may assume that what Cromwell had wanted to discuss with Harrison and certainly discussed with Hazlerigg in York was the collection and dispatch of reinforcements after him.

Meanwhile the Scots had been recruiting, and though their army was small at the outset it was destined to reach a total of thirty or even forty thousand. In effective command was David Leslie, the general who had fought with Fairfax, Cromwell and Ireton at the battle of Marston Moor and had no concern with the *débâcle* of 1648. He was operating on inner lines, close to his supply centres, and had every justification for engaging in a purely defensive strategy. For if he could hold out for three months, winter would embrace them all, and it seemed likely that, unless the invaders captured Edinburgh and its port of Leith, the rigours of nature would compel them to retreat. On the other side, the English had several advantages. In Cromwell, Lambert and Monk they had commanders whose records were outstanding and whose experience was ripe. They had as the nucleus of their army six regiments of the New Model and other regiments subsequently formed that had been welded together in battle and whose training had never been allowed to slacken. These hardened fighting men were familiar with their duties and their prospects of promotion; and their *esprit de corps* was high. Leslie's troops were mustered only for the one campaign. Very few Royalists had been permitted to join the Army of the Kirk and many of the officers, as a Royalist complained, were 'ministers' sons, clerks and such other sanctified creatures, who hardly ever saw or heard of any sword but that of the Spirit'. The other ranks had been hastily levied, and though often of excellent materials they were always liable to be dismissed for political reasons by the Presbyterian junta that now governed Scotland. Indeed the process of purging the Scottish army of unreliable elements continued until the eve of the battle of Dunbar.

It was because Leslie recognized that his soldiers were inferior both in training and morale to the veteran 'Roundheads' that he decided at first on a strategy of defence in depth. The inhabitants of the south-east of Scotland, which is so rich in arable land, were ordered to remove their corn and forage and take their cattle and sheep behind the walls of Edinburgh. The English concentration in Northumberland had made it clear that they were coming in by the road from Berwick, and Leslie therefore withdrew from East Lothian, which provides little natural protection, and prepared to man a fortified line covering Edinburgh and Leith. Cromwell's first aim was to capture a port, and on July 28th he duly occupied Dunbar, with its small all-weather harbour of Belhaven, 30 miles from Edinburgh. The need for having such a secure supply base was underlined by the success with which Leslie attained his first object of depriving the invaders of any chance of living off the country. One of Cromwell's officers reported: 'In the march between Mordlington [just north of the border] and Copperspath [a defile between the Lammermuir Hills and the sea] we saw not any Scotch man in Eyton and other places we passed through; but the streets were full of Scotch women; pitiful, sorry creatures, clothed in white flannel, in a very homely manner; very many of them much bemoaned their husbands, who, they said, were enforced by the lairds of the towns to gang to the muster.' As soon as the beacons heralding the invasion had been lit on the hills, all the able-bodied Scots had fled, driving their cattle before them. At Dunbar the

English found no male Scot over seven or under seventy except a few decrepit ones. But no plundering was permitted in the Cromwellian army. For stealing a cloak a sergeant of Colonel Coxe's regiment was later hanged in the Pentland Hills. On July 28th the English occupied the next northerly port or fishing village of Musselburgh after it had been reconnoitred by Major-General Lambert and Commissary-General Whalley with an advance guard. A small body of the enemy was surprised in the town by Lieutenant-General Fleetwood's regiment who took a few prisoners. On the next day the whole army drew up in sight of the capital of Scotland on the very spot where 103 years earlier the Lord Protector Somerset had won the battle of Pinkie Cleugh.

The English navy commanded the sea, and thus the capture of Dunbar and Musselburgh had been simplified, and on July 29th four warships began cannonading Leith. But Cromwell soon discovered that Leslie's position covering Edinburgh was too formidable to be attacked. The weather turned against the Parliamentary army which, owing to lack of tents, had to bivouac in the open. Scarcity of provisions obliged them to retreat to the sea; the Scots 'skulked into their dens and we marched with empty stomachs,' noted an English lieutenant. Cromwell ordered his army to fall back on Musselburgh. Major-General Lambert and Commissary-General Whalley were now in command of a rearguard formed out of their cavalry regiments. The retreat was so rapid that the rearguard became separated and the Scots fell upon them 'like a swarm of bees'. Captain Evanson, who commanded one of the columns (and who was himself a Presbyterian) was overpowered by a contingent of Scottish horse, but Cromwell's, Lambert's and Whalley's regiments came to the rescue, and the English army managed to draw away in fairly good order, even taking some prisoners. King Charles II who was on Castle Hill actually saw the Scots—whom he called his 'Green Horns'—being beaten off. But the Scots were by no means through. A picked force of cavalry was sent after the English rearguard to renew the fight on July 31st. With them went a few English Royalists who deceived an outpost of Colonel Lilburne's regiment by calling out to it in an English accent. This attack was repulsed by others of Lilburne's troopers and some of Lambert's and Hacker's musketeers and cost the Scots several officers, forty or fifty men killed, and eighty prisoners. During the first bout of these rearguard actions Lambert's own charger was shot under him and he himself was wounded by lance both in the arm and the body and taken prisoner for a while, but at once rescued. Commissary-General Whalley's counter-charge saved Lambert and was commended by General Cromwell in a dispatch. On August 6th the English had further to retire from Musselburgh to Dunbar, as the continued bad weather prevented supplies from Newcastle being landed on the exposed beaches.

Thus the first fortnight's fighting had favoured the Scots. Leslie's position before Edinburgh had proved impregnable and so soon were the English faced with difficulties of supply that they had been compelled to retreat and undergo humiliation from the harassing of their rearguard and the unhorsing of their Major-General. On the other hand, the actions between the English rearguard and the best Scottish troopers had spotlit the superiority of the English veterans.

As soon as his army had rested and collected its supplies Cromwell advanced again. This time, instead of attempting a frontal assault on Edinburgh, he decided to try to break through Leslie's lines of communication north and west of his capital. On August 13th the English army moved round west of the city into the Pentland Hills so as to threaten the roads to Queensferry and Stirling. By August 17th the bulk of the English army had been drawn up on its new front. But Leslie, whose knowledge of the ground, as Cromwell admitted, was infinitely better, retorted by occupying another unassailable position between two lakes at Corstorphine, south of the road to Queensferry, and, as Cromwell's supplies again gave out, and he felt himself in danger of being separated from his ships, he was once more obliged to retire to the sea. The English withdrawal this time was an entirely dismal affair unrelieved by glory. The weather remained wet and stormy and a number of men were lost through sickness and exposure. Only by protecting their retreat with clever placing of their guns along the hills were the men of the English Commonwealth, chased by the Scots, able to reach Musselburgh without disaster. But during that tempestuous August retreat the Scots almost succeeded in cutting off the English from their supplies. It was Cromwell himself who informed the Council of State on August 30th after he had regained the sea that only 'the Lord in mercy' had prevented a defeat.

Cromwell and his Generals now resolved to pull back into Dunbar, transform the port into an armed camp, and wait on Providence or, in modern terms, events. That was finally decided at a Council of War in Musselburgh on August 30th. In spite of their setbacks Cromwell, Fleetwood, Lambert and Monk had no thought of retreating to England. On the contrary, they hoped that the Scots would be tempted out of their fortified lines and away from their bases, while their own difficulties with commissariat would be eliminated. The situation was thus summed up by Cromwell:

> Upon serious consideration, finding our weakness so to increase, and the enemy lying upon his advantage, at a general council it was thought fit to march to Dunbar and there to fortify the town. Which (we thought), if anything would provoke them to engage. As also that the having a garrison there would furnish us with accommodation for our sick men, would be a good magazine — which we exceedingly wanted; being put to depend upon the uncertainty of weather for landing provisions, which many times cannot be done though the being of the whole army lay upon it, all the coasts from Berwick to Leith having not one good harbour. As also to lie more conveniently to receive our recruits of horse and foot from Berwick.

So, after 500 sick and wounded had been embarked at Musselburgh, the ships hoisted sail for Dunbar and the army resumed its march through a moonless night shrouded by a Scotch mist. This was the most difficult part of the withdrawal. The Scots harassed the rearguard which was saved from destruction only by the darkness on August 31st. Next day the English army drew up in order of battle fully expecting to be attacked. But so excellent was its lay-out, organized, it is said, by Colonel Monk, that Leslie, having seen it, decided not to engage. But he continued to pursue with pugnacity and the

English were thankful to reach Dunbar with their equipment more or less intact.

Meanwhile the Scottish General had used his knowledge of the topography to sever his foe from land communication with England. Marching inland parallel with the English as they clung to the sea he had encamped on Doon Hill, a wide eminence 500 feet high in the Lammermuir range, 2 miles south of Dunbar, and had sent a party to hold the pass at Copperspath on the road to Berwick-on-Tweed between the hills and the sea. Thus at the beginning of September the two armies faced the wrong way, the Scots with their backs to England, the English with the sea behind them on the coastal road to Edinburgh. Unless the Scots moved away or were conquered the English could receive no reinforcements or supplies by land from Newcastle. On September 2nd Cromwell wrote to Hazlerigg: 'The enemy hath blocked up our way at the Pass at Copperspath, through which we cannot get without almost a miracle . . . If your forces had been in a readiness to have fallen upon the back of Copperspath, it might have occasioned supplies to have come to us . . .' What Hazlerigg was doing at the time we do not know. But Cromwell and his army, now reduced by casualties to 11,000 men, had to fend for themselves.

The result of the battle of Dunbar, which began before dawn on September 3rd, 1650, was so extraordinary and overwhelming as to justify the many puritans who fought in it in believing that it was predestined by a quirk of the Almighty. The Scots outnumbered the English by more than two to one. They had the moral advantage of having outmanœuvred their enemy during the previous six weeks. Before the battle they had held yet another of the series of impregnable positions chosen by their General through his grasp of the local terrain. They had blocked the way home for the English and forced them to fight on hostile soil with the sea as their only life line. Between the two armies lay a long but narrow wooded glen through which ran a burn (the Brox) flooded by the rains and which could only be crossed easily at three points. To carry out an offensive the English had first to surmount this minor obstacle and then assault a Scottish line which, even after it came down off Doon Hill, stretched in an arc forbiddingly from the hills almost to the sea. Yet when the smoke of battle had cleared, the Scots had lost some 3000 men killed, 10,000 in prisoners, and 15,000 weapons, while the English losses were claimed as about thirty. No historian has been able to explain fully in purely military terms, on the basis of such evidence as remains, the bewildering completeness of the victory.

One thing at least is certain — that generalship counted heavily. The confidence of the English commanders was superb and unshakable. Though, as Cromwell informed Hazlerigg, they knew they were 'upon an engagement very difficult', they thought of nothing but attacking and defeating the Scots in the field. Leslie also intended to take the offensive if he could; but the Scottish commander, who was a weaker tactician than strategist, misread the situation. He imagined that the English, demoralized by setbacks and thinned by medical casualties, would try to force their way down the Berwick road with their cavalry and that he would be able to fall upon them from flank or rear as they passed. It was a Scottish pipe dream. He would have done better to have sent a contingent down from Doon Hill to outflank the English from the west and perhaps spike their guns. Instead he assumed that the English were intent on flight. Thus on September 2nd both sides prepared for battle.

That morning broke stormy and wet. The English were unable to pitch their tents and suffered much discomfort. But the Scots were even worse off on the wind-swept Doon Hill. Partly because their commanders found it insufferable to remain encamped there any longer, partly because they were exhorted by their Committee of Estates to fall, like Ehud, upon the Moabites, they ordered their men to move down on to the rich sloping grasslands below the line of the hills. As the horse of their right wing descended, the English stood to their arms expecting to be attacked at once. A small English outpost in a cottage on the south side of the Brox Burn was overpowered and a prisoner was taken and brought before Leslie for interrogation. The prisoner assured Leslie that the English army meant to attack, but he appears only to have reinforced the General's opposite convictions. 'Soldier,' he said to the prisoner, 'how will you fight when you have shipped half of your men and all your great guns?' By the early evening all the Scots had come down from Doon Hill. The bulk of their cavalry was stationed on the right covering the road to Berwick down which the English were expected to try to break out, their foot was in the centre, and a smaller body of horse was on the left with little space to manœuvre between the foot of Doon Hill and the deeper and wider part of the glen. Thus, in Cromwell's words — and they are significant — the Scots caused 'their right wing to edge down towards the sea'.

Meanwhile the English Generals had spent most of Monday drawing up their men in order of battle. They, for their part, had no doubt that the Scots were going to attack. At four o'clock in the afternoon they retired to Dunbar for supper and afterwards rode out to Broxmouth House, a mile and a quarter from Dunbar and less than half a mile from the sea, to reconnoitre the enemy's positions. After they had examined the new Scottish line below the hill, Cromwell turned to Lambert and said: 'I think it gives us an opportunity and an advantage to attempt upon the enemy.' To this Lambert replied that he had been thinking of saying the same thing to him. They then called up Colonel Monk who assented too. Later in the evening a Council of War was held with some of the colonels and 'they also cheerfully concurred'.

What was it about the Scots' position that induced these three officers to plan an attack at dawn on the next day? Cromwell never explained — any more than he disclosed the tactics he had in mind. The only surviving piece of evidence suggests that the Generals were struck by the fact that the left wing of the Scots was cramped and could be immobilized by a feint and by artillery fire, As, however, the Scots horse on that wing numbered under 2000, as compared with their heavily reinforced right, it may be doubted if this was a decisive argument. What may have been more important to them was that the Generals saw that the Scots were strung out in a wide arc between the Doon Hill and the sea — a distance of some 3 miles — and therefore had left openings between their forces. If surprise could be obtained, the English might exploit these gaps after they had crossed the burn.

During the late evening the English army was moved up close to the glen and two field guns placed with each regiment of foot. That was a precaution against a night attack by the Scots, and if it was marked by General Leslie, merely confirmed his notion, founded on false intelligence, that no offensive was intended by the English.

The night before the battle was sleety and tempestuous, 'a drakie nycht full of wind and weit', as a Scot put it. Each side stood to arms alerted. But towards morning the Scots who had lain tentless in the fields concluded that there was no immediate danger and orders were given that the men might bivouac as best they could. Some of them groped for cover among the shocks of corn and the lights of the musketeers were extinguished to save match. (The dowsing of their match put the Scottish infantry at a disadvantage when the English fell on them.) Horses were unsaddled and sent to forage and some of the officers sought shelter in the neighbouring farms. Leslie afterwards complained that they would have won the battle 'if the officers had stayed by their troops and their regiments'. The stormy night with clouds obscuring the light of the harvest moon made it virtually impossible for the Scottish pickets to detect the immense activity on the other side of the line. Moreover trees and bushes hid the way from Dunbar to the Brox Burn. Under such cover the English commanders were busy all night organizing for the attack. Their aim was to cross the glen, form up on the other side, and launch an offensive at dawn. One of the troopers recollected that Cromwell 'rid all the night . . . through the several regiments by torchlight, upon a little Scots nag, biting his lips till the blood ran down his chin without his perceiving it, his thoughts being busily employed to be ready for the action now at hand'.

The preliminary stage of the operation, the movement over the Brox Burn, began at about four o'clock in the morning (the sun was not due to rise until half-past five). Even to attempt as much as that in the pitch dark shows how the Generals must have relied on the discipline of their officers and men. The burn, even when flooded, cannot have been hard to surmount, but at points the sides of the glen were steep and slippery, and any noise might have given warning to the enemy and enabled him to interfere before the troops were all in line. The forces chosen to lead the assault were six cavalry regiments under Fleetwood, Lambert and Whalley, and three-and-a-half regiments of foot brigaded under Monk. Another infantry brigade under Colonel Overton and Okey's regiment of dragoons were kept on the Dunbar side of the Brox Burn to guard the guns and menace the Scottish left wing. Cromwell retained under his own command a reserve consisting of his own cavalry regiment and three foot regiments — his own, Colonel Pride's and that of Major-General Lambert.

The crossing of the burn was successfully carried out by the assault force while it was still dark without alarming the Scots, lulled by drowsiness and a mistaken sense of security after an advance by night had failed to materialize. But once the cavalry attack went in at about five o'clock in the morning 'the enemy', according to Cromwell himself, were 'in a very good posture to receive them, having the advantage of their cannon and foot against our horse'. The mounted men then fired their pistols at each other, the cannon sounded on the right, and most of the Scots awoke. 'Before our foot could come up,' Cromwell continued in his official dispatch, 'the enemy made a gallant resistance, and there was a very hot dispute at sword's point between our horse and theirs.' Lambert's cavalry recoiled before a line of lancers. Then the infantrymen under Colonel Monk came up in the second wave and attacked the Scottish foot in the centre, but they too were thrust back by superior numbers. Here was the crux of the battle. Cromwell now sent in his reserves — his own regiment of horse and three regiments of foot. 'And the sun appearing upon the sea, I heard Nol say, "Now let God arise and his enemies shall be scattered" ': thus recalled an infantry officer who was there, thirty years afterwards. 'The Lord General's regiment of foot', it is stated in the *True Relation* of the battle, 'charged the enemy with much resolution, and were seconded by Colonel Pride's men.' Lambert's foot regiment was also pushed into the battle under the General's own supervision. Cromwell's foot regiment repulsed the finest of the Scottish infantry at push of pike, while his cavalry regiment skirting the sea rolled up the enemy's flank. Lambert's horse now rallied and charged the enemy's horse with terrible effect, they being in Oliver's words 'made by the Lord of Hosts as stubble to our swords'. Leslie's right wing was routed, and the English cavalry now turned to the support of their foot, as they did at Marston Moor. One Scottish foot regiment which had been fighting well at push of pike and butt of musket was dispatched by a troop of horse. After but an hour's struggle the Scots panicked and threw down their arms in the centre, and their left, hemmed in at the foot of the hills, seeing the fate of their comrades, disintegrated and fled in every direction.

Thus the victory of Dunbar was won partly through the surprise achieved by the attack at dawn after the English had formed up undetected south of the burn, and partly by the skill with which Cromwell had thrown in his reserves at the right place and the right time. According to one account, some of the Scots were killed fast asleep in their tents. According to another, the Scottish army was outflanked both by the cavalry and the foot in the English reserve; but that is scarcely consistent with Cromwell's statement that the Scottish line stretched down almost to the sea, and no mention of a flank attack appears in Cromwell's reports or in any contemporary narrative. Indeed the Scots, who knew the English were in Broxmouth House, quite near to the sea, could scarcely have left themselves open to so obvious a manœuvre. What appears more likely to have happened is that Cromwell took advantage of one of the gaps in the long Scottish front and was able to send in his reserve of foot to the left of the enemy's main infantry positions while they were distracted by the first attack directed upon them by George Monk.

How did Cromwell's Generals behave in the battle? In the sparse surviving reports strangely little mention is made of his Lieutenant-General of Horse, Charles Fleetwood, but biographers of Monk and Lambert have vied with each other in claiming for their heroes a dominant role. As to Monk, it is true that his advice was sought during the planning of the battle and that he was given the command of the first wave of foot. But at that time he had little knowledge of the Parliamentary army's capabilities. On the other hand, Cromwell and Lambert were a tried combination who had together won a similar victory against the odds — and against the Scots — at Preston two years earlier. Lambert undoubtedly took a lead in working out the tactics, drawing up the line of battle, and placing the guns. His name comes before that of Fleetwood in Cromwell's report to Parliament. His rallying of the English horse after the initial repulse contributed materially to the victory. For six years on from the time of this battle he and Cromwell were bound together by an intimacy that derived from a comradeship in arms. Commissary-General Edward Whalley, whose horse was shot dead under him and was himself wounded in the wrist, also distinguished himself, as he had done before the battle. The bravery and confidence of all these officers — Fleetwood, Monk, Lambert and Whalley — were essential elements in a military triumph, rooted in discipline, nurtured by surprise, and crowned by courage. Yet there is no evidence worthy of the name to suggest that the mind behind it all was other than Cromwell's own: these men were his lieutenants and not his masters.

BIBLIOGRAPHY TO CHAPTER II

Besides the standard works on Cromwell, there is W. S. Douglas, *Cromwell's Scotch Campaigns: 1650-1651* (1899). *The Autobiography of Captain John Hodgson* (ed. Turner, 1882), the most popular original source, needs to be used with great care as it was written during the reign of King Charles II some thirty years after the events it describes — and what could a young subaltern be expected to know of grand strategy? The most detailed account of the battle of Dunbar is in *Transactions of the Royal Historical Society*, New Series, vol. XIV (1900) by C. H. Firth. The original authorities are listed in this article. The most valuable original account of the battle is not that of Hodgson but by Cadwell in 'Relation of the Battle between the Scots and Cromwell at Dunbar': *Ormonde Papers* (ed. Carte, 1739), I, 381 seq. Cromwell's letters are in Abbott, II, chap. VII. T. S. Baldock, *Cromwell as a Soldier* (1899) is illuminating, but most secondary accounts of the battle seem to me to contain errors. Harrison's letter quoted on page 15 is in *The Milton State Papers* (ed. Nickolls, 1743), p. 10. The quotations on pages 17 and 20 are from Hodgson.

CHAPTER III

WINTER IN SCOTLAND, SUMMER IN WORCESTER, 1650-1651

THE battle of Dunbar pulverized and abased but did not destroy the spirit of Scotland. Cromwell found it impossible to care for the 10,000 prisoners he had taken; so he released about half of them — the sick and the wounded — and dispatched the remainder under guard to Newcastle. The march across a land shorn of food was terrible even in the annals of war. At Morpeth in Northumberland the prisoners broke into a garden and devoured raw cabbages. Dysentery spread among them and before the wretches reached their goal many hundreds had died of disease or starvation. One can imagine how the incident exasperated feelings in Scotland against the invaders.

Otherwise the defeat at Dunbar divided and confounded Cromwell's enemies. The Royalists, mainly concentrated in the Highlands, blamed the Kirk; the leaders of the Kirk still distrusted the Royalists; and in the Lowlands around Glasgow an extreme Covenanting group under Colonel Archibald Strachan and Colonel Gilbert Kerr, soon to be known, because of a manifesto which they published, as the Remonstrants, aimed at inducing the English to leave Scottish soil on condition that they themselves undertook to rid their country of King Charles II. But in spite of differences with each other, none of the Scots were inclined to acquiesce in an English occupation, and Cromwell was to discover that neither his guns nor his blandishments could quieten clansmen entrenched on their native hills and moors, where from behind every rock or out of every ditch an ambuscader might pounce.

The day after Dunbar Major-General John Lambert was dispatched with seven cavalry regiments and one of foot to lay hold of Edinburgh. David Leslie with the shattered remnants of his forces had withdrawn as far as Stirling to guard the only practicable bridge over the Forth. Edinburgh surrendered to Lambert's courteous assurances and put at his disposal one of the churches where his chaplains and more theologically-minded soldiers might preach at each other. But in Edinburgh Castle, formidable and rockgirt, Sir Walter Dundas with ample supplies and ammunition still held out. When Cromwell, having marched by way of Leith, joined Lambert in Edinburgh with the bulk of the infantry on September 7th, he had therefore to take account of a strategic situation still fraught with difficulties. Behind him was the road to Berwick, beset by moss troopers, while the other way back into England through Carlisle was obstructed by the Covenanting force under Colonels Strachan and Kerr. Beside him were Dundas's men in Edinburgh Castle: he was emphatically reminded of their presence when at the time of his entry into the City one of his soldiers had his arm shot off by a cannon ball from the garrison. In front of him lay the width of the Forth and the screen of the Trossachs. In the middle was Leslie astride Stirling Bridge. All forbad his advance into the Highlands.

Nevertheless Cromwell and his Generals decided to thrust forward. After he had called up what reinforcements he could from Newcastle, knowing that at the most only about two months' good campaigning season remained, Cromwell on September 14th boldly led his army towards Stirling by way of Linlithgow and Falkirk. He had been compelled to leave four regiments behind to guard Edinburgh and Leith, Colonel Robert Lilburne being placed in command at Edinburgh. The weather was still shocking and the roads so clogged with mire that two of the siege guns had to be sent back. Cromwell himself also returned to Leith for a day in the hope of meeting his old friend General Richard Deane, a fighting man at home alike on land and sea, but he was a day late and Cromwell rode back to his army.

Cromwell's anxiety to meet Deane at Leith showed that he was intent on storming Leslie's position. For Deane, a Gloucestershire man of forty, was probably the greatest English expert on artillery in all the Parliamentary forces. He had commanded the guns at the battle of Naseby when his steady fire had helped to break Prince Rupert's charge, and had been appointed comptroller or second in command of the ordnance.

Afterwards he was General Fairfax's artillery adviser at the siege of Bristol, and when Parliament had wanted to send Cromwell to Ireland in 1647 Deane had been assigned to take charge of the artillery. Described by the Earl of Essex under whom he first served as an artillery officer as 'an honest, judicious and stout man', he was related on his mother's side to the Cromwells and became Oliver's 'trusted partisan'. Certainly he was conspicuous in the army's march on London in 1648 and forceful as a regicide. Since the execution of King Charles I, he had served in the navy as one of the three Parliamentary Commissioners at sea and, having convoyed Cromwell's expeditionary army to Ireland in 1649, was in 1650 the officer responsible for the naval support essential to the Scottish campaigns. General Deane soon joined the Council of War at the front.

Once in sight of Stirling on September 18th, Cromwell and his Generals conferred. Conciliatory overtures had been rejected by the garrison, the English trumpeter receiving his *congé* from a Scottish gentleman with a pike in his hand. All preparations were completed for an assault, but the English Generals hesitated. They had the men (outnumbering the Scots by two to one) and they had the scaling ladders. But they had not all the guns they needed. And even if they effected a breach, stormed and occupied the town, could they retain it? For the Forth was not navigable as far as Stirling so that the town could not be supplied by sea, while the communications by land from England were long and as yet insecure. Why court a repulse if once taken Stirling could not be held? Moreover the Scots were known to be quarrelling among themselves and victory might be won more cheaply. So the Council of War, though 'unanimous in resolution and courage', determined to retire. We may assume that Richard Deane's advice as naval and artillery expert was decisive and that George Monk too had his say. Thus the English advance on Stirling resolved itself into a reconnaissance in force. Yet it was a moral defeat. That same night King Charles II was reported to have entered Stirling and the guns in the town were fired for joy. The English fortified Linlithgow, 25 miles south-east of Stirling, and during the winter the area between

Stirling and Linlithgow, flat and devoid of cover, became a no-man's-land for the two armies.

Nevertheless Cromwell was reluctant to abandon every effort to push north before the winter, and played with the idea of an amphibious assault on the coast of Lothian, collecting men and boats for the purpose. But at the moment he had enough to do in clearing his communications and his Generals were all kept busy. General Deane was employed in fortifying Linlithgow. Commissary-General Whalley was ordered to Carlisle to collect forces ready to march against Strachan and Kerr. Monk and Lambert were sent back to reduce and garrison castles so that they should protect instead of interfering with the main line of communications through Berwick to Newcastle. Together they took the surrender of Dirleton House, not far from Musselburgh, in which dwelt a nest of moss troopers. There 'the great shot played, and the fourth shot of their mortar-piece tore the inner-gate, beat down the draw-bridge into the moat, and killed the lieutenant of the moss-troopers, so that they called for quarter'. Three Scottish officers were put to death, ten English prisoners were released, and the house was demolished. Then Monk subjugated Roslin House and Lambert fell on Borthwick Castle. Before this, Cromwell had cancelled Whalley's orders to march against the western army of the Scots and told him instead to make ready to open alternative lines of communications for the English army from Carlisle. But before he could do that, the western army had to be subdued.

In the third week of October Cromwell had paid a courtesy call on Glasgow accompanied by 9000 men. He was not without hopes that he might wean these fierce Presbyterians from the central Scottish Government at Stirling. At any rate all was sweetness and light. The English soldiers found Glasgow a more agreeable town than Edinburgh. Cromwell's suffered a long sermon from the Reverend Zachary Boyd in the High Church, although he was afterwards reported to have overwhelmed Boyd 'by a prayer of two or three hours duration'. An English officer was court-martialled for blasphemy as if to assure the Glaswegians of the Christian orthodoxy of the English commanders. But none of these gestures nor a stream of letters and proclamations titivated to meet the susceptibilities of the godly of Glasgow and its hinterland could induce the Lowlanders to believe that it was right for the English soldiers to stay encamped in their country. In the end Cromwell felt obliged to take action against Colonel Gilbert Kerr and his Covenanting stalwarts, Colonel Archibald Strachan having given up searching his soul and disappeared into prison or limbo.

Cromwell planned a three-pronged operation to stop Kerr's men from linking with the Scots at Stirling. Lambert was sent south of the Clyde towards Hamilton (12 miles south-east of Glasgow), which was believed to be Kerr's headquarters; Whalley was ordered up from Carlisle where he had been awaiting his call; and Cromwell with a main force of 8000 men advanced from Edinburgh towards Hamilton by way of Kirk o'Shotts. The rendezvous date for the three armies was November 29th. As Kerr had only some three or four thousand men his fate appeared to be sealed. However, Cromwell's elaborate plan broke down. When he spotted his enemy near Hamilton he found that the Clyde was so swollen by torrents and Bothwell Bridge so effectively obstructed and fortified that he was unable to cross the river. Moreover he had no intelligence of Lambert and disturbing reports from Edinburgh. So he withdrew. But Lambert arrived a day late for his appointment, and the Scots, who had been distracted by Cromwell's appearance in front of them suddenly discovered Lambert — and Whalley with him — behind them, in Hamilton. That night Colonel Kerr, whose numbers exceeded those of Lambert and Whalley, determined to attack. The English routed the Scots in a fight in the streets of Hamilton and wounded their commander. That was the end of the Remonstrants and a personal triumph for John Lambert.

If political warfare had played only a minor part in the overthrow of the western army, it seems to have contributed materially to the fall of Edinburgh Castle. Like Strachan and Kerr, Sir Walter Dundas felt dubious about the policy followed by the Committee of Estates (the organ of the Scottish Government) in allying themselves with King Charles II. Cromwell's blandishments had unsettled him. Yet his position in those days when siege warfare was still primitive was almost unconquerable. He might have held out for many months and interrupted English communications. Cromwell had collected miners from the Glasgow area and also from Derbyshire in an attempt to blast through the south side of the rock on which the Castle stood. Their task was unmanageable and was met by counter-mining, and having got his artillery into place, by the middle of December Cromwell was ready to storm the citadel. But before he ordered the storm he offered tempting terms. At last Governor Dundas yielded. Perhaps he had heard of Cromwell's massacres at Drogheda and Wexford. At any rate his fellow Scots thought he was a traitor. Colonel George Monk was one of the two officers who negotiated the capitulation and soon afterwards he was appointed English Military Governor of Edinburgh.

The bulk of Scotland south of the Clyde and Forth, except for a few castles, was now under English control and the battle line was clearly drawn between the two sides. The Royalists and the Scottish rulers came hesitantly to a working agreement, though the alliance was never firm. At first King Charles II had contemplated throwing off the tutelage of the ministers and putting himself under the protection of his friends in the Highlands. But after some embarrassing moments all was smoothed over. On January 1st, 1651, he was crowned a Covenanted King at Scone; and hereafter he instructed his followers to keep their tongues in their cheeks and obey the Kirk by acknowledging their repentence for the 'sinful and unlawful engagement' they had taken in the past when they had followed the first Duke of Hamilton into England in 1648. The second Duke of Hamilton and his rival, the Marquis of Argyll, were put on the same committee; but Hamilton was to die fighting for his King at Worcester, while Argyll stayed at home in Scotland. The temporarily united Scots now waited to see what Cromwell and his army would do next. In fact Cromwell's army, as General Lambert complained, was still puzzling how to subsist on a little cheese and a hope of horse meat.

During the winter Cromwell's Generals were dispersed on many duties. In February at the annual election of the

English Council of State Charles Fleetwood and Thomas Harrison were added to the members. Thereupon Fleetwood left the army in Scotland and returned to England. It is not known why Cromwell allowed his Lieutenant-General to depart while the campaign was still far from finished. If Fairfax had still been Commander-in-Chief, would he have let Cromwell go? Fleetwood, a much respected figure, was probably more of an administrator than a tactician. Cromwell may well have felt that with Lambert, Monk and Deane beside him, he could spare Fleetwood and indeed he may have preferred to have a man whom he trusted, less fanatical than Harrison, to supervise military matters in England. At any rate soon after Fleetwood returned to London, Harrison was ordered (in March) to collect 4000 men and leave the English capital for Lancashire, superseding Colonel Nathaniel Rich, a fellow Fifth Monarchist, who was moved to Leicester. Harrison was put in charge not only of Lancashire, but of Staffordshire, Cheshire, Derbyshire and Nottinghamshire and thus shared the command of the north of England with Hazlerigg who was still in Newcastle. One of Harrison's friends, the Fifth Monarchy preacher, Vavasour Powell, enlisted himself as a colonel, raised a regiment out of his Welsh congregation, and marched forth in support of his co-religionist. Harrison reached Lancaster on May 30th.

George Monk, having mastered his duties in Edinburgh, went in February to batter into submission the castle of Tantallon beside the Edinburgh-Dunbar road, on the sea, an ancient stronghold of the Lothians. After ten days the garrison beat a parley, the Governor came out and delivered a speech on the walls, and Monk led his prisoners back to Edinburgh. In the following month Monk by an amphibious operation, in which General Deane's warships took part, captured Blackness Castle on the south side of the Firth of Forth. Both these sieges exemplified Monk's skill in combined operations. For his services he was awarded with promotion. On May 6th Richard Deane was appointed Major-General of the Army by Cromwell as well as being given the colonelcy of Mauleverer's regiment of foot, Mauleverer having died in Scotland in the previous December. On the same day Monk took over the command of the artillery from Deane with the rank of Lieutenant-General of the Ordnance. During this period Cromwell was taken seriously ill, and Lambert commanded the army in his stead.

Cromwell had been reluctant to retire into winter quarters as was the practice among armies in the seventeenth century. During his campaign in Ireland he had fought on through most of the winter and he tried to do the same thing in Scotland. Hence there were a number of skirmishes between the two sides. But General January and General February were in more effective command in Scotland than they had been in Ireland. One squally night in January the Scots from Stirling had made a lunge at Linlithgow but had been sent about their business, and later in the same month Monk had tried to organize an amphibious assault on Burntisland, on the north side of the Firth of Forth opposite Leith. A winter gale and the alertness of the Scottish gunners put an end to that attempt. Early in February Cromwell himself had tried to cross into Fife east of Stirling, but again bad weather had compelled him to withdraw.

Thus in fact no change in the relative positions of the two armies occurred during the winter nor did much happen in the spring of 1651. Cromwell was taken ill again in May and the initiative momentarily passed to the Scots. In spite of the English victory at Hamilton they proved still able to interfere with the communications of the Parliamentary army through the west to Carlisle. Their cavalry carried out raids below the Clyde which were reported to have frightened the English garrisons as far south as Dumfries where Colonel Matthew Alured with his Lancashire regiment of foot was stationed. At the end of June the Scots marched out from Stirling and entrenched themselves in the hills at Torwood nearby, while parties occupied Falkirk and drove the English from Calendar House not far from Linlithgow. By this time the English had fourteen regiments of horse, twelve of foot, and sixteen big guns, a substantially larger army than that which had won Dunbar. Yet so excellent was the new Scottish defence line at Torwood that Cromwell retired after he had reconnoitred it.

But Cromwell was now determined to bring the long-drawn-out campaign to an end. There was only one way and that was once again to defeat the Scottish army in the field. Neither the victory of Dunbar nor the occupation of Edinburgh and most of the Lowlands had extinguished the patriotic ardour of his enemies, while his proclamations and manifestoes had failed to persuade them to break with their King. Though he had received reinforcements from England, his army was still too small to destroy the Scottish forces so long as they remained behind their fortifications. During the second half of June by demonstrations in force before Torwood he had vainly tried to provoke the Scots to battle. He had reconnoitred every conceivable way to cross the Forth east of Stirling. In the second week of July he dispatched Lambert, who, since Fleetwood's departure had commanded the cavalry, with three regiments of horse to explore the fords across the Forth west of Stirling. Lambert, who carried out a fine piece of reconnaissance north of Strathblane and even succeeded in crossing the Forth at one point, came back with the surprising news that the enemy had few defence works in that neighbourhood. But, as it happened, it was on the other side of Stirling that the decisive operation was now to be undertaken.

Whether the new operation was a deeply laid plan or just one of those instances in the history of warfare where a success was exploited beyond all expectation is not clear. At any rate on July 17th Colonel Robert Overton commanding a brigade of 1600 men was sent across the Forth by boats from South Queensferry to North Queensferry (where the Forth Bridge is now) with orders to effect a lodgement and entrench himself on the promontory there in yet another attempt to draw off the Scots army from their defence line south of Stirling. If the Scots had moved, Cromwell's main army would have attacked. Surprisingly enough, Overton crossed the river without difficulty, but failed to disturb the Scots. Lambert was now sent to follow him up and by July 20th he managed to push another 2500 men across the Forth. Now Leslie no longer dared ignore the threat to his flank and rear, but he was too wily to send more than a small portion of his army to deal with Overton and Lambert. It is likely that once again Leslie's intelligence was faulty and that he underestimated the number of men and weapons that the English had transported over the river. In any case he sent only some 3500 under Sir John Brown and Major-General Holborn to drive the English off the North Queensferry peninsula. As at Hamilton fight, nine months earlier, Lambert was entirely ready to receive them. He stood on the defensive until all his men, consisting of two cavalry regiments and two foot regiments, had come ashore and were in line. Then he ordered Colonel John Okey, now promoted from a commander of dragoons to being a colonel of cavalry, to attack the enemy as they appeared to be wheeling away. Both sides drew up in order of battle by the village of Inverkeithing, Lambert having a slight superiority in numbers but the worse of the ground since the English lay at the foot of the hills with the Scots musketeers manning the passes. But many of the English soldiers, notably in Lambert's and Daniel's regiments, were veterans, and on the right wing where their chief strength was concentrated they attacked uphill with spirit. Holborn fled, the Macleans of Mull made a last stand to be slain to a man, and altogether half of the Scots were reported to have been killed and most of the rest taken prisoners. Lambert led his men thus courageously to victory even though he had received a false report that Cromwell himself had again retired to Linlithgow. It was learned after the battle that a couple of bullets were found between Lambert's coat and his armour.

Cromwell now reinforced Lambert's success. First he sent two more regiments of horse and two of foot to join the Major-General, then he moved forward as if to pin Leslie in Stirling, feinting before him on the ancient field of Bannockburn. Thus Leslie, who had contemplated marching with all his strength against the victorious Lambert, was obliged to remain in Stirling so as to cover the bridge. That gave Cromwell the opportunity he sought to join Lambert; he rapidly countermarched to South Queensferry and started throwing across the bulk of his army in Lambert's wake. He kept only four regiments of horse and four of foot south of the Forth. The English Commander-in-Chief fully realized that by thrusting the bulk of his army north of the Forth he was giving Leslie the opportunity, should he wish to take it, of marching south into England.

The intelligence services of the Commonwealth were excellent. For example, that March Major-General Harrison had arrested a Royalist conspirator in a shop in the Strand and squeezed much information out of him. During the summer Cromwell had learned from half a dozen sources that King Charles II and the English Royalists in Scotland were eager to move into England, hoping to pick up in Lancashire, in the west of England, and in Wales reinforcements which would enable them to dash on to London and destroy the Republic. On the other hand, Cromwell had never been given — or been able to support — a large enough army in Scotland to attack the Scots on both sides of the Forth. By grasping his chance to cross the Forth he cut the Scots in Stirling from their own communications and gave them the alternatives either of fighting where they stood or undertaking the gamble of pushing forward across the border to England. There was no danger of the Scots being able to come far without being caught. The infantry laden down with their long pikes or lances, or with the elaborate paraphernalia of match, ball and powder needed to fire their muskets, could not hope to move at a rate of more than about ten miles a day and could not possibly expect to reach the English capital without prolonged halts. Meanwhile they would be chased by the English cavalry from Scotland under Lambert, obstructed by the northern forces under Harrison, and smothered by the militia directed upon them from every side by the organizing talent of Fleetwood. Yet some risk necessarily attached to Cromwell's grand strategy. And just as he might never have embarked upon it had it not been for Overton's *tour de force* in crossing at Queensferry or Lambert's overwhelming victory at Inverkeithing, so too he would not have chanced leaving the Commonwealth open to invasion had it not been that his Generals were all in place ready to stop it.

On July 23rd Major-General Harrison had been summoned from Lancashire to confer with Cromwell at Linlithgow; he was told to call up reinforcements from Nottingham and directed to watch the borders. Commissary-General Whalley was instructed to clear the Fife seaboard, after the main army had taken the port of Burntisland with its guns and warships.

Lieutenant-General Fleetwood was prepared to hurry north at a moment's call. Major-General Lambert with his tried cavalry and knowledge of vanguard tactics could ride south at a day's notice. Lieutenant-General Monk could be left behind to hold down the conquered territories. So, while pandemonium broke out in Stirling, Cromwell calmly moved north behind the enemy's back to Perth on the Firth of Tay and accepted its surrender on August 2nd. By that time he had learned for certain that King Charles II, now the official Commander-in-Chief of the Scottish army, with the Duke of Hamilton, the Earl of Loudoun, General David Leslie, General Massey, and a host of Highlanders but not the Marquis of Argyll, had taken the plunge; they had broken camp in Stirling, and were heading towards Carlisle, Lancashire and then — perhaps Whitehall.

Cromwell's Generals set about their duties with such composure that it appeared as if the Scottish invasion had long been foreseen by all of them. Overton was left in Perth; Monk with five or six thousand men (consisting of four regiments of horse and three of foot) was ordered to besiege Stirling and then take charge in Scotland. Lambert with three or four thousand cavalry rode out of Leith in pursuit of the Scots promptly on August 5th. Harrison, who was in Newcastle by August 5th, had by August 7th collected another 3000 cavalry and dragoons ready to strike across the Pennines and check the enemy's advance. Cromwell himself left Leith on August 6th with the rest of the horse, the foot (consisting of nine regiments) and the train to jog along at any easy pace, confident that his arrangements were all in order. He was accompanied by Major-General Deane in charge of the artillery. Lord Fairfax emerged from his retirement to assume command of the Yorkshire trained bands. Lieutenant-General Fleetwood in London ordered the militia of the home counties to concentrate at Banbury. And it was not until August 6th that King Charles II with some 16,000 men crossed the border.

Before he left Leith Lambert wrote to Harrison:

> My Lord General hath commanded me to desire you with all convenient speed to march with the horse and dragoons with you towards the enemy, where you may best flank

> them, straiten their provisions, and do service as you see opportunities upon them . . . I intend to keep as close in the rear as I can, yet something to the left hand [i.e. through Cumberland and Lancashire], so as I may be in a capacity to correspond or join with you, as occasion requires.

Harrison, thundering in the name of the Lord of Hosts, who would, he felt sure, put a 'mighty spirit of terror' into the enemy and enable the friends of Christ to break him 'in pieces like a potter's vessel', called on the northern counties to furnish men, horses and provisions. Then he led all the mounted men he had out of Newcastle after giving orders to the local foot to break down the bridges and occupy the passes. On August 9th Lambert was at Penrith in Cumberland and on August 11th Harrison was at Skipton in the West Riding. Harrison on that date told the Speaker that while he expected 'the terror of the Lord' would 'prove a sorer enemy to them than we', he knew that Lambert would 'dog their march' while he was hastening to 'get the van and if possible secure the middle parts of Lancashire before them'. By the middle of August Harrison came over from Ripon and joined Lambert near Preston in Lancashire, Lambert having ridden 200 miles since he left Leith on August 5th, caught up the enemy, collected their stragglers, and overtaken them on their left flank, as he had promised Harrison.

Together Cromwell's two most daring Generals had a fair-sized army, consisting of 9000 horse and between three and four thousand foot. Yet they decided against trying to halt the progress of King Charles II, as they might well have done, in country that Lambert knew well, at Warrington Bridge across the Mersey, which they were too late to destroy though they had, as Harrison reported on August 16th, spoiled passes and fords elsewhere on the river as far as Manchester. Instead, after a rearguard action by the foot, they drew back to Knutsford Heath, their object being, in Lambert's words, to 'amuse the enemy, and to flank and front them till the General come up to us'. Indeed though Lambert and Harrison excused themselves to the Council of State for not fighting at Warrington Bridge because of their lack of infantry in country better suited to it than to cavalry it is likely enough that they refrained only on Cromwell's express orders. For his purpose was not merely to defeat King Charles II in the field, but to annihilate his army and prevent the Scottish forces, split asunder by the very fact of their march into England, from ever returning home.

King Charles II and his army safely crossed Warrington Bridge on August 16th and next day the King conferred with the Earl of Derby who had arrived with a very small force from the Isle of Man. The second Duke of Hamilton had begged the King to press on to London at all costs, but he was asking the impossible of the already exhausted troops. Instead the King turned into the Midlands, hoping to find rest and recruits, and left the Earl of Derby behind to exercise his influence on Lancashire. On August 22nd Charles II and the Scots came to Worcester. Three days afterwards Colonel Robert Lilburne and his regiment, reinforced by three companies of local foot soldiers and a handful of dragoons, detached from the army under Lambert and Harrison, defeated Derby at a battle in Wigan, though the Earl, who was wounded, narrowly escaped with thirty horse to join his master in Worcester and radiate despondency among his fellow Royalists.

The English Council of State had long directed its attention to the City of Worcester. As early as March the Council had been ordered by Parliament to make the City 'untenable' and to keep a watch on the many Royalists there. When Lambert reached Coventry on August 23rd, after leaving Warrington, he had received orders from the Council to pay regard to the safety of Worcester and he had hurried 500 cavalry to reinforce the militia in the City. However, when King Charles knocked at the gates the small Parliamentary garrison prudently withdrew to Gloucester. On the following day the King was greeted deferentially by the Mayor and on the Sunday (August 24th) attended service in the cathedral. The Scots were pleased to find so congenial a place to stop after marching 300 miles in three weeks. But to his surprise the King was unable to enlist more than a few inhabitants in the supposedly loyal neighbourhood to strengthen his army.

The reason for the King's disappointment is clear. As soon

as he left Scotland for England the weight of nationalist fervour shifted to the other side of the scales. In Scotland the English appeared as invaders fighting to deprive the country of its Covenanted King and to fasten their alien rule and religion on an independent nation. But once the Scots crossed the frontier they became the aggressors and from every side patriots rallied to the colours of the Commonwealth. However restrained in their conduct — and King Charles had done what he could to prevent plunder and pillage — the Scots could expect no welcome in their venture to impose *their* monarch and *their* faith on the people of England. By allowing the Scots to break through to the south Cromwell in fact gained not only a military but a political advantage.

As the Royalists marched on Worcester by the western route through Nantwich, Lichfield, Wolverhampton and Kidderminster, Cromwell came after them by the eastern route through Durham, Chesterfield, Burton and Coventry to Warwick. At Warwick on August 24th Cromwell met Fleetwood and his own brother-in-law, Colonel John Desborough, who had come up from the south. On August 27th the Parliamentary army concentrated at Evesham which for the time being became Cromwell's headquarters. Thus King Charles II had less than a week after he arrived in Worcester to prepare for the wrath that was to come. On August 25th the Royalists sent out parties to break down the bridges across the Severn, on which Worcester stands and which runs due south from the City, and on the Teme, which meets the Severn at right angles a mile south of Worcester. At the same time work was started on restoring the fortifications of Worcester and a star-shaped earthwork, named Fort Royal, was quickly thrown up at the south-east angle of the walls. But the outlook was gloomy. The time to organize against a siege was short. Few Cavaliers answered to the appeals of their King and the Scottish generals quarrelled with one another.

There were no quarrels in the Parliamentary camp. Every officer knew his task and his place. Fleetwood's men who had been ordered to rendezvous at Banbury now joined him in Evesham. And by that time Lambert and Harrison had united with the main army. On August 28th Lambert with a party of horse and dragoons was dispatched to Upton on the Severn, 10 miles south of Worcester, with instructions to get across the river, though there it flows fast and wide. When he arrived he found the bridge destroyed and the town in Royalist hands, but at dawn on the next day he ordered eighteen dragoons to creep over planks laid or left on the surviving piers of the bridge so as to surprise the sentries and hold the bridgehead on the other side until the rest of his men could make their way across. The eighteen men straddled over the planks, but the 300 Scots who had been posted in Upton soon detected them and drove them into the church near the bridgehead. Lambert took at once a characteristically bold risk and sent the rest of his dragoons to ford or swim the river which was nearly 100 yards wide as best they could and relieve their comrades besieged in a now burning church. The Scots were outnumbered and overwhelmed and their commander, General Massey, was wounded. Thus the English gained a foothold to the west of the Severn. That afternoon Cromwell himself rode over to Upton to thank Lambert's men for what they had done and Lieutenant-General Fleetwood later arrived in the town with a brigade of horse and foot to make it his headquarters for an attack on Worcester from the south. Cromwell himself kept more than half of his army, with Lambert and Harrison, on the high ground immediately east of Worcester, having advanced from Evesham to his new headquarters at the village of Spetchley, about 2 miles east of the City.

Cromwell's plan had both a political and a military purpose. The political purpose, which was inspired and blessed by the Council of State, was to prevent the Royalists from moving on towards London, to cut off the King from his supporters in Wales, and to prevent the Scots from reaching home again. The military purpose was to defeat the enemy without undertaking a full-scale siege of Worcester which might take a long time and be costly in casualties. Once Fleetwood had established himself on the right bank of the Severn, the Royalists were shut off from Wales and the West, while a force under Colonel Lilburne was ordered north of Worcester to obstruct the road back to Scotland at Bewdley Bridge. Moreover as soon as Fleetwood's threat to the City from the south developed, it was hoped that the Royalists would come out and fight in the open. It was for this reason that Major-General Deane was instructed to join Fleetwood at Upton and by September 2nd the Lieutenant-General had eleven or twelve thousand men at his disposal. Nevertheless the plan meant that Cromwell had to take the unusual risk of dividing his army. But he seemed to be justified by the fact that it was superior in numbers to that of his enemy, as he had under his command, including some competent militia, over 30,000 men against some 16,000 under King Charles II. The Royalists did not divide their army to anything like the same extent. On the tongue of land to the south of the City, stretching about a mile from the walls down to the River Teme they had about three reinforced foot regiments under the command of Major-General Robert Montgomery who were apparently covered by the natural obstacles formed by the Severn and its tributary. Under Montgomery was Colonel Sir William Keith, who held Powick on the Royalists' right in front of the only convenient bridge over the Teme (which had been at least partially broken down) and Colonel Pitscottie on the left occupying the meadows along the line of the Teme to where it meets the Severn. Colonel Dalziel was in immediate support. But the bulk of the Royalist army with the King and the Duke of Hamilton remained within the walls of Worcester, although General David Leslie, with most of the Scottish cavalry, was posted in the area known as the Pitchcroft (now a race course) just outside the City. When the battle began the main defences south-east and east of Worcester were far from completed and were confronted by Cromwell's artillery which had been admirably posted on Red Hill and in Perry Wood, north of Red Hill, a mile to the east.

On the night of August 29th the Scots launched an unavailing attack on Cromwell's guns. On the same day Cromwell and his Generals had held a Council of War and put the finishing touches on their plan of battle.

That plan, as we have seen, was for Fleetwood to attack the City from the south and thereby try to draw the Scots out of their positions behind the walls and earthworks into the open. Cromwell's main body, covering the City from the east, would then be able to converge on the enemy and envelop them while Lilburne stood ready to cut off their exit northwards.

In readiness for Fleetwood's attack two bridges of boats had been collected and towed up the Severn from Gloucester, one to enable a crossing to be made over the Teme near its confluence with the Severn, the other, within pistol shot of it, to be thrown across the Severn itself just above the confluence so as to provide a link between Cromwell's forces on the eastern side of the Severn and Fleetwood's men to the west of it.

After four days' labour the boats were ready and assembled under cover of artillery fire, and about two o'clock in the afternoon of September 3rd, 1651, Fleetwood, after advancing from Upton that morning, ordered a general assault. His left wing was to attack at Powick and his right was to move across the bridge of boats near the mouth of the Teme. The crossing of a river in the face of the enemy is one of the most difficult operations in war and both left and right were met by the stiffest resistance from the Scots. They do not appear to have interfered with the boats as the English drew them into position, but the Scots must have seen them being made ready that autumn afternoon and must have fired on the English foot as soon as they landed. The King himself visited Powick Bridge to put heart into the men of Colonel Keith's brigade which was hotly contesting the English attempt to cross on its right. Here Fleetwood's men had no bridge of boats and the fighting must have taken place in front of the bridge, possibly in Powick village. The fight on the river line was the first crisis in the battle of Worcester.

At this point one notices a startling similarity between the tactics of Dunbar and Worcester. In each case the battle began by the English overcoming a water obstacle in order to fight the Scots: at Dunbar it was the flooded Brox Burn, at Worcester it was the two rivers. At Dunbar, since the battle began at dawn, almost complete tactical surprise was gained, but at Worcester since the bridges of boats necessary for the crossing were not in place until the early afternoon the Scots were ready and resisted with violence and success. Now, as at Dunbar, at the right time and place, Cromwell himself came up and threw in his reserve. He had under his command his lifeguards and own regiment of horse, together with two experienced foot regiments of the New Model (Ingoldsby's and Charles Fairfax's). While Fleetwood's right was being held up after crossing the Teme, Cromwell pushed first his foot and then his horse across the second bridge of boats over the Severn, thus coming in against the Scots on their left flank. Cromwell himself led his foot across the bridge. Pitscottie and his men, though they fought splendidly among the hedges, were overpowered and slowly driven back on Worcester. The defeat on their left inevitably affected the Scottish right which was stubbornly resisting the English attempts to cross the river by Powick Bridge. But there too superior numbers gradually told. Yet it was not until some hours later that Fleetwood's division finally pushed Montgomery's men back into Worcester. If David Leslie had reinforced Montgomery at this juncture the battle might have lasted even longer than it did, though it could scarcely have changed the result. According to one account, Leslie disobeyed orders from King Charles II to go to Montgomery's aid, but if so, he had plausible military reasons for refusing. For it would have seemed foolish to jeopardize his cavalry among the hedgerows while the City of Worcester and the main Royalist force was still intact.

Watching from the tower of the cathedral the struggle swaying to and fro along the line of the Teme, the young King himself made up his mind to lead a sally against Cromwell's army on Red Hill. Whose advice he sought or took we do not know, but it was not Leslie's. Under the King's own command the Royalist horse poured out of St. Martin's Gate and Sidbury Gate (to the east and south-east of the City) and under cover of their own artillery on Fort Royal attacked up hill. The struggle lasted for three hours, the Royalists continuing the battle at push of pike and butt of musket even after their ammunition was exhausted, But once again numbers and discipline decided; and Cromwell himself was able to bring back his reserves from the other side of the Severn to take part in the final contest. Thus the second part of the battle was lost and the Royalists, thrust downhill into the City from the east as well as retreating from the south, jammed each other in the streets and perished in thousands. A party of militia from Essex seized Fort Royal, put the garrison to the sword, and turned the Royalists' own guns on the fugitives. Major-General Harrison reported: 'What with the dead bodies of men and the dead horses of the enemy filling the streets, there was such a nastiness that a man could hardly abide the town.' Yet a large number of Scots took little or no part in the fight; at any rate 4000 fled through the northern gate. Harrison and Whalley went after them and Colonel Lilburne was waiting to cut them off. Harrison was vigorous in the pursuit and on September 7th had reached Preston whence he announced his hope that hardly any Scots would escape from England. In the end at least eight or nine thousand prisoners, including David Leslie, were taken and most of the rest of the invading army was slain.

There are some obscurities about the battle of Worcester. Though we have several accounts of it, the intentions of Cromwell and his Council of War can only be pieced together. We do not know what part (if any) Leslie played on the Royalist side nor do we know for certain what either Lambert or Harrison did on the Parliamentary side. According to an unconfirmed story in the memoirs of Lieutenant-General Ludlow (who was in Ireland at the time) both Lambert and Harrison were with the main army at Red Hill. Lambert had earned credit by his seizure of Upton and afterwards joined Cromwell at his headquarters in Spetchley. After that we lose track of him. He must have been to the fore in the fighting for his horse was shot under him. Harrison, we learn from his own letter of September 7th to the Speaker, was put in charge of the pursuit and it seems almost certain that he was on Red Hill and followed the retreating army into the City. He rounded up at least 3000 prisoners. But again it was Cromwell's battle. Fleetwood directed the attack across the Teme from the south, but without Cromwell's help might have been defeated there. Deane, we may suppose, was responsible for posting the guns which covered the assembly of the bridges of boats. Meanwhile Lieutenant-General Monk, left in Scotland — 'some one must be left in the post of peril to play Cromwell's part while he was gone', as one of his biographers flatteringly put it — accepted the surrender of Stirling on August 14th and later in the month stormed Dundee.

Of all Cromwell's Generals who served in the campaigns of Dunbar and Worcester John Lambert won most glory as a fighting man. At Hamilton, at Inverkeithing and at Upton he had shown daring and initiative and like Cromwell himself he was always in the thick of the fighting, being once taken prisoner, three times wounded, and twice unhorsed. At Dunbar he led the first assault on the Scottish line in the attack at dawn. After Fleetwood had returned to England he had taken over command of all the cavalry in the army and when Cromwell was ill he had acted as Commander-in-Chief. In the pursuit to Worcester he led the van. Whether he was in command on Red Hill when Charles II sallied out of Worcester or, as another account avers, led the right wing of Fleetwood's advance across the Teme, he was certainly well to the fore in the battle of Worcester. In the whole of the civil wars no General, apart from the two Commanders-in-Chief, outshone him.

Harrison had proved himself a reliable independent commander. His enthusiasm had been of value both before and after the battle of Worcester, making him a veritable angel of destruction chasing and chastising the foemen of the Lord. The measure of Cromwell's confidence in him was shown when he left him in charge in England while Fleetwood, Lambert and the rest were in Scotland, and when he summoned him up to Scotland and then ordered him back to England as soon as the danger of a Royalist incursion was realized.

In spite of the exaggerations of his biographers, the part taken by Lieutenant-General Monk should not be overlooked. Unquestionably his profound knowledge of the art of war was appreciated by Cromwell, who ignored his dubious past and unpopularity with the veterans of the New Model Army and insisted on placing him in a series of responsible posts. He was in command of the foot at Dunbar, was consulted by Cromwell at all times, and was sufficiently trusted by him to be left in charge in Scotland during the Worcester campaign. Cromwell's relatives, Commissary-General Whalley, Major-General Deane and Colonel John Desborough, had also proved themselves brave soldiers and reliable subordinates. And yet among all these officers it seems to have been Charles Fleetwood, whose military career on paper is far from outstanding, in whom Cromwell and the Council of State of the Commonwealth had most faith. During Cromwell's long absence in Scotland it was for Fleetwood that the Council of State had sent (and even during Cromwell's illness, when Lambert had asked for Fleetwood's return to Scotland, the Council of State had refused to let him go). And whatever Fleetwood's exact part was at Dunbar, he was unquestionably Cromwell's second in command at Worcester. To him we may attribute the surprising success of the militia regiments called up for the Worcester campaign. And it was largely because Fleetwood had been so good in organizing and training these militiamen and bringing them from the south when they were wanted that Cromwell had been able to take the risk of dividing his army and thereby turning the last battle into an 'absolute victory' — a 'crowning mercy'.

Cromwell's Generals had their rewards. Offices were distributed to them and lands assigned to them by a grateful Commonwealth. But while all this was going on in England, one of Cromwell's Generals and closest friends — a man who had never sought rewards or glory but served the Republic with devotion and faith, had died across the sea in Dublin: that was his son-in-law, Henry Ireton.

BIBLIOGRAPHY TO CHAPTER III

For the Scottish campaign see besides Douglas's and Gardiner's standard works, C. H. Firth, *Scotland and the Commonwealth*, papers edited for the Scottish History Society in 1895. The most detailed account of the battle of Worcester is in J. W. Willis Bund, *The Civil War in Worcestershire* (1905), but it is almost certainly wrong on some points, e.g. the part played by Lambert. The newsletters in the *Perfect Diurnall* and *Mercurius Politicus* are among the most important original sources for the battle. Cromwell's letters are in Abbott, II, chap x. The bullet marks still to be seen on Powick church suggest that the fighting on the English left took place in Powick village and not at the bridge which was partly broken down. Once the Scots were driven back the English presumably forded the River Teme, which is not deep at this point. The correspondence of Lambert and Harrison is in H. Cary, *Memorials of the Great Civil War* (1842), vol. II. There is a *Life of Richard Deane* by J. B. Deane (1870).

CHAPTER IV

MAJOR-GENERAL HENRY IRETON AND THE CONQUEST OF IRELAND

Henry Ireton was born in 1611 and died in 1651

HENRY IRETON was five years older than Thomas Harrison and seven years older than John Lambert. Like them, he was transformed into a soldier by the civil wars. He was a Nottinghamshire man, born in the village of Attenborough in 1611. His family were modest but reasonably well-to-do gentry and the household was of a puritan turn of mind. Not only was his mother, three years before he was born, presented to the Archdeacon of Nottingham's Court 'for refusing to be churched according to the rites and ceremonies of the Church of England', but when he was four his father, German Ireton, with other inhabitants of Attenborough, pleaded guilty to 'not receiving the Holy Communion kneeling'. Henry was the eldest son in a family of eight children and, like Cromwell, was a boy when his father died. We may suppose that this experience gave him a habit of leadership. It has not been established whether he was educated at Nottingham Grammar School, as is likely, but at the age of fifteen he was certainly entered as a Gentleman Commoner at Trinity College, Oxford, where he took his B.A. degree, and when he was eighteen he became a student at the Middle Temple. Afterwards he lived the life of an unmarried but impeccably behaved country gentleman until the war broke over his county when he was thirty.

The people of Nottinghamshire were not on the whole critical either of the Court or the Church, though the northern half was more inclined towards parliamentarianism and puritanism than the southern. The Iretons belonged to a puritan circle and three young men in particular, Henry Ireton himself, and his two friends, Francis Thornhagh of Fenton, and John Hutchinson of Owthorpe, who was also Ireton's cousin, formed the nucleus of a parliamentarian movement there.

Mrs. John Hutchinson was therefore in a position to know what manner of person Henry Ireton was. She wrote of him in her *Memoirs:*

> Having had an education in the strictest way of godliness, and being a very grave and solid person, a man of good learning, great understanding, and other abilities, to which was joined a willing and zealous heart in the cause and his country, he was the chief promoter of the Parliament's interest in the county. . . .

Ireton's profoundly religious outlook was a permanent feature of his character. 'I think', he said later in life, 'the main thing is for every one to wait upon God, for the errors, deceits, and weaknesses of his own heart.' The other side of the medal is provided by a remark of Anthony à Wood who says of Ireton's behaviour at Oxford that 'he had the character in that house [Trinity College] of a stubborn and saucy fellow towards the seniors and therefore his company was not at all wanting'. Thus we may picture the young Henry Ireton as an excellently educated country gentleman with a natural gift for leadership, a headstrong frame of mind, and a severely puritanical point of view.

In the spring of 1642 Francis Thornhagh, the most attractive of the three vigorous puritan leaders in Nottinghamshire, a tall dignified youngster with tawny hair and beard, and Henry Ireton, who was dark and spare, promoted a petition from the county urging King Charles I to return to London. In June Ireton joined the Mayor of Nottingham and others in petitioning Parliament to take precautions against the Royalists laying hold of the county capital and the magazine. However, it was at Nottingham that the King in fact raised his standard on August 22nd and all that Ireton could do (in Mrs. Hutchinson's words) was 'to gather a troop of those godly people whom the Cavaliers drove out, and with them to go into the army of my Lord of Essex', who had been appointed the first Parliamentarian Commander-in-Chief. 'Which', added Lucy Hutchinson, defending her husband's more leisurely procedures, 'he [Ireton] being a single person, could better do.' Captain Ireton had been given authority to raise a troop in July and it appeared in the thick of the fighting at the battle of Edgehill, but afterwards it was sent back to protect the county.

The three friends, Ireton, Thornhagh and Hutchinson, all served on the Parliamentary county committees, and Thornhagh, who was now about to succeed his father as a baronet, became lieutenant-colonel of a cavalry regiment in which Ireton served as major. Thornhagh's regiment, or part of it, joined Cromwell at Grantham and fought in the battle of Gainsborough on July 28th, 1643. Sir Francis Thornhagh was taken prisoner in Gainsborough and afterwards escaped, ultimately to be killed by a Scottish lance at the battle of Preston. John Hutchinson became the Parliamentarian Governor of Nottingham, and died as a prisoner in the Isle of Wight after the Restoration, but lives yet in his wife's *Memoirs*. Ireton's abilities were recognized by Cromwell who appointed him as his Deputy Governor in the Isle of Ely and embodied Ireton's troop of horse in his own cavalry regiment.

This was the time, at the beginning of Cromwell's career as a soldier, when he was exceedingly strenuous and resourceful. He was therefore not often in Ely, where his family had dwelt for the last seven years. And his decision to leave Ireton there in command underlined his appreciation of Ireton's quality and sympathy. While Ireton was stationed at Ely, he began to court Cromwell's eldest daughter, Bridget. He was a suitor almost as congenial to the lady as he was to her parents. But they did not marry until the first civil war was nearly over in the summer of 1646 when Ireton was thirty-five and his bride was twenty-two. A striking letter written by her father to Bridget Ireton, some three months after she married, is still in existence, in the course of which he wrote:

> Dear Heart, press on; let not husband, let not anything cool thy affections after Christ. I hope he will be an occasion to inflame them. That which is best worthy of love in thy husband is that of the image of Christ he bears. Look on that, and love it best, and all the rest for that.

Bridget was not destined to see much of her first husband. She was married to a soldier. He was to die far away from her, serving his country as he saw fit.

Under Cromwell's patronage Ireton advanced. He was

appointed Quartermaster-General in the Earl of Manchester's army, though he was not given a regiment of his own until after the battle of Marston Moor where he still had only a troop. When Cromwell and Manchester were quarrelling because Cromwell accused Manchester of not really wishing to prosecute the war until victory had been won, Manchester's Quartermaster-General testified against the Earl before a House of Commons committee. He told the committee that he had heard Manchester say that he wanted the war ended not by the sword but by an accommodation, and he accused the General of delays and of neglecting his opportunities. Having delivered this back glance, Ireton returned to his duties and affections in the Isle of Ely where he had been instructed to raise and train fresh troops and which, according to an unfriendly contemporary account, he had helped to convert into a veritable 'Amsterdam', his soldiers occupying the pulpits at the Sunday morning and afternoon services while the ministers dared not attempt to preach. After the quarrel between Cromwell and Manchester was resolved in February 1645 by the passing of the Self-Denying Ordinance, Ireton was given a Kentish regiment in the New Model Army.

Yet higher honours awaited him. When the New Model set out on its first campaign in the summer of 1645 Ireton was given command of a vanguard of horse instructed to attack the flank of the Royalist army which had captured and sacked Leicester and was dominating the Midlands. On July 13th, 1645, Ireton's men fell on the Royalist headquarters in the village of Naseby taking several prisoners and giving warning to Prince Rupert of the coming of Fairfax and Cromwell. Though his numbers were much inferior, King Charles I determined to fight, and at Cromwell's request Ireton was appointed Commissary-General, that is to say second in command of the New Model cavalry with five regiments at his orders on the left of the battle line. But General Ireton, quickly promoted from the mere captaincy of a troop at Marston Moor to command of the left wing at Naseby failed to shine. His charge was poorly delivered and inadequately followed up. Prince Rupert, who led the Royalist right, recovered from his initial check, drove Ireton's cavalry from

MAJOR-GENERAL HENRY IRETON

the field, and captured his train and baggage. Ireton himself was unhorsed, wounded and for a while taken prisoner, though he escaped and 'fought like a lion'. But his personal courage was not in question.

Ireton served with Fairfax for the rest of the campaign, being present at the siege of Bristol. And in the autumn of 1645 he was elected M.P. for Appleby. Before he took his seat he found himself in hot water with his superior officer. For he had been sent by Fairfax with his own and other regiments from the west country to Oxford to take part in the siege. While Ireton was in camp before the City he received a message to the effect that the King was now ready to surrender himself to Parliament. Instead of reporting this dramatic information to the Speaker or to General Fairfax, Ireton wrote to his friend and patron, Cromwell. Cromwell read his letter to the House and publicly rebuked Ireton for not dispatching it direct to Parliament. However, all that was on the political plane. Cromwell did not at that stage want the army to be accused of meddling in politics. On the very day that he rebuked Ireton in the Commons, he was signing the marriage settlement. On June 15th, 1646, Henry Ireton and Bridget Cromwell were married. Five days later as one of the commissioners for the surrender of Oxford (like Lambert), Ireton signed the capitulation that virtually brought the first civil war to its close.

It was in 1647 in the intervals between the first two civil wars that Ireton revealed his gifts as a political philosopher which mark him out as one of the ablest Englishmen of his time. Up till that date he had shown himself simply as a brave soldier, pushed forward by the patronage of Cromwell, but not nearly as capable a commander as his junior, John Lambert.

Nevertheless he had spent the seven most active years of his life in the army and he perfectly understood the point of view of the puritan soldiers. They had won a war; they wanted peace and quiet; but at the same time they demanded fair treatment. But when Ireton entered the House of Commons he found that a very different atmosphere prevailed; the majority of members there, since the Royalists had withdrawn, were Presbyterians. They regarded the New Model Army as an instrument to oblige the King to consent to a Presbyterian settlement. And now that the King was their prisoner they had no further use for the army which they said must be disbanded forthwith or be sent over to Ireland to restore order there. In the spring of 1647 Commissioners from Parliament had gone down to Saffron Walden in Essex to see General Fairfax and give him their commands. But the rank-and-file of the army did not intend to be shouldered aside with their arrears still unpaid. None of them would volunteer to serve in Ireland until they knew more about the terms they were being offered and they framed and sent petitions to the Commons saying as much. The leaders of the Commons were indignant at such impertinence. The petitioners, declared Denzil Holles, were 'enemies to the State and disturbers of the public peace'. Army officers, including Ireton, were roughly ordered to stop such petitioning and make the army do as it was told. Noisy scenes took place and Ireton, who defended the petitioners, was challenged to a duel by Holles. Ireton was of the opinion that a duel was not the right method of settling political differences, but was ready to make a gesture to satisfy honour. The Speaker had to rebuke these lively M.P.s and Ireton agreed to accompany Cromwell and other Generals to Saffron Walden to examine and report on the situation. Cromwell reported back to the House that the army would disband if their pay claims were met, but would not go to Ireland. In spite of this the Commons ordered that the regiments were to be separated from each other and the soldiers were then given the alternative of being at once demobilized or serving in Ireland. On May 27th Ireton, who had stayed with the army, wrote to Cromwell in London: 'I doubt the disobliging of so faithful an army will be repented of . . . It shall be my endeavour to keep things as right as I can, but how long I shall be able I know not. Unless you [i.e. the Commons] proceed upon better principles and more moderate terms . . . I cannot but imagine a storm.' Thenceforward Ireton devoted himself to drawing up a constitutional arrangement which would reconcile the King, the Parliament and the army. As a sanction Cornet Joyce was sent with a party of horse to lay hold of the person of Charles I. According to one of Cromwell's officers, Joyce received his orders from Ireton, who had entered into secret communication with the King some weeks earlier. Ireton met the King for the first time in the village of Childerley, 6 miles north-west of Cambridge, on June 7th.

Ireton's intention was to use the sword to impose a reasonable settlement on King and Parliament. On June 5th he drew up a 'Solemn Engagement of the Army' which stated that it would not disband nor divide without satisfaction and security. On June 10th he signed a letter to the Lord Mayor and Common Council of London explaining the aims of the army. Finally on June 14th was published a 'Representation of the Army', composed by Ireton with the help of Cromwell and Lambert in which more detailed notions of the future government of the kingdom were expounded. The scheme thus outlined and finally published in the document called 'The Heads of the Proposals' set out a written constitution for the nation which should make the King's power subservient to that of Parliament, but also reduce the power of Parliament itself by making it more amenable to the constituencies, and by establishing 'liberty of conscience' as a fundamental right. New Parliaments were to be elected every other year, to sit for at least 120 days, the constituencies were to be rearranged in a more equitable way, and 'rotten boroughs' were to be abolished. To ensure that there should be no renewal of the civil war the King was to be deprived of all control over the militia for ten years and Royalists were not to be eligible as Members of Parliament. As to the Church, the coercive powers and jurisdiction of the bishops were to be taken away and a less contentious method of paying the clergy than by tithe was to be found. Certain other reforms were promised and the soldiers' arrears of pay were to be provided. Such broadly were the terms for a constitutional agreement worked out by Ireton and Lambert in the summer of 1647. 'We do but take the King as a man with whom we have been at a difference,' Ireton explained. 'We propound terms of peace.'

Cromwell pressed for this settlement and even complained of Ireton's slowness in drawing it up. But the trouble lay not so much in the scheme itself, which contained every ingenuity, but in fulfilling it. Charles I was evasive. Ireton warned him bluntly: 'Sir, you have an intention to be arbitrator between the Parliament and us [the army] and we mean to be so between you and the Parliament.' Ireton found he had to contend not only with an attempt by the monarch to play off the army leaders, the English Presbyterians and the Scots against each other, but with a revolutionary and republican movement that was beginning to sweep the ranks of the New Model. On July 16th when he described his proposals to the General Council of War at Reading Ireton met with sharp opposition from the Agitators or agents who represented the private soldiers. Ireton pleaded for enlightened statesmanship. We must not act, he argued, as if our only object was to obtain power in our hands by force: 'to give the kingdom satisfaction is the thing we desire'. But the Agitators wanted to march on London at once and expel the Presbyterian leaders from Parliament.

As it happened, all Ireton's reasoned oratory, all his prudence and balancing, were vitiated by the play of events. While he, Lambert and Harrison were conferring with the Agitators about the 'Heads of the Proposals', the London mob invaded the House of Commons and compelled the Speaker to defy the army. Thereupon the army moved on the capital, the Presbyterian leaders in the Commons fled, and Ireton resumed his seat in the House, and exerted himself there as well as at army headquarters to obtain assent to his constitutional programme. In debates held at Putney, where the army had now stationed itself to overawe London, Ireton's political philosophy was displayed for the benefit of his contemporaries and of posterity.

Ireton was a conservative reformer who thought logically and powerfully about the nature of government. But he has been neglected by historians. There is only one biography of him and that no more than painstaking. His ideas have been discussed but incidentally by writers on political thought. In the twentieth century so far the Levellers and millenarian pamphleteers have monopolized the limelight. Only recently have more conservative thinkers been seriously examined, as, for example, in Mr. Peter Laslett's essay on Sir Robert Filmer. Even Thomas Hobbes, Ireton's contemporary who published his *Leviathan* in the year when Ireton died, has been undervalued as a political scientist, although his ideas are unfortunately widely prevalent in the world today. In their desperate sense of realism Hobbes and Ireton had much in common, but with one notable difference: Ireton accepted the importance of political freedom — as distinct from economic or religious freedom — which Hobbes's logic did not permit him to do. That freedom Ireton hoped to secure by balancing various parts of the constitution, the executive, the legislature and the electorate, against each other.

As Hobbes thought man's natural condition of life to be short, brutish and nasty, so Ireton remarked that mankind was corrupt and likely to remain so. Like Hobbes, too, Ireton was obsessed, as was understandable in the sixteen-forties, with a dread of anarchy. His opponents in the army debates, for their part, were concerned less over preserving the safety of the State than with protecting individual rights. They were suspicious of all government; he was aware that liberty might degenerate into licence. When Ireton reminded the representatives of the rank-and-file that they had already engaged by the declarations which he had drawn up in their name to maintain the framework of the existing constitution, though amending it radically, they retorted that unjust engagements need not be kept. Ireton was shocked. The notion that 'no engagement is binding further than that he [who makes it] thinks it just or no' cut at the very root of civilized society. 'I account that the great foundation of justice,' he said, 'that we should keep covenant one with another'; and again: 'any man that makes a bargain and does find afterwards 'tis for the worse, yet is bound to stand by it'. The rule of doing to another as he would be done by, he added, was 'the only rule of justice'. 'Covenants freely made, freely entered into must be kept with one another. Take that away and I do not know what ground there is for anything you can call any man's right.'

Such was Ireton's common-sense view of the *basis* of the State; human justice, in his opinion, had nothing to do with either 'natural rights' or Biblical precepts. The *purpose* of the State, he considered, was to preserve peace and defend property. He therefore believed in a property franchise, since he thought that representation should be founded on the possession of a stake in the country and not on the assumption that all men are equals. That was why he repudiated the democracy of the Levellers. If by the 'right of nature' every man might vote, he said, 'by the same right of nature, he hath the same equal right in any goods he sees — meat, drink, and clothes — to take and use them for his sustenance'. By introducing manhood suffrage, 'we shall plainly go to take away all property and interest that any man hath either in land by inheritance, or in estate by possession, or anything else . . .' Democracy, he argued, would lead to communism in goods and anarchy in government.

Ireton was also opposed to another demand of the Levellers — that magistrates should be forbidden to concern themselves with matters of religion. For, he argued, if any such general ruling were made, that would prevent justices from maintaining order wherever a breach of the peace was committed in the name of religion. Just as equality in the franchise would result in an attack on property, so unqualified freedom of conscience for the individual believer would mean the destruction of order.

As with Hobbes, granted Ireton's premises, it was difficult to gainsay his conclusions. The principal difficulty about his theory is that it permits little room for change. If government and parliament are thought about in terms of the existing distribution of property and if a covenant once entered into must be kept, then how is political improvement possible? One reply no doubt is that while inflexibility is the weakness of all written constitutions it can be surmounted. Another is that Ireton was not a pure theorist; he was a practical man trying to solve a particular problem. Though he was a provocative debater and first class at exposing the faults in the arguments of his critics, Ireton, like Cromwell, was anxious to compromise. He was ready to extend the franchise, although he thought that its traditional limitation to the forty-shilling freeholder went far enough. 'All the main thing that I speak for,' he explained in the course of the Putney debates, is 'because I would have an eye for property.' In the later debates at Whitehall on the eve of the King's execution he showed that he was willing to warn magistrates against interfering with Christian worship provided that the public peace were not endangered. Nor did Ireton quibble over forms of government. He would have agreed with Cromwell that he was not 'glued' nor 'wedded' to any one form. Indeed it would be unwise when we reread these constitutional debates of 1647, in which Ireton and the Levellers took part, to distinguish too boisterously between the outlook of Ireton and of Cromwell. We must remember that Cromwell was taking the chair and that he wanted to promote an understanding so as to preserve unity in the army. Ireton, on the other hand, was the spokesman of the general officers, including Lambert, who had drawn up the 'Heads of the Proposals'. Yet, as Professor Woodhouse has written: 'Ireton, who was probably the ablest political thinker that the revolution produced, sympathized with many of the Levellers' pleas for practical reforms.' All he contended against was an extreme individualism that would undermine the fabric of the State.

On the immediate question in the summer of 1647 whether they were willing to preserve the monarchy and the House of Lords Ireton felt that he was committed. Like Cromwell, he defended these two institutions, though he proposed that the King's veto should be abolished for at least ten years and that the Commons should be allowed if necessary to pass legislation without the concurrence of the Upper House. These proposals, more even than his condemnation of universal suffrage, brought on him the wrath of the Levellers. He was described as 'the cunningest of the Machiavellians', as a man who sold himself to the King in return for promises of rewards and honours. But the truth was the opposite. Ireton had toiled to produce a constitutional settlement on which all parties could agree. But once he discovered that the King was insincere, he had no wish to maintain existing institutions for their own sake. In December of 1648 he was sedulous in bringing the King up for trial. He assented to the idea of a one-chamber legislature. After Charles I had been executed, he was appointed to various committees to defend the proceedings of Parliament and expatiate on the 'benefits redounding to the people of the nation' by the establishment of a Republic.

The 'people of the nation' were not lightly convinced. The Levellers with whom Ireton had argued in 1647 and 1648 'in one long and tedious tug' reckoned that they had been betrayed by him. There was some substance in their case, for Ireton appears to have accepted in principle their constitution known as the second 'Agreement of the People' on the eve of the King's execution, but the new Commonwealth was oligarchic in character. John Lilburne, the Leveller leader, demanded that Ireton should be cashiered, and five troopers, who had been sentenced for mutiny in March 1649, asserted that Ireton, with Cromwell and Harrison, now ruled the Council of Officers, and the Council of Officers ruled the State. That was an exaggeration; indeed neither Ireton nor Harrison was a member of the Council of State.

In June 1649 Cromwell was appointed Lord Lieutenant and Commander-in-Chief in Ireland and Ireton was originally selected to be his second in command, but later that position, which carried with it the rank of Lieutenant-General of the Horse, was conferred on Colonel Michael Jones, an Irish Protestant who had been Governor of Dublin and defeated the twelfth Earl of Ormonde, the Royalist Lord Lieutenant, at the battle of Rathmines before Cromwell and Ireton arrived. But early in the campaign Ireton was promoted Major-General.

On August 15th Ireton with the larger part of the expeditionary army embarked at Milford Haven to take part in the Irish campaign. Two days before Cromwell had sailed for Dublin to meet Michael Jones. It seems that Ireton had intended to sail to Munster, but he was unable to land there and joined Cromwell in Dublin on August 23rd. With Cromwell he fought at the sieges of Drogheda and Wexford, where the whole garrisons were slaughtered after the walls had been breached. The terror inspired by those sieges, the disunity of the enemy, the discipline of the Parliamentary army, which was maintained in spite of medical casualties and some setbacks, and the supremacy of the navy in close support meant that when Cromwell left Ireland in May of the following year no large Irish or Royalist army was left in the field and only Connaught and a few sizeable towns had still to be subdued.

At the end of 1649 Ireton was appointed President of Munster by Parliament and after he had bade what proved to be his last farewell to his father-in-law at Youghal on May 26th, 1650, when Cromwell was recalled to England on account of the threat from Scotland, he became Deputy to the Lord Lieutenant and acting Commander-in-Chief.

Cromwell had left the enemies of the English Commonwealth in Ireland shattered. The Earl of Ormonde was unpopular with the Irish because he was not a Roman Catholic; and before the end of 1650 he left the country, together with some of his best officers, after handing over his responsibilities to Lord Clanricarde, who was a Catholic. But the Irish, aware that King Charles II had now sold himself to the Scottish Presbyterians, cooled from their loyal fervour. They clung instead to the consolations of their religion and their hopes of independence. The Ulster Catholics, who had the only useful army left, appointed a bishop to command them who promptly led them to destruction at the hands of Sir Charles Coote (who had formerly been President of Connaught under Charles I) in the battle of Scarriffhollis on June 21st. The remainder placed their trust in the Almighty. So, incidentally, did Ireton; but he had also guns and reinforcements. But he was in no hurry to conclude the campaign by siege warfare and in fact relied at first less on the military art than on Irish treachery. After he had taken Waterford on August 6th he vainly summoned Limerick and Athlone. Owing to the lateness of the season he had to abandon both.

During the winter of 1650-51 Ireton was joined at Waterford by his wife, who later returned to England, and by Lieutenant-General Ludlow who came to take up his appointment as second in command. Sir John Reynolds was made Commissary-General of Horse. Reynolds, a Cambridgeshire man who was popular with the troops, had received his colonelcy in 1648 and been in Ireland since July 1649, fighting with Michael Jones at Rathmines. Roger Boyle, Lord Broghil, an Irish Protestant Royalist (being a son of the first Earl of Cork), who had changed sides on the persuasion of Cromwell, was annoyed that he had not been given Ludlow's post, but was soothed with the office of Lieutenant-General of the Ordnance, though Ireton is believed to have distrusted him. The other Parliamentary Commissioners landed along with Ludlow and before the campaigning season opened, arrangements were completed for the civil administration. Broadly the Commissioners carried on Cromwell's policy, which was to confine the native Irish to the remoter parts of the island and make ready to colonize the strategic Irish towns with English settlers of Protestant faith. Thus, after the surrender of Waterford, Ireton had warned the inhabitants that they might be ordered to leave their homes for ever at three months' notice.

On May 10th, 1651, Ireton convened a Council of War at Clonmel in Munster. It was decided to attack the towns guarding the Shannon (Limerick, Athlone, Killaloe and Portumna) so as to advance to the final conquest of the country by subjugating Connaught, the last centre of resistance. Sir Charles Coote and Commissary-General Reynolds, with some 4000 men, were ordered into Connaught from Ulster, while Ireton himself and Ludlow attempted to surround and capture Limerick. After feinting further up the River Shannon Ireton managed to force a crossing by boats, though the way from the English camp to the projected crossing was beset by bogs, which had to be covered with hurdles and by timber to bear the gun carriages. However, the enemy were intimidated by the English artillery posted on the far bank from them and obliged to fall back and permit Ireton's men to establish themselves on the north side of Limerick. At the same time Coote succeeded in pushing round the Irish under Clanricarde and later occupied Athlone and Portumna. Delighted with these successes, Ireton ordered a day of thanksgiving, attributing the fright or surprise of the foe to the active intervention of God. But when on June 23rd Ireton tried to seize the upper end of King's Island on which the city of Limerick stands his amphibious assault was beaten off. June 24th therefore was assigned as a day of humiliation so as to 'bewail the sins of the army which might occasion the Lord's displeasure against us'. When on July 15th Ireton recounted the defeat to the Speaker he wrote:

> God hath taught us also (in dreadful language) who it was that gave us passage over this river [the Shannon] by his outstretched arm, and taught us how to value such a mercy and reproved our understandings and unmindfulness of it.

Ireton now aimed at starving the recalcitrant city of Limerick into surrender. Meanwhile he ordered Ludlow to go in support of Coote and in his absence was himself nearly killed in an unexpected sally by the Limerick garrison, which remained defiant, hoping to survive another winter. The soldiers inside the walls boasted that while the English 'laboured to beat us out with bomb-shells . . . they would beat them away with snow balls'. But Limerick was in a desperate condition, for not only were supplies scarce but the plague was spreading. Ireton would not allow civilians to leave the town partly because he did not wish the garrison to be relieved of useless mouths and partly because he feared lest they brought contagion to his own men. Hence he gave notice that any who attempted to escape and were caught should be executed. Three were hanged as examples, including a girl, whose father vainly offered to redeem her life with his own, and the rest whipped back into the town. A gibbet was also erected within sight of the walls by way of warning. Yet it was not until Ireton landed guns from his ships and brought up batteries from other parts of Ireland that the brave defenders at last surrendered on October 27th. Military historians are of the opinion that Ireton might have thought of deploying his guns earlier.

The truth was that Ireton was not a very good General. There is little doubt that a Cromwell or a Marlborough — or even a Ludlow or a Deane — would have completed the Irish campaign sooner. But he was a tireless, conscientious and, according to his lights, godly administrator. On more than one occasion he punished subordinate officers for killing enemy soldiers after they had surrendered on an assurance of mercy. Colonel Daniel Axtell was deprived of his command and ordered back to England for this crime, though it appears that he was not directly responsible. On another occasion Ludlow described Ireton as 'much troubled' because a boatload of Irish were slaughtered on the Shannon. Does all this imply that Ireton in his heart disapproved of Cromwell's conduct at Drogheda and Wexford? Certainly Ireton strove to be scrupulous in obeying the rules of war. After the fall of Limerick a number of prisoners excepted from mercy by the articles of capitulation were tried for their lives. Among them was the

Governor, Colonel Hugh O'Neill. Ireton at first thought that he ought to be executed, but deferred to the recommendations to clemency put forward by the other members of the Court. Ludlow, who was there, significantly observes that Ireton 'was now entirely freed from his former manner of adhering to his own opinion, which had been observed to be his greatest infirmity'.

On November 5th Ireton ordered a day of thanksgiving for the taking of Limerick. Though it was so late in the year he then sent Lieutenant-General Ludlow with a party of horse into County Clare on the far side of the Shannon to reduce the towns in that area. Ireton, however, would not impose on another any duty that he would not undertake himself and so shortly afterwards he himself joined his Lieutenant-General there. While the two Generals were in Clare they received a visit from Lady Honoria O'Brien — 'a lady that went for a maid though but few believed it' — who was accused of protecting the goods and cattle of the Royalists while enjoying a safeguard from Ireton. When she was charged by the Lord Deputy with this offence she burst into tears and begged forgiveness. Then she sought Ludlow's intercession, which she obtained. Ireton told Ludlow: 'As much a cynic as I am, the tears of this woman moved me.' Even puritans had their moments.

In Clare both Ludlow and Ireton were taken ill, Ireton catching cold owing to the heavy rain, snow and high wind that chilled the county. Ireton was indeed a martyr to his tasks. Ludlow, who knew him well, wrote of him in retrospect that 'he was so diligent in the public service and so careless of every thing that belonged to him, that he never regarded what clothes or food he used, what hour he went to rest or what horse he mounted'. Nor would he accept any reward. After the battle of Worcester Parliament offered to settle £2000 a year in land upon him, but he refused it saying 'he should be more contented to see them doing the service of the nation than so liberal in disposing of the public treasure'. When that bleak November he was taken ill he declined to go to bed until after he had sat in a court martial on an English officer 'who was accused of some violence done to the Irish'. He ordered that the officer be cashiered, although he was a useful man. Soon the Lord Deputy was laid low with fever, but though he was let blood, he did not cease working, arranging for the garrisons, and planning the winter quarters of his army. On November 26th he expired. In Dublin when the news was heard it was noted by the English reporter there that 'we see neither piety, wisdom, valour nor worldly greatness are able to protect a man from the sudden stroke of death and destiny'. He was only forty. His remains were taken to London and buried in Westminster Abbey after a spectacular ceremony, the 'vain pomp' of which was said to have been 'very offensive' to many puritans. Undoubtedly he himself would have thought such adulation uncalled for, and might, as Ludlow said, 'have preferred to find a grave for his body where his soul left it' in that unhappy alien land where, far from his wife and children, he killed himself by overwork.

The affinity between Ireton and his father-in-law was a spiritual and intellectual one. Ireton's grave puritanism — which made him, for example, regard it as an offence to be punished by demotion if one of his officers or soldiers married an Irish girl 'in pursuit of carnal lust' — appealed to Oliver Cromwell. Hence he pushed him forward by favouritism, but, if we may judge by results, it was scarcely an unjustified favouritism. Yet Ireton was not cut out to be a soldier, and though highly conscientious as an administrator, his very conscientiousness undermined his powers of decision. He was a thinker who, like not a few English thinkers, forced himself to become a man of action.

It has often been said that Ireton's translucent intellect made him Cromwell's mentor in political questions. 'None', wrote Bulstrode Whitelocke who served on the Republican Council of State, 'could prevail so much nor order him so far as Ireton could.' Clarendon wrote that he 'was often thought by his obstinacy to prevail over Cromwell and to extort his concurrence contrary to his inclinations'. Another contemporary maintained that 'Cromwell only shot the bolts that were hammered in Ireton's forge.' From all this it has been further deduced that had Ireton lived longer Cromwell would never have dismissed the Protectorate Parliaments, experimented with his Major-Generals, or been tempted by the plan to become King himself. But that is pure speculation. We know from the Putney debates that they sometimes differed, but only on points of emphasis. As we have seen, Ireton was eclectic in his choice of forms of government so long as they protected property and secured order. There is no solid reason to suppose that he would have disapproved of Cromwell's constitutional experiments.

There were naturally differences between the two men. Cromwell, having long been a Member of Parliament, was perhaps slower than Ireton to abandon all attempts at compromise with the old order. Ireton, however obstinate intellectually, was the more merciful of the two, never allowing his sense of duty to be deflected by anger. And though it would be wrong to assume that the course of English history would have been materially changed if Ireton had survived the snowstorms of County Clare, his death was the severest blow Cromwell was to suffer among all the Generals he lost or was yet to lose.

BIBLIOGRAPHY TO CHAPTER IV

A biography of Henry Ireton by R. W. Ramsey was published in 1949. For Ireton's youth and friends in Nottinghamshire see A. C. Wood, *Nottinghamshire in the Civil War* (1937) and *Memoirs of the Life of Colonel Hutchinson* (ed. Firth, 1906). Reports of the debates in which Ireton took part are in the *Clarke Papers*, vol. I (ed. Firth, 1891), and A. S. P. Woodhouse, *Puritans and Liberty* (1938). Discussions of Ireton as a political thinker are in Woodhouse's introduction and Gooch and Laski, *The History of English Democratic Ideas in the Seventeenth Century* (1927). For Ireton in Ireland see Ludlow's *Memoirs*; J. T. Gilbert, *A Contemporary History of Affairs in Ireland* (1880); and R. Bagwell, *Ireland under the Stuarts* (1916). Contemporary reports from Ireland and some of Ireton's letters are to be found in *Mercurius Politicus*, *Perfect Diurnall*, *Several Proceedings*, etc., which also include newsletters describing Ireton's last days. The officer who stated that Ireton gave Joyce the order to seize the King was Major Huntingdon, *Sundry Reasons* (1648).

CHAPTER V

MAJOR-GENERAL THOMAS HARRISON AND THE DISSOLUTION OF THE RUMP PARLIAMENT

Thomas Harrison was born in 1616 and died in 1660

AFTER Major-General Ireton had taken the surrender of Limerick, Lieutenant-General Monk had stormed Dundee, and Cromwell's other Generals had completed the 'mopping up' operations to end the Worcester campaign, the English Republic seemed at last to be safe from all its enemies. But the Rump Parliament had still to reconstruct the nation under a constitution that would endure. Understandably enough, there was fear among the politicians at Westminster, as after Caesar's return from Gaul and later Napoleon's return from Egypt, that the victorious Commander-in-Chief would now attempt to become a dictator.

But just as Ireton in Ireland and Monk in Scotland had shaped their policies solely in the light of military needs, so Cromwell at first conducted himself simply as a soldier who modestly received his plaudits on his return to the capital. He was not then thinking of grasping power, but he and his Generals were anxious to promote a settlement. They considered it was time that Parliament should be dissolved and a new one chosen 'to reap the fruit of all the blood and treasure that had been spent'. Originally it was expected that the constituencies would forthwith be remodelled and a different franchise introduced. These were regarded among the Independents in the army as first steps towards other reforms in Church and State that should herald the New Jerusalem for which many had fought and some had died. On the other hand, the majority of the Members of Parliament were sceptical about how an electorate, however constituted, was likely to behave after war and revolution, and preferred to devise some scheme which would at least enable them to retain their own places in the government of the country.

Thirdly, a movement was forming amongst those Christians who believed that the destruction of the monarchy presaged the return of the Son of God to earth, to impose a government by saintly men elected by the churches rather than suffer the rule of sinners who might find their way into Westminster under a system of free elections. Six weeks after the battle of Worcester a pamphlet entitled *A Model of a New Representative* was published advocating their point of view.

On November 14th, 1651, the Rump Parliament determined by a majority of four votes to fix a date for its own dissolution, but four days afterwards it resolved that elections were not to be held for another three years, that is to say until November 1654. This was hardly calculated to gratify any of the parties in the army. Nor was a decision reached by Parliament on the following day to omit two of Cromwell's leading Generals, Harrison and Lambert, from membership of the annually elected Council of State. A further blow was aimed at Cromwell himself with a vote on November 28th that there should be no permanent chairman of the Council of State but that a new chairman should be elected every month. The dissatisfaction of Cromwell's officers with these affronts was expressed when on December 10th Cromwell summoned them to attend a meeting, to which he also invited a number of lawyers, at the Speaker's house to talk about the future government of the country. At that meeting (from which Lambert was absent as he had been sent back to Scotland) Major-General Harrison opened the discussion by saying that they had gathered to consider 'a settlement both of our civil and spiritual liberties . . . so that the mercies which the Lord hath given to us may not be cast away'. The lawyers wanted to restore some form of monarchy, possibly with King Charles I's youngest son, the Duke of Gloucester, as the titular king. But the officers present, especially Harrison and Cromwell's relatives, John Desborough and Edward Whalley, were opposed to any such a solution. They all stood four-square for a Republic, but not the Republic ruled by the existing Rump Parliament and circumscribed Council of State. From the date when the Rump chose to prolong its life for another three years and the time of the meeting at the Speaker's house,

MAJOR-GENERAL
PHILLIP SKIPPON

MAJOR-GENERAL
JOHN DESBOROUGH

MAJOR-GENERAL
THOMAS HARRISON

LIEUTENANT-GENERAL
EDMUND LUDLOW

Cromwell's Generals began to contemplate the overthrow of the Rump so that they might create a satisfactory system in its place. Among those whose opinions on the subject were the most clearly defined was Major-General Harrison. We shall now therefore look more closely at his record and character.

Thomas Harrison was born in Newcastle-under-Lyme in the summer of 1616 and was the son of a butcher in that town who was four times elected mayor. He received an inferior education to that of Cromwell, Ireton or Lambert. After leaving his school (presumably the local grammar school) he was apprenticed clerk to an attorney in Clifford's Inn where, together with some of the young men reading for the Bar in the Inns of Court (such as Charles Fleetwood and Edmund Ludlow, later both to be Lieutenant-Generals), he enlisted in Essex's lifeguard in 1642. Previously these young men had undergone military training in the Artillery Ground and although when they obtained their baptism of fire at Powick Bridge they retreated in disorder, they fought gallantly enough at Edgehill. At this battle Harrison may have met Cromwell for the first time.

When Fleetwood formed a cavalry regiment in Manchester's army in 1644, it was natural that he should appoint his friend from the Inns of Court as one of his captains, and by the time of the battle of Marston Moor Harrison had been promoted major in the regiment, which became celebrated for its Christian soldiers. 'Looke on Col. Flettwoods regiment,' exclaimed a contemporary critic, 'with his Major Harreson, what a cluster of preaching offecers and troopers there is.' At Naseby Fleetwood's regiment fought under Ireton on the left wing and Harrison was with Ireton when he carried out his reconnaissance before the battle. Part of Fleetwood's regiment with Harrison in command was employed in a force detached under Cromwell to reduce Royalist fortresses in Hampshire and Wiltshire during 1645. Before that at the battle of Langport Harrison (according to the Reverend Richard Baxter) distinguished himself 'with a loud voice breaking forth in to the praise of God with fluent expression, as though he had been in a rapture'. In 1646 he was elected M.P. for Wendover and married Katherine, the daughter of a London woollen draper, named Ralph Harrison.

After sitting on a committee to deal with the question of the army's arrears of pay, Harrison sailed to Dublin in February 1647, but within three months he was back in England taking part in the army debates. In June 1647 Fairfax appointed him colonel of a regiment of horse that had served in the New Model under the command of Colonel James Sheffield, a son of the first Earl of Mulgrave. Sheffield was on the side of Parliament in its quarrel with the army during 1647; but his regiment objected violently to his views and 'dismounted their dissenting officers and seized their horses and arms'. In Harrison they found a colonel more to their taste. Indeed in the army debates that November Harrison showed that he wanted to prosecute the King as a 'man of blood', abolish the House of Lords, and substitute a government of Saints, and was supported in his argument by the Fifth Monarchist, Colonel Nathaniel Rich, and by Colonel Thomas Rainborough, an extremist who was killed during the second civil war; Rainborough's brother, William, was the major in Harrison's regiment. Something of the flavour of Harrison's arguments in the debates of this time may be seen by this extract from a later speech in a discussion on 'The Agreement of the People':

> The Word of God (he then said) doth take notice that the powers of this world shall be given into the hands of the Lord and His Saints; that this is the day, God's own day, wherein he is coming forth in glory in the world, and he doth put forth Himself very much by His people, and He says in that day wherein He will thresh the mountains he will make use of Jacob as that threshing instrument . . . and He will work on us so far that we are to be made able in wisdom and power to carry through things in a way extraordinary, that the works of men shall be answerable to His works.

And the Lord and His Saints were not to be interfered with: earlier Harrison had argued, as against Ireton, that magistrates should have no right to impose restrictions over the exercise of religion.

If Harrison stood to the left of the general officers in his political opinions, his regiment was even more radical than he was. When it became obvious in the autumn of 1647 that

Fairfax and Cromwell were not going immediately to compel the King and Parliament to accept the Levellers' programme, Harrison's regiment again mutinied. Although we have no details, we may assume that it was the sympathetic attitude of their colonel which induced the troopers to put a stop to their demonstrations and revert to discipline.

In May of the following year Harrison's regiment was ordered north to fight in the second civil war by opposing the invasion of the Scots led by the first Duke of Hamilton. Major-General Lambert, who was in command in the north before Cromwell arrived, employed Harrison's regiment as part of his rearguard when he was obliged to withdraw before the advance of the Scots, whose numbers were superior to his. On July 17th the regiment was surprised by a night attack near Appleby in Westmorland. Harrison successfully counter-charged the enemy; but in doing so he received three wounds and was therefore unable to take any further part in the campaign. In November, however, he had sufficiently recovered to attend meetings of the council of officers at Windsor and in December Cromwell and Ireton entrusted him with command of the cavalry guard that conducted King Charles I from Hurst Castle in Hampshire to Windsor and afterwards from Windsor to London: he had given proof that he would be strict in that duty.

The King had heard that the army intended to murder him and credited rumours that Harrison was the officer who was going to do it. But when he saw Colonel Harrison he was reassured, for he saw that 'he looked like a soldier and his aspect was good . . . and that having some judgment in faces, if he had observed him so well before, he should not have harboured that ill opinion of him'. But although Harrison was not a murderer, he held out to the King no prospect that he would escape punishment. 'The law', he told him when they supped together, 'was equally obliging to great and small, and justice had no respect to persons.' Indeed after much prayer and heart-searching he was convinced that it was the will of the Lord that Charles I should die. He closely questioned Mrs. Elizabeth Poole of Abingdon who obligingly visited the Army Council in December 1648 to advise the officers against executing the King, but he evidently concluded that his own visions or inspirations were better founded than hers. 'No man indeed,' wrote Sir Charles Firth, 'was personally more responsible for the trial and execution of the King.' And Harrison saw no need to conceal his part. What they did, he proclaimed after the restoration of Charles II, 'we did not in a corner' but in the light of day for every man to see. Finally he was ordered to take care that there should be no demonstration when the body of the martyred King was buried.

Soon after the Commonwealth had been set up Thomas Harrison was made a Master of Arts by the University of Oxford for helping Cromwell to suppress the Leveller mutinies and then in July 1649 General Fairfax sent him to take charge of South Wales and its neighbouring counties while Cromwell's expeditionary army was being embarked for Ireland. In an Act of February 22nd, 1650, his name appeared first among a large number of commissioners who were instructed to appoint preachers to propagate the Gospel in Wales and if necessary to discharge any ministers who were failing to do so properly. The task of these commissioners was not simple, as Wales was then among the least puritan and most Royalist quarters of the country. However, Harrison and Colonel Philip Jones, supported by such flaming preachers as Vavasour Powell went energetically about the business and soon it was said that 'the gospel is run over the mountains between Brecknockshire and Monmouthshire as a fire in the thatch'. Harrison (as we have already noted) left Wales to take command in London when Cromwell rode into Scotland in 1650.

A scholar who specialized in Harrison's career in Wales has argued that we do wrong to exaggerate Harrison's fanaticism in his younger days and invokes in his support a statement by the great historian, S. R. Gardiner, that it was not until 1653 when Harrison was thirty-seven that he 'drifted into the ranks of the Fifth Monarchy Men', who regarded the Second Coming of Christ as imminent and all human conduct subject to that event. Of course it is perfectly true that several of Cromwell's Generals — for example, Ireton and Fleetwood — used strong biblical language to sustain them in the line of duty. They were none the worse, and some would say they were the better, soldiers for that. But a study of such letters and speeches of Harrison as have survived leads to the conclusion that he was indeed a God-drunk man, the most consciously religious of all Cromwell's Generals, that even more than Cromwell himself he was under the constant and indeed hourly impress of being guided in all his actions by an omnipotent power that was near to him and that he felt was coming nearer still. Both in the meetings of the Council of the Army in 1647 and during his sojourn in Wales in 1650 he was intimately associated with avowed Fifth Monarchy men like Rich and Powell. And though the evidence is not clear about when he actually joined that sect, his outlook does not in fact seem to have undergone any fundamental change between the end of the civil wars and the year 1653.

It is not difficult to understand the attraction which Thomas Harrison for a long time exerted over Oliver Cromwell. He did not enjoy the intellectual equipment of Ireton or the military brilliance of Lambert. Yet he had qualities that appealed both to the practical and to the mystical side of Cromwell's nature. In the first place, Harrison was a thoroughly reliable officer. Clarendon noted that 'there were few men with whom Cromwell more communicated, or upon whom he more depended for the conduct of anything committed to him'. But he was more than a competent subordinate. He had a fervid personality and an inexhaustible stock of Scriptural phrases. He was outspoken in his convictions of providential guidance. Roger Williams, an able puritan, described him as 'a very gallant, deserving, heavenly man, but most high flown for the kingdom of saints'. His name is said to have been interpreted as meaning 'a clear burning lamp of the mountain of battle' and that interpretation suited his character well. Like Cromwell Harrison was convinced that the God of Battles intended their victories for a purpose. After the battle of Worcester Cromwell had written to the Speaker in Parliament:

> I am bold humbly to beg that all thoughts may tend to the promoting of His honour who hath wrought so great a salvation... and that justice and righteousness, mercy and truth may flow from you, as a thankful return to our Gracious God....

Three days afterwards Harrison also wrote to the Speaker:

> The Lord grant the parliament . . . may improve this mercy . . . according to the will of God, in establishing the ways of righteousness and justice, yet more relieving the oppressed, and opening a wider door to the publishing the everlasting Gospel of our only Lord and Saviour, who is worthy to be loved, honoured, exalted, and admired by all His people, and will be so through the Spirit that He will give them and all his enemies shall be made his footstool.

Thus they were then men very much of one mind.

One curious facet of Harrison's character was his love of conspicuous clothing. Mrs. Hutchinson has a story that he persuaded her husband and others to come to the House of Commons on one occasion in plain black suits, but then himself appeared 'in a scarlet coat and cloak, both laden with gold and silver lace, and the coat so covered with clinquant [tinsel] that one scarcely could discern the ground'. This is confirmed in Sir Thomas Herbert's memoirs (Herbert was with the King when Harrison was his guard). 'The captain', says Herbert, 'was gallantly mounted and armed; a velvet montero [peaked cap] was on his head, a new buff coat upon his back and a crimson scarf about his waist richly fringed.'

By 1651 Harrison was said to have been a wealthy man, having received the lucrative appointment of Lieutenant of the Ordnance, and could afford to indulge his taste for gay clothes. It was his only known weakness, for his heart was not in earthly things. According to one of his biographers, 'having worked his will in Wales, he was anxious to set up the rule of the Saints upon earth in London'. Such was the General who, after the death of Henry Ireton, exerted a profound influence on Oliver Cromwell.

During the first half of 1652 the movement initiated by Cromwell the previous December and seconded by Harrison to induce Parliament to work out a constitutional settlement was in abeyance, and Cromwell and his Generals concentrated on military affairs. A number of Commissioners had been sent to Scotland to restore order and work for union, including Major-General Lambert and Major-General Deane, and on

January 30th Lambert was appointed by Parliament as Lord Deputy and Commander-in-Chief in Ireland to take the place of the dead Ireton. Lieutenant-General Ludlow, who had been acting as Commander-in-Chief since the end of November must have had hopes of the succession, and the acid remarks he made in his memoirs about Cromwell and Lambert may have been induced by his failure to obtain it. Lambert was also to be disappointed. In February he returned from Scotland to London to prepare for his new appointment and spent a large sum of money in buying the equipment he thought he needed. But on May 19th Parliament changed its mind. It abolished the post of Lord Lieutenant of Ireland, held by Cromwell, and with it vanished the well-paid office of Lord Deputy. Cromwell was retained simply as Commander-in-Chief of Ireland, as well as of England and Scotland, and the existing Commissioners were left in charge of civil affairs.

There is no evidence that Cromwell himself engineered the decision which blighted Lambert's fortunes. On the contrary, to abolish these posts was to insult the General himself, though no doubt Parliament's aim was to save money when expenses were severe. The proposal to reverse the previous vote was carried only by a narrow majority and, significantly, Harrison was one of the Tellers against it. Lambert afterwards averred that Cromwell had assured him that 'nothing troubled him more than to see honest John Lambert so ungratefully treated' and to compensate him Cromwell gave up the balance of pay due to him as Lord Lieutenant — some £2000 — to reimburse the Major-General for the money he had wasted. Thus far from alienating Lambert the incident drew the two men closer together.

Lieutenant-General Charles Fleetwood was made acting Commander-in-Chief in Ireland under Cromwell on July 9th. Fleetwood, as we have seen, had long been one of Cromwell's most trusted Generals, having been his second in command at the battle of Worcester. But now their relationship was strengthened by another tie. Mrs. Hutchinson relates a story, which may or may not have been exact, that Mrs. Lambert, like her husband, was upset by his failure to obtain the post of Lord Deputy in succession to Ireton and wreaked her wrath, somewhat gratuitously, on Ireton's widow, Bridget, who was Cromwell's daughter. A scene is said to have taken place in St. James's Park which not only gave offence to Cromwell but also caused Fleetwood to extend his sympathy to the young widow. Thence, Mrs. Hutchinson concluded, blossomed romance. Be that as it may, on June 8th, 1652, Charles Fleetwood and Bridget Ireton were married.

Fleetwood arrived in Ireland in September to take over his command and settled in Dublin with his family in November. Meanwhile the war between England and the United Netherlands had started and Lieutenant-General George Monk was withdrawn from Scotland to serve at sea. Colonel Robert Lilburne was left in charge in Scotland, but scarcely appears to have been equal to the task, for letters from junior officers in Scotland complained about disturbances breaking out in the Highlands and suggested that either Lambert or Monk ought to have been kept there. At one time (in April 1653) it was proposed that Lambert should go back to Scotland for six months, but Lambert, like Harrison, remained with Cromwell in London; and it was not in fact until April 1654, after Cromwell had become Lord Protector, that Monk returned to Scotland armed with wide powers. Meanwhile the very fact of the Anglo-Dutch War, which Cromwell, Harrison and Lambert all disrelished, gave a fresh impulse to the movement among the army leaders that had died down at the beginning of the year to press the Rump Parliament to dissolve itself and introduce a new form of government in its place.

For nine months the army malcontents had waited with a good deal of patience to see if anything concrete would come from the deliberations at Westminster. Parliament had indeed gone so far as to resolve itself into a Grand Committee to discuss the question of a 'new representative'. But the debate stuck and now councils of officers began to meet again regularly in London to air the many grievances of the army against the politicians. On August 13th, 1652, a petition was presented to Parliament by Cromwell's cousin, Commissary-General Edward Whalley, supported by five other officers (Barkstead, Worsley, Goffe, Hacker and Okey) advocating an ambitious programme of reforms, though it omitted, at Cromwell's own request, a specific demand for the immediate dissolution of Parliament. Lambert, but not Cromwell, was among the signatories to the petition. Once again, as in 1647, Cromwell himself was trying to mediate between Parliament and the army. But his forceful lieutenants, Lambert and Harrison, were each for his own reasons out of temper with the Rump and eager to petition with their swords in their hands as the best means of inciting progress.

Both Cromwell and Harrison, being M.P.s, were named members of the large committee appointed by Parliament to consider General Whalley's petition, and prolonged discussions ensued. On September 14th this committee recommended that in order to hurry along the preparation of a bill to arrange for elections a small select committee should be set up in place of the Grand Committee that had hitherto literally sat on the matter. On January 6th Parliament acquiesced to the extent of putting Harrison (who was now again a member of the Council of State) in charge of the Bill in place of the civilian, Sir Henry Vane. But the Generals were now tiring of committees, and discontent was infecting the entire army. The council of officers began to meet every day during January 1653, and somewhere about this time Cromwell told Quarter-Master Vernon that 'he was pushed on by two parties to do that, the consideration of the issue whereof made his hair to stand on end'.

> One of these [he continued] is headed by Major-General Lambert, who in revenge of that injury the Parliament did him, in not permitting him to go into Ireland with a character and conditions suitable to his merit, will be contented with nothing less than a dissolution. Of the other Major-General Harrison is the chief, who is an honest man, and aims at good things, yet from the impatience of his spirit will not wait the Lord's leisure, but hurries me on to that [i.e. the forcible dissolution of Parliament] which he and all honest men will have cause to repent.

Yet throughout the late winter and early spring Cromwell still held his hand. But the pressure upon him was extreme. Thomas Harrison had become the acknowledged leader of the section of the army that was calling for action. He had convinced himself that the majority of the Members of Parliament were corrupt sinners. Two years earlier he had accused a member, Lord Howard of Escrick, of taking bribes from the Royalists and had obtained his expulsion from the House. Colonel Rich and Colonel Pride supported Harrison with enthusiasm; and Lambert agreed with him. It was widely reported in London that if Cromwell refused to move soon, Harrison intended to deprive him of his command, exerting his influence in Wales to raise a force against him: on March 25th there was a rumour that 'a plot of Harrison's had been discovered in North Wales'. Harrison's friend the Reverend Vavasour Powell appeared in the capital and exercised his gifts as a revivalist to stir up the mob. Yet Harrison and Powell had enemies in Wales. Colonel Edward Freeman, M.P. for Hereford, promoted a petition from South Wales and Monmouthshire, which was said to have been signed by 15,000 persons, protesting against the way in which the Act of 1650 had been administered and claiming that the Commissioners had unfairly deprived existing clergy of their dues, had been guilty of peculation, and had failed to replace those ministers whom they ejected with efficient preachers. Vavasour Powell retorted that 'no generation since the Apostles' days had such powerful preachers'. On the whole, the case against Harrison's handling of the conversion of Wales (assuming that Wales needed converting) does not appear to have been sustained. Nevertheless the majority in Parliament refused in April 1653 to renew the Act, thereby openly defying Harrison and all his friends. Cromwell, who thought highly of Harrison's work as an evangelist, was also upset. And so the crux was reached.

For months Cromwell had hesitated as to his course of action, and contemplated every conceivable scheme of constitutional reform from making the Duke of Gloucester King to becoming King himself. For Cromwell's instincts were conservative, whereas Harrison, stirred by his conviction that the Day of the Lord was nigh, was in a revolutionary mood. The leaders in Parliament — or some of them — took the offensive against Cromwell, thrust forward by Harrison, by attempting to intrigue with Lord Fairfax, Lambert and others to depose the Commander-in-Chief; and the majority in the House had now settled on a scheme whereby there should, after all, be no complete dissolution, but instead they should keep the management of the nation's affairs in their own hands, only filling up the vacant seats, while they themselves decided upon the qualifications of those who were to be newly elected. To that plan most of the army leaders were opposed. They did not of course demand a free general election; that was inconceivable, for it might have proved fatal to the Republic; but they were concerned over the kind of new blood that was to be introduced. Cromwell (in Gardiner's words) 'had now to choose between Vane's scheme of recruiting the existing Parliament and Harrison's scheme of erecting an assembly of pious and virtuous men'. Yet as late as April 19th it seemed as if a compromise might be arranged.

But on the morning of April 20th, 1653, when the majority in Parliament were hurriedly trying to push through Vane's plan, Harrison, who was sitting in his place as Member for Wendover, warned them of the provocation they were giving to the army. For the Independent soldiery feared that Vane's Bill would be followed by the dismissal of Cromwell, the reappointment of Fairfax, and the fastening of an all-embracing Presbyterian rule on the nation. No doubt these fears were much exaggerated, but at least to Harrison and his friends, burning with ardour to destroy the ungodly, they seemed real enough. Harrison sent a messenger to Cromwell, who with a number of his officers was in his lodgings at the Cockpit, warning him of what was on foot. Thereupon Cromwell (though he was not himself in uniform) came down to the House accompanied by a file of musketeers, whom he left outside. He sat down by Harrison and listened silently to the debate. At last when the Speaker put the Bill to the vote, Cromwell whispered to Harrison: 'Now is the time. I must do it.' His patience was exhausted. He was provoked beyond endurance and now did what Harrison wanted. After Sir Peter Wentworth had replied to the accusations that poured in fury from Cromwell's lips, charging the astonished Members with every conceivable injustice, form of corruption, and lack of virtue, the Commander-in-Chief ordered Harrison to call in the guard. Thereupon Harrison instructed the Speaker to leave his chair, pulling him down by his gown when he resisted. The mace was taken away and the Members shepherded from the chamber by the soldiers. That same afternoon, accompanied this time by Lambert as well as by Harrison, Cromwell visited the Council of State and dissolved it also.

Thus the Rump Parliament and the Council of State that had governed England for ten years and had conquered Scotland and Ireland came to its end. Having raised the sword against Charles I, it perished by the sword it had raised. But the sword was the sword of the New Model Army and not the angry act of a single man.

A distinguished American historian, writing in 1938, when the minds of men in the free world were under the impress of successful dictatorship, argued that the breaking of the Rump was a deeply laid plot on the part of Oliver Cromwell; that he had pretended to agree with Harrison, had squared Lambert, and extracted the consent of Monk before he attacked Vane and his friends, even though they had gone some distance to meet the wishes of the army. This interpretation of history does not accord with Cromwell's character or with his own account of what happened. For Cromwell was a man who long hesitated over taking decisions; he meditated and he prayed and he looked for dispensations from on high; it was only at the end of his travail of spirit, when the Seeker at last became the Finder, that he was moved to wrath. We have already shown that up to the spring of 1653 Cromwell had restrained Harrison and others in the army who were urging the dissolution of the Rump. Not until the last moment when he fancied that Vane intended to rush through a constitutional bill distasteful to the army as a whole did he break the Government with his musketeers.

Afterwards at least two reports confirmed this sequence of events. On May 6th it was reported to the exiled Royalist court:

> Harrison hath lately written to an intimate friend that the Lord had now *at last* made the General the instrument to put the power into the hands of His people (meaning the fanatic gathered churches) *contrary to his intentions*; that it was the Lord's work and no thanks to his Excellency.

On May 17th Sir Edward Nicholas, Charles II's Secretary of State, wrote to a correspondent:

> I understand . . . that Cromwell did rather join with Lambert and Harrison to preserve himself than that he did frame this great alteration of the Government in England and that he had *no such absolute power* in England or in the army *as some apprehend.*

Nevertheless the precipitation with which Cromwell and his Generals put an end to the rule of the Rump meant that they carried through their *coup d'état* before deciding what to do next. Thus Oliver Cromwell had then to take another choice: he had to resolve whether he would follow the advice of Major-General Thomas Harrison, the principal agent of the dissolution, or of Major-General John Lambert as to what form of government he should introduce in place of the Long Parliament.

BIBLIOGRAPHY TO CHAPTER V

There are two good biographies of Thomas Harrison, by C. H. Firth (1893) and by C. H. Simpkinson (1905) in which Harrison's letters are printed *verbatim* from various original sources. For his conduct in Wales see also Thomas Richards, *A History of the Puritan Movement in Wales* (1920). The quotation on page 93 is in Ludlow, I, 346; the American historian referred to on page 96 is the late W. C. Abbott; and the quotations from the Royalist correspondents are given in the *English Historical Review* for 1893, but the italics are mine.

CHAPTER VI

MAJOR-GENERAL JOHN LAMBERT AND THE ESTABLISHMENT OF THE PROTECTORATE

John Lambert was born in 1619 and died in 1684

THE character of John Lambert contrasted sharply with that of Thomas Harrison. In Lambert's letters we find none of the all-pervading religious inspiration that gripped Harrison and animated Cromwell, Fleetwood and Ireton. Lambert's religion is unknown, but his wife was said to have been an Independent and they were both friendly with Lord Fairfax and his Presbyterian circle in Yorkshire. Political, and not ecclesiastical, reform was Lambert's interest: the two best constitutional schemes invented during the Cromwellian period are associated with his name. He was an extremely ambitious man. Perhaps even more than Cromwell he was a natural-born soldier, as skilful as he was brave. He was an excellent administrator and very popular in the army. His early career was a success story without parallel in his times. But his tragedy was that he reached the summit too soon. Like many another young man who has sped towards the heights, he could not understand why any cup should be dashed from his lips. But understandably others did not sympathize with his resentment, but rather rejoiced in his discomfiture.

Lambert was born at Calton in the Craven Highlands in north-west Yorkshire on September 17th, 1619. His great-grandfather, a lawyer, acquired all the lands in the parish of Malham which had formerly belonged to the monks of Bolton at the time of the dissolution of the monasteries. It was grazing country: when in 1656 Lambert introduced into the Commons a bill for 'the better ordering and governing the makers and workers of broad sized woollen cloths within the West Riding of Yorkshire', he told the House that 'the most of my poor fortune there depends upon the rate of wool'. He was probably educated at Kirkby Malham grammar school and at Trinity College, Cambridge, and afterwards studied at one of the Inns of Court. These facts are not certain, but it is likely that such was his education: the analogy with that of Cromwell and Ireton is marked. Lambert lost his father when he was thirteen and married when he was twenty: his wife was Frances, the seventeen-year-old daughter of a neighbour, Sir William Lister. Through the Listers he was connected with the Fairfaxes, and soon after the civil war began, by the end of 1642, John Lambert was serving as a captain in the cavalry regiment of Sir Thomas Fairfax. We have already noted the rapidity of his rise in the Parliamentarian army. By the close of 1643 he was colonel of a cavalry regiment of his own, which, after taking part in the relief of Nantwich in Cheshire, returned to Yorkshire to fight at Bradford.

It was at Bradford that Lambert first earned honour as an independent commander. A battle was fought between a Royalist force under Colonel John Bellasis, who was related to Lambert's wife, and Lambert's men, who were said to be much inferior in numbers. The contest lasted for eight hours and at length the Parliamentarians ran out of powder:

> Hereupon [related the chronicler, John Vicars] a council of war was suddenly called, and it was agreed that before they would offer any parley to the enemy the horse should charge once more, which in that desperate exigence was performed with such undaunted courage and resolution of spirit that the enemy's horse, not able to withstand the shock, began a little to give ground, which our cavalry soon observing, they followed the advantage with so much impregnable courage that they forced them to a very disorderly retreat . . . And thus this valiant Colonel Lambert, after this defeat and brave victory so fortunately achieved, presently entered Bradford, and regarrisoned it for the use of Parliament.

In July 1644 he was with Fairfax on Marston Moor. In January 1645 Fairfax appointed him Commissary-General of the northern army, and in the New Model he commanded not only his own cavalry regiment, originally raised in the north, but also a foot regiment which he took over from Colonel

Edward Montagu, the future Lord Sandwich of Pepys's diary. Though Lambert was not present at the battle of Naseby, he took part in the pursuit and afterwards accompanied General Fairfax during his campaign in the west of England, becoming with Ireton, one of the Commissioners who negotiated the surrender of the Royalist army under Sir Ralph Hopton. Lambert and Ireton were again among the commissioners who took the surrender of Oxford in June 1646, and Lambert was then appointed temporary Governor of the City. He boasted in later years that his conduct as Governor prevented damage being done either to the City or to the university, and, although the Roundhead soldiers could not restrain themselves from preaching in the pulpits, no injury was done to the fabric of the Oxford churches. Thus this more ancient university owes a debt to a Cambridge man.

In July 1647 Lambert returned to his native Yorkshire, now with the rank of Major-General, and apparently acquired another regiment, the cavalry regiment previously commanded by Sydenham Poyntz, a poor disciplinarian, whom he superseded. In December, however, he gave up the command of his foot regiment, although (as we have already seen) he was to obtain another foot regiment, at Monk's expense, when on his way to Scotland in 1650. Thus at the age of twenty-eight Lambert stood in rank and prestige the third most important figure in the Parliamentary armies, after Fairfax and Cromwell. He was loved by his men. After Parliament and the army quarrelled in 1647 he was chosen as the spokesman of the committee of officers who represented the grievances of the common soldiers when they were resisting the demand that they should either serve in Ireland or disband. Together with Henry Ireton he had drawn up the 'Declaration of the Army' and the 'Heads of the Proposals', and he had been one of the signatories of the army's 'Remonstrance' which was presented to Parliament in that year. His university and legal training had made him, like Ireton, an obvious compiler of constitutional schemes, but he seems to have been somewhat more democratic than the elder general in his outlook: at any rate he favoured a broader property qualification for parliamentary voters.

Soon after the 'Heads of the Proposals' had been completed, Lambert rode north with the duty of reorganizing or disbanding the regiments which were discontented and unruly now that the war was over and their arrears were still unpaid. His task was delicate. When he first addressed the men of the northern army his speech, though tactful and conciliatory, was greeted in silence. But as soon as they understood that he intended to meet their complaints and treat everyone fairly, he had his reward: discipline was restored and the grumblers were pacified. Yet though his 'civility' and 'sweetness' exacted much praise, he was not soft, and soldiers found guilty of plundering were promptly punished. Thus the citizens of Yorkshire were reconciled to the quartering of a large army: one pamphleteer wrote that he 'gaineth the love of all people wherever he goes, keeping his soldiery in excellent order and discipline'. At the same time he averted in the northern army those mutinous outbursts with which Harrison and other commanders had to contend in the south of England.

When the second civil war broke out in the north a Royalist general, Sir Marmaduke Langdale, occupied Carlisle and an adventurer named John Morris, who was afterwards executed for treason, betrayed Pontefract in Yorkshire. Lambert, who soon collected an army of some 8000 men, aimed at preventing these two Royalist strong points from linking up. He ordered the investment of Pontefract and he himself contained Langdale in Carlisle. With Harrison's help he defeated Langdale in the field and reduced the garrison of Carlisle to extremities. But immediately afterwards the Scots under the Duke of Hamilton crossed the border and Lambert had to retire into north Yorkshire, leaving the Scots to overrun Cumberland and the north-west. Like Lambert, Cromwell at first assumed that the enemy forces would aim at thrusting into Yorkshire from the west and after his arrival in the north with his army to join Lambert in August 1648, the two armies rendezvoused at Leeds. It is surmised that Cromwell may then have visited Lambert's home, Calton Hall, and met his wife and children. Frances Lambert, who was now twenty-six, was a woman of charm and beauty, and in later years Royalist scandalmongers did not scruple over associating her name with that of the Lord Protector. It would be pleasing to think that the great man was so human. But, apart from the fact that Cromwell is reported to have shown her little courtesies in public when her husband was his chief executive during the Protectorate, the evidence of any more exciting relationship between the two, we must confess, does not exist.

Lambert's campaign in the early summer of 1648 had ensured ultimate victory for the Parliamentarians. Together Cromwell and Lambert fought and won the Preston campaign and afterwards Lambert accompanied Cromwell to Edinburgh where he came to terms with Argyll and the Covenanters. After Cromwell returned to London, Lambert remained in Yorkshire to take charge again as Major-General of the siege of Pontefract, which Cromwell had vainly summoned and was the last fortress in England to hold out for King Charles I. One of Lambert's predecessors as commander of the besieging force was Colonel Thomas Rainborough, the democratic friend of General Harrison. While Rainborough had been preparing to undertake his duties a party of Cavaliers broke into his room in a Doncaster inn and killed him. The Parliamentarians regarded this 'commando' action, as we might call it, as murder. Consequently Colonel John Morris, the Royalist Governor of Pontefract and others, were down on a list of war criminals who were to be tried for their lives. But Lambert was a merciful man. As soon as it became plain that Pontefract could resist little longer, he was persuaded to allow the castle gates to stay open for forty-eight hours during which the defenders might do what they could to assist Morris and five other 'excepted persons' to escape. On March 21st, 1649, the gates were opened; the besiegers drew up all their horse and foot as close as they could to the castle and at sunset the garrison made a sally during which Governor Morris and one other managed to break through the ring on horseback; another of the excepted persons was killed in the sally, and the other three were hidden by their comrades who bricked them up inside one of the walls, and Lambert's Commissioners were then informed that all the six had got away. Morris and his comrade were later caught near Chester and executed at York; but the three self-immured prisoners are said to have ultimately escaped and survived the Restoration. To the rest of the garrison Lambert granted generous terms, though the castle was destroyed. Lambert's gentlemanly treatment of his enemies was unusual in the later stages of the civil war; it is to be noted that the terms he allowed to the first Duke of Hamilton and others at the close of the Preston campaign subsequently came in for criticism in the Army Council. General Fairfax was, however, so pleased with the way in which Lambert had conducted the siege of Pontefract that he wrote a letter of commendation to the Speaker; whereupon Parliament voted Lambert an award of £300 a year in land to be granted to him and his heirs for ever.

After the Restoration Lambert claimed that he was deliberately kept by Cromwell in the north of England during the trial and execution of King Charles I because it was known to the other leaders of the army that he disapproved of regicide. On the face of it the argument was disingenuous, for no one was better qualified than he was to carry out the siege of Pontefract and wind up the campaign in Yorkshire. On the other hand, Lambert was certainly on intimate terms with Fairfax, and it is reasonable to suppose that Lambert shared his patron's political opinions. Lambert, as we have shown, was not revengeful and he had none of that compelling spiritual fervour which drove men like Harrison and Ireton to don the mantle of the Almighty and condemn Charles I as a Man of Blood. Lambert ranged himself on the Parliamentary side not because of religion but because of politics. Belonging, as he did, to that rising or expanding middle class which began asserting its claims to power in the reign of Queen Elizabeth I, he had sympathized with the movement directed by John Pym to restrict the prerogatives of the monarchy. He had signed the petition which Fairfax had tried to present to King Charles I on Heyworth Heath begging him to return to London. His young brother-in-law, Captain William Lister, had been killed by his side in one of the first battles of the civil wars; and we may guess that this personal tragedy hardened his heart against the Royalist cause. Lambert had been named one of the Commissioners at the King's trial. But his fortunate absence from the capital during January 1649, when Charles I

MAJOR-GENERAL JOHN LAMBERT

met his death in Whitehall, was to gain for John Lambert nearly another twenty-five years of life.

In the early weeks of 1649 Lambert had devoted much of his time and energy to securing proper pay and decent treatment for the soldiers under his command. He had even levied taxes in Yorkshire without the consent of Parliament rather than let his troops go without their pay. On other occasions he had found money for them out of his own pocket. Thus it was scarcely surprising that he was the idol of his men. He was also happy in his marriage. In the course of the campaign in 1651 when he was collecting more laurels as a General Frances Lambert had come up to Scotland hazarding the dangers of the front line to be near him. Some of her letters have survived and, within the conventions of the time, express the tempered ardour of married love. But it is to be discerned that neither she nor her husband took overkindly to the puritan pattern of conduct. In none of Lambert's letters do we detect anything more than the businesslike language of the professional soldier. Frances wrote to one of her husband's captains:

> I pray remember my dear love to your wife, . . . Desire her to let me have the yard of French lawn and the scollop . . . for I have nothing to wear about my neck, and I dare not go bare, for fear of giving offence to tender saints. . . .

One has the feeling that both the Lamberts, had chance designed it so, would not have felt ill at ease in the gay court of King Charles II.

After the battle of Worcester Lambert was at the peak of his success, if not yet of influence. Parliament now voted him another £1000 a year. He was offered, and could afford to refuse, the position of Commander-in-Chief both in Ireland and in Scotland. He invested large sums of money in confiscated lands and extended his properties in Yorkshire. He also speculated largely in the soldiers' debentures, that is to say, their claims on the State for arrears of pay. In May 1652 he purchased for some £7000 the splendid mansion of Wimbledon House in Surrey, which had formerly been a royal residence. In this handsome building with its high turrets and gilded weathercocks, girt by long elm tree avenues and orange and pheasant gardens, John and Frances Lambert dwelt during the months preceding the breaking of the Rump: we may suspect that they watched with sardonic eyes Thomas Harrison's 'Assembly of Saints' being planned, after Cromwell had rejected Lambert's own more realistic advice to establish a small workable council of twelve to govern the country.

Oliver Cromwell had not in fact made up his mind when he dissolved the Long Parliament what form of government he intended to put in its place. Both among the lawyers and among the Generals themselves there was much discussion of the value of monarchy. It is, however, necessary to appreciate that when the phrase 'monarchy' was employed the speakers were not thinking in terms of reviving the prerogatives and trappings of the Stuarts. But since 1649 the administration had been carried on by a small and unrepresentative body of men which used the Council of State simply as its executive agent: the Council had been in no way similar to a modern Cabinet. The system was a clumsy one: everybody recognized, and particularly the soldiers, that day-to-day decisions, such as appointments to high executive posts — as in the case of Lambert — could not suitably be made by a debating society. That was why Cromwell, the lawyer, Bulstrode Whitelocke, and others had seriously considered a form of government with 'somewhat of monarchical power' in it. And Cromwell himself could not help wondering whether, now that he as Commander-in-Chief was left as the only legally constituted authority in the nation, he ought not to assume full executive powers. For the time being he was persuaded otherwise. It is all the more remarkable — and a proof of his cautious political outlook — that he resisted the temptations of military dictatorship because there is a consensus of evidence that the breaking of the Rump had been a popular move and that his own stock stood high both with the army and the London mob.

On April 22nd, 1653, the Army Council published the first declaration of its intentions: 'the supreme authority', it said, 'should be by the Parliament devolved upon known persons, men fearing God, and of approved integrity, and the government of the Commonwealth committed unto them for a time'. This temporizing statement reflected differences of opinion behind the scenes. General Lambert, supported by some of the lawyers, including the Lord Chief Justice, Oliver St. John, and John Selden, was pressing for a small executive council with clearly defined rights and duties: there should, they suggested, be an 'instrument of government' drawn up and published which would remove from Cromwell all the temptations of dicatorship. When on April 29th a small Council of State, consisting of only ten members, was established it looked for the moment as if Lambert had won the argument. On the other side, General Thomas Harrison and his followers, the men who, more than any others, had induced Cromwell to destroy the Rump Parliament, wanted power to be handed over to a large but select puritan group — the example of the Jewish Sanhedrim of seventy was what they had in view — keeping the Council of State, as before, merely as an executive instrument and not as a policy maker. The day after the Council of State was set up, that is on April 30th, a proclamation was published to the effect that 'persons of approved fidelity and honesty were to be called from the several parts of the Commonwealth to the supreme authority'. On the same day Harrison wrote to a friend that while it was

> resolved to have in power men of truth fearing and loving our Lord, His people and interest: the difficulty is to get such: whether my Lord [Cromwell] only shall call them or the Saints choose them.

If Harrison is to be believed therefore the subsequent debates in the Council of Officers cannot have been concerned about whether or not an Assembly was to be called but who was to call it. Eventually Harrison's point of view won the day. On May 6th it was announced that an assembly of 129 members were to meet at Westminster, not elected by any new franchise but chosen by the Army Council from lists of persons recommended by the independent puritan congregations in each county.

Although one imagines it can scarcely have been a matter of significance to Harrison and his friends among the Baptists and Fifth Monarchy men that this Assembly of Saints was to contain 129 instead of seventy members (though numerology played then, as it does yet, an important part among the superstitious) the Harrisonians were still, it seems, suspicious. Some of his admirers openly said that Harrison and not Cromwell ought now to take the lead in the Commonwealth. Christopher Feake, a Fifth Monarchy preacher, instructed his congregation 'that although the General had fought their battles with success, yet he was not the man that the Lord had chosen to sit at the helm'. Another friend of Harrison, Vavasour Powell, had declared from his pulpit in Whitehall after the dissolution that now 'law should stream like a river freely, as for twenty shillings what formerly cost twenty pounds', and plainly thought that Harrison was the man to arrange it. Outside observers were conscious of a growing rivalry between Harrison and Lambert. The Royalists were informed that Harrison was preaching that the Spirit had told him that the Government must be settled in a monarchical way and was supposed to be thinking of himself as the monarch. On the other hand, Lambert was described to them as a gentleman born, learned, well qualified as to courage, conduct, good nature and discretion. He was said 'cunningly and tacitly' to oppose Harrison, knowing himself 'hard enough for Harrison' and 'some thought, hard enough both for Harrison and Cromwell'. This report continued:

> He hath the present vogue as a person that would (or might at least) do something considerable for the dissolved Parliament, some hope for the King also. I conceive the inducements to this opinion are that he had not his hand immediately in the last King's blood, that he is not severely of any opinion in religion inconsistent with monarchy, neither is his interest made up of any such. . . .

The letter-writer concluded: 'I pray you think of what I have above mentioned concerning Lambert. The observations come from a person of quality and a confidant of his.' But all these accounts must have been largely guesswork. No one at that time seems to have known exactly where Lambert stood. Cromwell is alleged to have called him 'Bottomless' and another contemporary report, though also of low value, described him as an 'unfathomed person'. We may compare with the contradictory stories about Lambert what the Venetian agent in London had written home about Harrison. At first he had reported that 'so much bad blood exists between Cromwell and . . . Harrison who both covertly and openly seeks to deprive the former of his command of the army,' yet later he confessed that he was quite wrong and that Harrison's opposition to Cromwell was 'a blind'. Historians are sometimes tempted to call these reports of the Venetians and such foreigners in London 'well informed' because they lack other information. But one cannot make bricks without straw. The only hard kernel of truth that seems to remain from all these travellers' tales is that Harrison was suspicious of Cromwell's intentions and Lambert was opposed to Harrison's scheme of government as being better suited to cloud-cuckoo-land than to the English Commonwealth. However, when the Nominated Assembly gathered in London on July 4th, 1653, it must have appeared as if the dreams of Harrison and his friends had come true. The apocalyptic, dithyrambic speech in which Cromwell welcomed the Assembly was attuned to the mood of the Fifth Monarchists. Quoting copiously from the Old Testament, he dilated upon the theme of a Chosen People, led by their prophets and saints. He went out of his way to justify the dissolution of the Rump on the ground of necessity and to condemn its members for having put a stop to Harrison's activities in Wales. Amid the flow of rhetorical extemporization there was perhaps one phrase of significance from Lambert's point of view when Cromwell said: 'I would *all* were fit to be called.' It was an astonishing performance. Even Thomas Carlyle, Cromwell's most effective apologist, remarked of this speech that 'The Editor has had his difficulties' and then interpreted it to his readers by more incomprehensible word-spinning than Cromwell himself had used. But in the heat of that July day, 300 years ago, it must have appeared to Cromwell's audience as if a new era had begun, a gorgeous prelude to the Millenium. It was but a mirage that beckoned them on. After the Long Parliament had been overthrown in April a puritan naval contractor had written from Portsmouth: 'I wish those who succeed may learn from their predecessors that as he has overturned, so he will overturn, till He come whose right it is. Even so, come Lord Jesus quickly.' But within six months the Assembly of Saints was overturned.

The first action of the Assembly of Saints was to co-opt Cromwell, Harrison and Lambert and two others. George Monk, perhaps an odd figure to be there at all, was already among the members. What Lambert thought about the new administration by the puritan notables is not hard to imagine. Up till the meeting in July he had been assiduous in the Council of State. In April, May and June he had attended seventy-five meetings; but he attended only twice in July, and on July 22nd a newsletter reported that he was living in retirement in Wimbledon. For the following three months he was absent both from the Council and the Assembly. Cromwell also confined himself to military matters. 'The persons that led in the meetings', as Cromwell observed afterwards, 'were Mr. Feake and his assemblage in Blackfriars, Major-General Harrison and the rest that associated with him at one Mr. Squib's house. There were all the resolutions taken that were acted in the House day by day.' The programme of Harrison and his cronies was to abolish the payment of clergy by tithe, to reform the Court of Chancery, and remodel the marriage laws: they embarked on their legislation with appetite. Their first two projects rapidly foundered because of the resistance of vested interests: only the civil marriage law, whereby men over twenty-six and women over twenty-two were allowed to wed by simple declaration before a magistrate was passed. The Saints earned especial unpopularity in the City of London when, after John Lilburne, the Leveller hero, who returned to England from exile, had been acquitted by the jury at Old Bailey, they ordered that, for reasons of public security, he should be sent back to the Tower of London.

Thomas Harrison and his followers did not in fact command a secure majority within the Assembly. It was only their vigour, single-mindedness, and diligence that enabled them to direct proceedings. But they pressed too hard. By November they had raised influential antagonists. They made the mistake of objecting to peace with the Dutch Republic, with which the Commonwealth had been at war for eighteen months, and of striking terror into the hearts of property owners and of the powerful group of lawyers which was unrepresented among them. Meanwhile in his palace in Wimbledon Lambert was biding his time and working on his 'Instrument of Government'. It was not until November that Lambert and his friends came out into the open and prepared their counter-offensive. Harrison had received a check when on November 1st he had received only fifty-eight votes against Cromwell's 113 votes in the new election to the Council of State. Later in the month a decision to renew heavy taxation at a war-time rate far in excess of anything paid under King Charles I caused an outcry in the capital and grumbling in the counties; yet it was the price that had to be paid for the continuation of the Dutch War. Then at the end of the month an act to erect a new high court of justice, to which Harrison was opposed on prudential grounds, was pushed through the Assembly by a snap vote. The tide was beginning to run so fiercely against Harrison that a few days afterwards he retired into the country while Lambert returned to London and presided over a meeting of officers.

In spite of his prolonged absence from the Assembly and the Council of State John Lambert had remained in close touch with Cromwell during the early autumn and presumably kept him informed of the progress he had achieved on the 'Instrument of Government'. But Cromwell, though he had already been disappointed by the perfervid behaviour of the minority in the Assembly, was, as usual before a crisis, hesitating. He had not yet decided to reverse his attitude of the previous May by throwing in his lot with Lambert instead of Harrison. At the beginning of December, however, it was Lambert's turn to sustain a setback. Like Box and Cox, Lambert now left London and Harrison returned from the country. The two parties within the Assembly — the Moderates and Harrison's followers — began fighting a ding-dong battle over the reorganization of the Church. Harrison and his adherents were against any form of state control whatever, any patronage, any payment of tithe, any selection or ejection of preachers — in a word they wanted anarchy tempered by enthusiasm. On December 10th they defeated a scheme sponsored by Cromwell's chaplain, Dr. John Owen, and advocated by the Moderates. It was a pyrrhic victory. For two days afterwards by an ingenious conspiracy planned by Lambert and other officers the Moderates met early in the morning before their opponents realized what was happening, and as soon as the Speaker had taken the chair, voted to resign their powers as a 'parliament' 'unto the Lord General' from whom 'they had received them'. Lambert sent along two colonels and an armed contingent to close the shop. Next day the General from Yorkshire himself marched into the Council Chamber and produced the 'Instrument of Government' on which he had laboured for so long. After a few days' discussions, of which we know little, the 'Instrument' was accepted.

Thus although Cromwell must have suspected what was afoot it was Lambert who destroyed the Assembly of Saints and was the architect of the Protectorate.

In accordance with its terms General Oliver Cromwell was on December 16th, 1653, declared Lord Protector of the Commonwealth of England, Scotland and Ireland and of the people assembled in Parliament. Major-General Lambert drove in the Protector's coach to the installation ceremony at the Court of Chancery, the Court that had now survived intact the fire of the Fifth Monarchy men. General Monk also rode in Cromwell's coach. After the Instrument had been read, 'Major-General Lambert, kneeling, presented Cromwell with a sword in a scabbard, representing the civil sword, which Cromwell accepting put off his own, intimating thereby that he would no longer rule by the military sword.' The ceremony was impressive, but lower down the river the dogs were barking.

Three days had passed. Harrison's supporters, the Fifth Monarchy preachers, Powell and Feake, were thundering at Blackfriars against the new Protector as being the 'dissemblingest perjured villain alive'. They were summoned to Whitehall, cross-examined and placed under arrest. Powell remained unrepentant. 'Let us go home and pray,' he retorted defiantly, 'and say, Lord, wilt Thou have Oliver Cromwell or Jesus Christ to reign over us?' At the same time 'Major-General Harrison being treated with to know if he would own and act under this present power, and declaring he could not, had his commission taken from him.' He spurned all offers of posts under the new Government, but surprisingly, as it seemed in view of his influence in the army, did not attempt to resist. It could not have offended his faith to fight it out, and he was said to have had 20,000 adherents. Presumably Lambert had taken every precaution. Or did Harrison after all feel in his heart that an England ruled by Cromwell might not be such a bad place? At any rate, in February 1654, orders came from the new Council of State that Major-General Thomas Harrison was to be banished to his home at Newcastle-under-Lyme, which he had inherited from his father, the butcher; and Major-General John Lambert, maker of the third revolution, became Cromwell's 'vice-regent'.

BIBLIOGRAPHY TO CHAPTER VI

A biography called *Cromwell's Understudy. The Life and Times of General John Lambert and the Rise and Fall of the Protectorate* by W. H. Dawson appeared in 1938. Lambert's letters, which Dawson did not publish in full, are to be found in Cary, op. cit., *Letters of Roundhead Officers written from Scotland to Captain Adam Baynes, 1650-1660* (1856), which includes at page 36 Frances Lambert's letter quoted in the text. *Thurloe State Papers, Historical MSS Commission Reports, Mercurius Politicus*, etc. The letter quoted on page 109 is in *Calendar of State Papers* (*Domestic*), *1652-1653*, p. 292. *The Calendar of State Papers* (*Venetian*), *1647-1652* and *1653* contains some of the reports quoted on the relations between Cromwell, Lambert and Harrison.

CHAPTER VII

ROBERT BLAKE AND THE GENERALS-AT-SEA

Robert Blake was born in 1598 and died in 1657

BEFORE Major-General John Lambert arranged for the Assembly of Saints to commit suicide, Cromwell, acting on behalf of the Council of State, had been seeking to conclude peace with the Dutch Commissioners in London. Because of General Blake's victories over the Dutch at sea Cromwell had been able to negotiate out of strength, but the severe terms he tried to obtain were intended to gratify the anti-Dutch feeling rampant in the Assembly. As soon as he became Lord Protector he grew more conciliatory. And the hope that the Protectorate meant peace abroad as well as at home was influential in determining Lambert's *coup d'état*. Thus Cromwell owed his aggrandizement in some measure to General Robert Blake. And Blake's triumphs shed prestige on the new Government.

Yet it has been argued that Blake himself disapproved of the Protectorate; that he was a stern, unbending republican. Nothing in Blake's own conduct or correspondence sustains such a view and it is not accepted by any of his modern biographers. His relations with Cromwell were cordial, if not intimate. We know that Cromwell admired him and soon after he took command in Ireland tried to persuade Blake to serve directly under him. When in January 1655 Cromwell prorogued his first Protectoral Parliament Blake wrote him a letter in which he condemned the conduct of its members as showing a spirit of prejudice and animosity and as therefore being unpatriotic to the Commonwealth. Nor can Blake have been much concerned over the earlier dissolution of the Rump since he accepted membership of the Assembly of Saints. If he had in fact disliked Cromwell's policies, he could have laid down his commission; if Cromwell had suspected him of disaffection (as in the case of Thomas Harrison) he would not have scrupled to dismiss him. Although he was a member of three parliaments, Blake was not a politician, but a loyal officer of the Commonwealth. He once declared that 'it is not for us to mind State affairs, but to keep foreigners from fooling us'. Blake may thus fairly be regarded as one of Cromwell's Generals.

Blake was born a year before Cromwell and also died a year before him. The careers of this great sailor and soldier covered nearly the same span. Almost alone among his Generals Blake belonged to Cromwell's own generation and he carried in his veins the blood of the Elizabethan sea-dogs. Yet like Cromwell, he discovered his fighting qualities late in life. He never married, he never intrigued, he never dabbled in affairs of state. He left the west of England to win fame and returned to the west to die. He served his nation with a devotion that towers above the centuries.

Blake's grandfather had settled in Bridgwater in Somerset, where he was three times elected mayor, after he had found prosperity as a merchant. He owned a number of ships that traded to different parts of the world and his business was afterwards carried on by his son, Humphrey, and his grandson, Robert, who was born, the eldest of seventeen children, at Bridgwater about September 1598. Having attended the local grammar school, Robert Blake went at the age of sixteen to St. Alban's Hall, Oxford, which was afterwards incorporated in Merton College, where he matriculated, but later he transferred to the new foundation of Wadham, and took his B.A. degree there in February 1618. Strange stories attach to Blake's career at Oxford. It is said that he was rejected for a scholarship at Christ Church and for a Fellowship at Merton. His failure at Merton is ascribed to his not being tall enough to satisfy the Warden. Where Blake was unique was in being one of our few admirals who in their youth contemplated the academic career. Successful admirals and generals are more accustomed to end their lives in universities than to begin them there.

Blake evidently left Oxford with reluctance (who does not?) but returned to Somerset to take over his father's business when he died in 1625. Nothing is known with assurance about what Blake did in the next fifteen years. But we may safely assume that just as Cromwell became a farmer, so Blake became a merchant and, as likely as not, crossed the seas in his own ships. Unless he gained some experience of seamanship during those years it is hard to understand why he subsequently took to a naval career, so to speak, like a duck to water, why he was appointed an Admiral when he was over fifty, or how he so rapidly mastered the technique of his new profession. There are indications that his family was of a puritanical turn of mind — a story survives about a Blake who was churchwarden of St. Mary's, Bridgwater, being reprimanded by Archbishop Laud — and his election to the Short Parliament at the end of King Charles I's 'Eleven Years' Tyranny' suggests that he associated himself with the grievances and desires of the burgeoning middle classes. He was not originally a member of the Long Parliament, being replaced by a neighbour who later became a Royalist, but when the civil war broke out he raised a troop in the dragoon regiment of Colonel Alexander Popham.

The Pophams were a leading Somersetshire family. Alexander's grandfather had been Lord Chief Justice in the reign of Queen Elizabeth I. They were the kind of men who were invariably deputy-lieutenants of their county and members of parliament for its boroughs. Alexander, seven years Blake's junior, was M.P. for various constituencies, and later served in the Council of State. Alexander Popham's younger brother, Edward, who was born about 1610, succeeded his father as M.P. for Minehead, and afterwards became Blake's colleague in the Parliamentarian navy. The Pophams were a cut above the Blakes and it was with their help that Robert rose during his military career.

Our first absolutely authentic glimpse of Robert Blake during the civil wars was when he was nominated member of a Somersetshire committee appointed to seize (or sequestrate) Royalist estates so as to raise money for Parliament. Next he appears as lieutenant-colonel in command of part of Popham's regiment (now seemingly a foot regiment) when Prince Rupert besieged Bristol in July 1643. The Roundhead Governor, Nathaniel Fiennes, agreed to terms in a hurry (like Prince Rupert himself later, he regarded Bristol as indefensible) but he omitted to notify Blake, who was in charge of one of the forts, that he had surrendered. Blake therefore continued fighting even after the capitulation, which pardonably irritated Prince Rupert, who is said to have contemplated hanging him. However, in the end Colonel Blake and his men were allowed to withdraw on the same terms as the rest of the garrison. Blake was next to the fore in the defence of Lyme in Dorset which was besieged by Prince Rupert's younger brother, Prince Maurice, in the spring of 1644. A collateral descendant of Sir Francis Drake who was present at this siege has a story about Blake's behaviour:

> This day [recorded Edward Drake in his diary] Lieutenant Colonel Blake (who was officer in chief of Colonel Popham's regiment in the town) told a commander of the enemy's who . . . was treating with him just under the line of the town, 'Here you see and behold how weak our works are; they are not the things wherein we trust; therefore tell the Prince that if he desires to come into the town with his army to fight, we will pull down ten or twelve yards so that he may come in with ten in a breast, and we will fight with him.'

The answer that was given to this bravado or bluff was that 'they would come in where they could and was most for their advantage'. But the town was soon relieved by the navy and on this occasion Blake rowed out to sea to meet the Earl of Warwick, who was the Lord High Admiral appointed by Parliament. Blake's service at Lyme was sufficiently valued to bring him the tough assignment of Governor of Taunton and promotion to the rank of full colonel.

The siege of Taunton is an epic of the civil war in the west of England. Blake held out there against the Royalists from October 1644 until July 1645. The town was thrice invested and thrice relieved. When first summoned by his neighbour, Edward Wyndham, Blake retorted: 'We . . . do much wonder upon what ground . . . you should conceive it possible to prevail over us by a mere paper project, either by threats to affright us from that duty we owe to God and our Country, or by artificial persuasions to induce us to a treaty so dishonourable, so unwarrantable.' There was a flourish about that letter (printed in the newspapers) that had to be maintained. Wyndham was driven off, but Lord Hopton launched a terrific assault: 'nothing was heard but thunder, and nothing seen but fire'. In answer to Hopton's summons Blake retorted that he had four pairs of boots left and he would eat three of them before Hopton entered the town. As it turned out, Blake did not have to eat his boots, but before the town was finally relieved thatch had been taken from the housetops to feed the horses and cords from the beds to provide match for the musketeers. After the relief of Taunton bonfires were lit in London and Parliament voted Blake £500.

In April 1646 Blake occupied Dunster Castle and with its surrender the civil war in Somerset came to its end. Blake was elected M.P. for his native town of Bridgwater and played an undistinguished, or at least indistinguishable, part in the Rump Parliament. Colonel Edmund Ludlow, who was at the same time elected M.P. for Wiltshire, met Blake when he arrived at the House of Commons and they took the oath together, Ludlow assuring himself that as Blake had been 'faithful and active in the public service abroad, we should be as unanimous in the carrying it on within those doors'. But, as in his early years, Blake now vanishes almost without a trace from history until after the execution of King Charles I.

Enough is known of Blake's early years for the historian to say that he was a keen parliamentarian and, like John Lambert, a soldier as brave as he was generous. We owe the following description of him to an eighteenth-century historian who claims to have obtained the information from his family:

> Admiral Blake, as to his person, was of a middle stature, about five feet and a half, a little inclining to corpulence; he was of a fresh, sanguine complexion, his hair of the frizzled kind, and, as was then much the mode, he wore whiskers, which he curled when he was any ways provoked. He was commonly very plain in his dress, but when he was abroad and appeared as General, was always as became his rank, with a reserve of moderation. He was religious, according to the profession he made....

This author added with surprise that Blake was never heard to swear, even when he was at sea. Hardly any of Blake's private letters have survived, but his official dispatches disclose a simple and not verbose religion, a dry humour, and a straightforward outlook on life. He was modest, grave but not austere (he would drink a cup of Sack or Canary wine), with pleasant manners and a clement and scholarly frame of mind. His early biographer asserts that 'there was in this gravity of his nothing of that pride, that haughty over-bearing spirit, that rough and forbidding air, which is too much affected by modern sea officers'. Such was the man who on February 27th, 1649, along with Colonel Edward Popham and Colonel Richard Deane, was appointed 'General-at-sea' of the new English Commonwealth.

Did Blake approve of the execution of King Charles I? It has been argued that his assumption of the post of General-at-sea less than a month afterwards is proof that he did. The argument is inconclusive. General Fairfax, as we have seen, also accepted a high position under the Commonwealth, although he disapproved of the execution and even refused to take an oath of loyalty to the Republic. Still, it is doubtful if an officer whose loyalty was in any way suspect would have actually been promoted to an important post at such a time. An equally plausible argument has been put forward about Blake on the other side: it is pointed out that he was not named a member of the commission set up to try the King, even though he was a Member of Parliament, a colonel in the army, and prominent in the victorious party in the State. His omission is therefore held to suggest that he was known to have been opposed to punishing the King. But this argument again is not convincing. Blake might, for example, have been excluded from the Commission because he was out of London at the time, as was John Lambert. Nearly all the colonels in Fairfax's army who had not changed sides in 1648 had favoured the King being brought to trial, though not all of them thought that he deserved the supreme penalty. Blake had the reputation of being an early republican. Clarendon, writing in 1650, claimed that Blake had said that 'monarchy is a kind of government the world is weary of'. Indeed the Royalists always regarded him as one of the most dangerous of their enemies.

GENERAL ROBERT BLAKE

Command of the sea was essential to the survival of the English Commonwealth. It was surrounded by enemies. Foreign Powers, some of which expressed shock at, and even disapprobation of, the regicides' rise to power, had to be forced or persuaded to acknowledge the new government. Many of the surrounding islands, such as the Isle of Man, the Scillies and the Channel Islands, were still in Royalist occupation and had to be subdued. Ireland was unconquered. The warships which had revolted in 1648 and were now under the command of Prince Rupert needed to be captured or sunk. Finally the loyalty and discipline of the fleet must be assured under officers who were completely trustworthy. Up till 1649 Parliament had enjoyed the services of an excellent admiral in Robert Rich, second Earl of Warwick. And Warwick had commanded a first-class navy which had been largely formed, ironically enough, by King Charles I himself. It contained over forty-two warships of different sizes and gunpower and was supplemented from time to time by armed merchantmen. Its pressure on the various ports had contributed more than is generally realized to the defeat of the Royalists in the first Civil War. But Warwick's Vice-Admiral, William Batten, had resigned in September 1647, and had gone over to the King in 1648. Warwick's own brother, the Earl of Holland, had also fought for the King in the second Civil War and was now on trial for his life, and thus since Warwick's own position naturally became untenable, a clean sweep had to be made of the higher command. But it is not clear why the obviously unsatisfactory solution of appointing three officers jointly to replace Warwick was fixed upon. A possible explanation is that it was out of deference to Warwick's dignity, three commoners being reckoned the equivalent of one peer. The three men appointed had all served successfully as colonels in the army; they all came from the west of England, the traditional nursery of English seamen, and they all seem to have had some knowledge of the sea. Their order of seniority was determined by the date when they received their commissions as colonels: Edward Popham came first, then Blake, and thirdly Deane. A concession to realism was that one out of the trio might be appointed to take a naval command by the other two. Blake was twelve years older than his two colleagues and in fact soon outstripped them as an Admiral by reason of his genius and diligence.

Edward Popham in fact probably had the widest knowledge of the sea. The fifth and youngest son of Sir Francis Popham of Littlecote he was perhaps, like his father and brother, educated at Balliol and the Middle Temple. As a young man he went to sea, serving first as a lieutenant under the Earl of Northumberland aboard the *Henrietta Maria* in 1636. In the following year, when he was twenty-seven, he became captain of the *Fifth Whelp*, an aged ship which sank in the open sea at the end of June, having sprung a leak. Seventeen of her crew went down with her, but Captain Popham and others escaped by boat and after rowing for fifty miles in the North Sea were rescued by an English ship bound for Rotterdam. Unchastened by this adventure, Popham in 1639 took command of the *Unicorn*, a hired merchantman in Sir John Pennington's fleet. When the civil war began he soon became a colonel. In 1643 he relieved Dorchester in Dorset and in 1644 was instructed to raise troops in Somerset. After the battle of Naseby he took part in the western campaign, raised forces for the relief of Taunton, and fought at Bridgwater. In July 1648 he received orders to accompany Warwick to sea, but the orders were afterwards countermanded. He was described by a fellow officer who knew him well as 'a gallant man, and steers as right at sea, and marches as fair at land as any man I know'. He seems to have proved himself a good captain, though, like Nelson, he suffered from sea sickness. The town of Yarmouth on one occasion presented him with three sheep for the excellence of his convoy work, and he earned honour for looking after the needs and pay of his men. He was married to Anne Carr, a daughter of a Groom of the King's Bedchamber, by whom he had three children.

Colonel Deane we have already met during the Worcester campaign. Richard Deane was the younger son of Edward Deane of Temple Guiting in Gloucestershire and was born in the summer of 1610. His uncle, Sir Richard Deane, who was Lord Mayor of London in 1628, had been a leading City merchant and it is likely that Richard became a shipowner himself and, like Blake, made some trading voyages in that capacity. Related both to Cromwell and to John Hampden, he was absorbed in fighting throughout the civil wars, beginning as a volunteer serving in the Gravesend garrison and ending as the principal expert on artillery in the New Model Army. He was present at the battles of Edgehill, the first battle of Newbury, Naseby and Preston; he was at the siege of Bristol and the surrender of Lord Hopton at Truro; and his regiment was among those which condemned King Charles I as a Man of Blood, while his own signature appeared twenty-fifth among the fifty-nine who signed the monarch's death warrant. He was a strict disciplinarian; like Lambert and Harrison, he condemned any form of pillage or extortion. So far as experience as an officer and politician went he out-topped his colleagues as Generals-at-sea; yet in seniority he ranked third.

Blake's appointment had come to him as a complete surprise. It was, he observed modestly, 'extremely beyond my expectations as well as merit'. It is presumed that he owed it largely to the recommendation of his friends the Pophams, Alexander being now a member of the Council of State and Edward pressing him to accept.

The pay of the Generals-at-sea was £1095 a year. Their first task as 'commissioners for ordering and commanding the fleet during the ensuing year' (1649) was to put it into fighting trim. There was an Admiralty Committee of the Council of State, of which Sir Henry Vane was the most active member, but the detailed work fell on the Commissioners of the Navy, whose secretary was Robert Coytmor, a civil service busybody who enjoyed pinpricking Generals.

During the first three months of their service Blake and Deane were hard at work organizing in Westminster, but when at the outset of the campaigning season of 1649 the Council of State heard the news that Prince Rupert with four warships and five ships which he had captured off the Scillies was lying in the mouth of the Channel on the look out for further prizes Popham was chosen by lot to take command in the Channel. Popham managed to capture two of Rupert's frigates and the Prince then withdrew to his base of Kinsale in southern Ireland. In May all three of the Generals-at-sea sailed from Plymouth with a squadron of some ten or twelve ships to blockade Prince Rupert in Ireland and, if possible, bring him to battle.

While Admiral Sir George Ayscue and Vice-Admiral William Penn kept guard over the Irish seas from their base in Dublin and Vice-Admiral Robert Moulton and Rear-Admiral Badiley guarded the Channel, Blake and Deane began a weary blockade of Prince Rupert in Kinsale. (Popham after seeing them in place at once returned to Plymouth and thence to London.) For over a fortnight bad weather drove the squadron away from Kinsale back to Milford Haven in Wales and the two Generals were relieved to find after they had battled their way against the gales back to Kinsale that 'providence which kept us by ill-weather hence, hath by the same kept all the revolters still in here'. At the end of June the two Generals having drawn lots, Richard Deane returned to England to make preparations for convoying Cromwell's army to Ireland and Robert Blake stayed at Kinsale to maintain the blockade of Prince Rupert's fleet. Prince Rupert was now intent on escape, for the pressure upon him had become severe, and he had already lost one of his frigates through the watchfulness of Blake and Deane. In spite of constant bad weather and murmurings from London and Dublin General Blake hung on. In the middle of October his squadron was once more driven back from Kinsale to Milford Haven by the tempests and this time Rupert effected his escape, disappearing into the void amid the November fogs. It was a disappointing end to Blake's long vigil, but the sea power of the Commonwealth had asserted itself and with Cromwell's victorious land campaign nearly completed, Ireland was doomed.

Soon after his arrival General Cromwell as Lord Lieutenant of Ireland had offered Colonel Blake the post of Major-General of Foot in his army. Deane wrote to Popham on August 23rd: 'My Lord Lieutenant will write to the Council of State to move for Colonel Blake to be Major-General of the Foot. I wish we may have as honest a man in his place, if it be so.' Blake was perturbed at the offer, which he was anxious to refuse. He wrote to Popham asking him to use his influence to prevent the proposal being put forward in Parliament so that he should not suffer the embarrassment of having to refuse an order promulgated on so high a level, as he was determined to do. Indeed he told Popham he would return to private life rather than accept. Nevertheless the offer was made by Parliament, though not in compelling terms, and Blake did refuse. It was after his refusal that Cromwell gave the post to Henry Ireton.

This episode sheds a fascinating sidelight upon the relations between Cromwell and his Generals. In the first place, it shows that Cromwell had discerned the genius of Blake. For Blake was not an obvious candidate; he was now fifty-one and his experience of land warfare had been limited. Ireton, on the other hand, was younger, was Cromwell's son-in-law, and had commanded the left wing at the battle of Naseby. Ireton was, as we have seen, not a first-class soldier and perhaps Cromwell knew this. But it is open to speculation what would have happened if Blake had become Lord Deputy of Ireland and Ireton had returned to England with Cromwell in 1650. Secondly, why did Blake refuse the post? Had he, even after the boredom induced by the siege of Kinsale, sensed that sea fighting and not land fighting was his *métier*? It is surprising if it were so. After all, he had distinguished himself in the defence of Lyme and of Taunton and he had still to prove himself at sea. Or is it possible that Blake disapproved of Cromwell's handling of the Irish campaign? The massacre of the Drogheda garrison took place on September 12th and Blake's letter to Popham begging him to spike the offer is dated September 16th. So that is a not unlikely explanation, for Blake was a humane man.

A final point is worth noting. Just as in the autumn of 1649 Cromwell tried to persuade Blake to leave the sea and take command on land, so in the spring of 1651 Cromwell was actually to induce Deane to abandon his naval duties in order to become a Major-General in the army. Does that mean that Cromwell, fine strategist though he was, underestimated the importance of sea power or did he only, like most high-ranking officers at all times, want to seize the best men for his own service?

After Prince Rupert escaped from Kinsale Blake shifted his base in southern Ireland to Cork, but soon afterwards he returned to England and having consulted his fellow Generals-at-sea it was decided that he should prepare a squadron to seek out the Royalist fleet. The decision that Blake himself should take command of the expedition shows that it was recognized how essential it was for the Republicans to destroy or disable Prince Rupert's fleet. For so long as Rupert was afloat seizing prizes and menacing the trade routes, so long would foreign powers be reluctant to bestow recognition on the English Commonwealth. Early in March 1650 Blake left Portsmouth for Cascaes Bay off Lisbon where it was now known that Prince Rupert was based. Blake carried with him special envoys to the Kings of Portugal and Spain and thus his mission had a diplomatic as well as a war-like character. On May 26th Popham joined Blake off Lisbon. Deane, who had been taken ill after he had convoyed Cromwell's army to Ireland, was left behind, but in the course of the campaigning season of 1650 he assumed command in the Downs and cruised in the North Sea so as to cut communications between King Charles II in Scotland and the United Netherlands which were then friendly to the Royalist cause.

Blake had been instructed to 'pursue, seize, scatter, fight with, or destroy, all and every of the ships and vessels of the revolted fleet' and 'in case foreign ships shall assist the said revolters, or fight against you, that you likewise fight against them'. All that was easier said than done. King John of Portugal had not recognized the Commonwealth and refused to order Prince Rupert out of the sheltering waters of the Tagus. When two French men-of-war turned up in the midst of Blake's fleet he was embarrassed and thought it politic to let them go. However, eventually Blake decided on strong action to bring the Portuguese to his own point of view. Late in September he met a large Portuguese convoy which had come from Brazil and captured seven of the vessels and the person of the Rear-Admiral. That caused King John to order Prince Rupert to go and on October 12th, 1650, he and his companions set sail, 'being destitute of a port', as one of them wrote, 'we take the Mediterranean for our harbour, poverty and despair our companions, and revenge our guide'. Refused victualling facilities in Portugal, Blake had been obliged to use Cadiz as his base, but never relaxed his watch on Prince Rupert. As soon as the news of his departure was reported to him, General Blake gave chase through the Straits of Gibraltar and into the Mediterranean. Early in November Blake caught Rupert's fleet near Carthagena, and although he was unable to bring his enemy to battle, four of the Royalist warships were driven in by storms and battered to pieces.

Meanwhile in England the Council of State had grown impatient with Blake (Popham had left him again early in September). Indeed — it is hard to place any other interpretation on the order — they had determined to supersede him in favour of Vice-Admiral Penn. William Penn was a professional naval officer. Born in Bristol, son of a naval captain, he himself had become a captain at the age of twenty-one. If Blake ever received the order to hand over his command to Penn he ignored it with a Nelson touch. Moreover as soon as the Council of State learned of Blake's successes it hastened to cancel its instructions. And by the time Penn arrived with his fresh squadron to deal with the remnants of Prince Rupert's fleet, Blake could return home to receive the thanks of a now grateful Parliament and an award of £1000 for his pains.

'Blake's journey into the Mediterranean,' observes one of his biographers, 'marked a new era in English policy . . . Since Blake's expedition the Royal Navy has with very short lapses, continuously maintained a Mediterranean station.' Prince Rupert withdrew to Toulon to refit and then managed to deceive Penn about his intentions. But once again he escaped from a Republican admiral only to meet punishment from the ocean gales. His flagship was sunk off the Azores and after many other adventures and misfortunes in the West Indies he limped back to Europe in the spring of 1653, never to fight against Cromwell's Generals again.

In 1651 while Cromwell was campaigning in Scotland with the support of Lambert, Monk, Deane and Harrison, General Blake and the main fleet, besides engaging in convoy duties, were cleaning up the Royalist outposts in the islands. On June 3rd Blake obtained the surrender of the Scilly Islands after granting generous terms to the garrison and in October he supervised the naval side of the invasion of the Channel Islands, the army being commanded by Colonel James Heane, a gallant officer who was to die fighting as a Major-General in the West Indies. A landing at St. Brelade's Bay was the turning point in the campaign which owed as much to Blake as anyone.

On August 19th, 1651, General Edward Popham, who had worn himself out in the service of the Commonwealth, had died of fever at Dover. Since Deane was now serving as a Major-General of Foot in the Worcester campaign, Blake became in effect the Lord High Admiral, republican style. When he returned to England from the Channel Islands he was elected a member of the Council of State, and in March 1652 on the eve of the Dutch War he was appointed to command the fleet for nine months.

We shall not detail the events of the Anglo-Dutch War of 1652-54, the struggle between heroes which is one of the best documented campaigns in the seventeenth century. In it Blake's genius flowered as fully as Cromwell's had done at Dunbar. The war began obscurely and accidentally with the battle of Rye Bay in May 1652. The Dutch resented the claim of the English Navy to search their merchant ships for enemy goods and their Admiral, Tromp, had instructions not to dip his flag to the English in the Channel. Blake, with thirteen ships encountered Tromp, with forty men-of-war off Dover when Tromp was coming to the aid of a Dutch merchantman. When Tromp refused to haul down his flag, Blake fired three times across his bow and a battle ensued in which, in spite of inferior numbers, Blake sank one Dutch ship and captured another. In reporting such damage as he had suffered to the Speaker of Parliament Blake wrote:

> We must needs acknowledge a great mercy that we had no more harm, and our hope the righteous God will continue the same unto us if there do arise a war between us, they being first in the breach, and seeking an occasion to quarrel and watching as it seems an advantage to brave us upon our own coast. . . .

Thus the war began. On July 12th Blake with a fleet of over sixty vessels did execution among the unfortunate Dutch fishermen, though after he had deprived them of their catch he sent them home. When Tromp attempted to intervene his fleet was damaged and scattered in a tremendous storm and afterwards he was superseded by Admiral De With, a man of high courage and uncontrollable temper. On September 28th-29th Blake, whose fleet included the superb 100-gun warship, the *Sovereign of the Seas*, crushed De With, and Tromp was hastily recalled. In November Tromp, with a fleet outnumbering that of Blake by about two to one, won the battle of Dungeness. Blake's defeat was excusable, but he blamed some of his captains and hired merchantmen and even condemned the conduct of one of his own brothers. Thus honours between Blake and Tromp were even at the end of 1652.

In 1653 Major-General Richard Deane was restored to his command of the fleet and Major-General George Monk was also appointed General-at-sea. Soon after the battle of Worcester, when Monk returned to London, Deane had been nominated Commander-in-Chief in Scotland and president of the Commissioners for Scotland. In that capacity he had come to an agreement with the Earl of Argyll, had pacified the Highlands, reconciled Edinburgh, reduced Arran, and captured the Bass Rock. Among his notable administrative decisions was his refusal to allow witches to be tortured. Thus he and Monk now turned with admirable versatility from ruling the Scots to fighting the Dutch in the North Sea. These appointments were intended to help Blake and not to affront him; indeed they were decided upon before his defeat at Dungeness. The three Generals fought together in the first battle of the New Year, the battle of Portland (February 14th). Soon afterwards Blake was taken ill and went to London 'much discontented' according to common report — not, however, with Cromwell's action in dissolving the Rump Parliament but with his own health and failure conclusively to defeat Tromp. Just before the battle of Portland he and Monk had drawn up a set of instructions 'for the better ordering of the fleet in fighting' in the course of which they advocated the method of fighting in line ahead. In the next naval battle — the battle of the Gabbard, on June 2nd, General Richard Deane, standing beside Monk on their flagship the *Resolution*, was killed by the first Dutch broadside, his body being cut to pieces by chain shot. Though drenched with the blood of his colleague, Monk took off his cloak and covered the remains before resuming the direction of the battle. The struggle persisted until dark and was continued the next day and finally the superior tactics and heavier metal of the English prevailed and when Blake's squadron hove into sight in the last stages Tromp withdrew defeated. That was almost the end of the war. After the battle De With declared to the States General: 'Why should I keep silent any longer? I am here before my Sovereigns and am free to speak, and I can say that the English are at present masters both of us and of the seas.' Two months later at the battle of Scheveningen Tromp himself was killed by a musket ball and in April 1654 peace was made on Cromwell's terms.

General Blake and General Monk received thanks and gold chains from the Assembly of Saints. Vice-Admiral Penn and Rear-Admiral Lawson had smaller chains and all were given gold medals. On July 9th Cromwell wrote to Penn: 'I often think of our great loss in your dear General Deane, my most near friend.' Thus before the Protectorate was established Cromwell had lost two Generals, both related to him and completed trusted by him, Henry Ireton and Richard Deane.

Victory over the Dutch had left Cromwell in a splendid diplomatic position. With the ships that had been taken from the Dutch he had the finest navy as well as one of the best armies in the world. The Protestant nations hastened to make treaties with him; though France and Portugal were still nominally at war with the Commonwealth, they did not fancy the menace of Blake's guns, and the French and Spanish Ministers were soon vying with each other in search of an alliance with England. Cromwell did not hurry over taking his choice. 'There is not a nation in Europe', he told the first Protectorate Parliament, 'but is willing to ask a good understanding with you.' But first there were insults to avenge.

In the autumn of 1651 Vice-Admiral Sir George Ayscue had been dispatched with a squadron of twenty ships to reduce Barbados in the West Indies, which was in Royalist hands, to obedience to the Commonwealth. The detachment of that force had had its repercussions on the Dutch War. Like Penn, Ayscue was a professional sailor. Son of a Lincolnshire gentleman who was an official in the privy chamber of King Charles

I, he had served as a naval captain for many years. When Vice-Admiral William Batten revolted against the Long Parliament and joined the King in 1648 it was Ayscue's influence that had kept part of the navy loyal to the Parliamentarian cause. After serving under Blake off Ireland and the Scillies, he had successfully reduced the Barbados to obedience and then returned to fight in the Dutch War. He is described as 'an honourable gentleman with a high sense of duty'. He is said to have made a fortune out of privateering and prizes. He retired to enjoy his gains at his house of Ham Haw in Surrey, but in 1658 was to be persuaded by Cromwell to accept an appointment in the Swedish navy. Thus he kept out of trouble's way during the Restoration. Ayscue imposed awe on the French and Spanish merchantmen off the West Indies and in 1654 Blake did the same thing in the Mediterranean.

Cromwell had by then determined to employ the large and victorious Commonwealth fleets to make England the greatest power in the world. But no one knows to this day exactly what his detailed intentions were or the nature of the instructions that were given to General Blake. It seems, however, that as early as June 1654, the Council of State had decided to attack the Spanish Empire 'beyond the line' in the West Indies and the Americas, and Admiral Penn and General Robert Venables were chosen heads of a commission to undertake the necessary preparations. Meanwhile Blake, like Ayscue earlier, was to intimidate the French and Spaniards, and after he had sailed from Plymouth in October and entered the Mediterranean it was at first made to appear as if his objective was the destruction of the French fleets. However, in the end he neither attacked the French nor the Spaniards (whom Cromwell had bamboozled) nor even the smaller states of Italy that had given comfort and shelter to Prince Rupert. Instead he turned his attention to the piratical Moors of North Africa. Partly to exact recompense for a British merchant of dubious character, partly to aid the Republic of Venice in its current war against the Turks (a belated Crusade that appealed to the English puritans) Blake sailed to Tunis and on April 5th, 1655, he silenced the land batteries at Porto Farina and burned nine galleys belonging to the Sultan of Turkey. Impressed by this feat of arms the

Dey of Algiers proved himself more amenable than the Dey of Tunis. This combination of realistic politics with Christian crusading was agreeable to Cromwell, who upheld Blake's conduct.

Meanwhile the expedition of Penn and Venables had set out for the West Indies. Penn had some forty warships; Venables, formerly the British commander in Ulster, had about 2500 soldiers of very second-rate quality raised by drafts. On January 29th they arrived at Barbados and enlisted some more and even worse soldiers and on April 14th they launched an inept assault on San Domingo, then known as Hispaniola. In the following month to offset their failure to take Hispaniola they had occupied what was then regarded as the barren island of Jamaica. War with Spain thus became inevitable and on his return from North Africa Blake was instructed to blockade the Spanish mainland and to lay hold of any Spanish treasure fleet he could. He was unable to do so and brought his fleet home to England in October, after a year's absence, empty-handed. On their arrival in London Penn and Venables, who from the very outset had spent much of their time quarrelling with each other, were imprisoned in the Tower for returning home without orders. But in spite of his inability in 1655 to inflict any blow on the Spaniards Blake was not punished. Thus Cromwell's gift for assessing the relative merits of his Generals remained unimpaired.

Robert Venables was in fact a brave and hard-working officer but he was a poor general, deficient in strength of character and over-confident in his own judgment. He also committed the mistake of shipping his own wife, a lady of mature charms, with him, which caused him to be accused of petticoat rule or alternatively of a self-gratification denied to the rest. Admiral Penn was far less to blame for the failure of the expedition. General Venables alleged that the Protector's own brother-in-law, Major-General John Desborough, was as guilty as any man for the poor results of the 'western design' because of the inferior soldiers and indifferent victuals that he provided for the expedition. Desborough had been appointed a General-at-sea along with Blake, Monk and Penn in December 1653. There is no reason to suppose that Desborough went so far as to put to sea or exercise his military skill upon the uncertain elements. But he was active on land. In November 1654 he had visited Plymouth along with Penn in order to try to assuage the grievances of the sailors there who complained not only about their food and drink but also about the press gang system. Afterwards he busied himself in victualling the ships destined for the West Indies. General Venables objected to the inferior quality of the supplies arranged by Desborough. Desborough said that Venables was trying to delay the departure of the fleet. Venables retorted that Desborough was a profiteer, enjoying his 'cut' from the contractors. Blake also complained bitterly of the provisions that were supplied to the fleet, which contributed to the undermining of his own health. Of course when things go wrong, everyone blames everyone else. Still there is a striking contrast between the efficient administration of the navy during the Dutch War and its shortcomings in the winter of 1654-55. Blake had warned Cromwell of the impossibility of keeping the fleet afloat with 'our ships extremely foul, winter drawing on, our victuals expiring, all stores failing, our men falling sick through badness of drink, and eating their victuals boiled in salt water for two months' space'; 'though supply come timely,' he added, 'yet if beer come not with it, we shall be undone that way'. Cromwell wisely gave him a free hand and told him to return 'at such time as you shall judge for the safety of the fleet'.

The Spanish War was now in full flame and Blake was a sick man. Nevertheless in the following February, with General Edward Montagu to assist him, he again set sail with forty-eight warships in the service of the Commonwealth. Montagu's was an odd appointment: he was only thirty, was a Commissioner of the Treasury, and had no previous experience of the sea; he appeared to have been intended as a kind of political commissar, in place of Vice-Admiral John Lawson whose left-wing political leanings had just brought about his resignation. After securing a base at Lisbon Blake imposed a blockade on Cadiz and the other Spanish ports. In August Cromwell recalled Montagu, but Blake continued the blockade with the smaller warships throughout the winter, an achievement almost without parallel in the early history of naval warfare.

Blake endured the vigil with commendably few complaints: 'We are altogether', he wrote to Montagu, 'and behold one another's faces with comfort.' At last his patience was rewarded when the news came that the Spanish Plate fleet from South America was on its way and had anchored at Santa Cruz in the Canary Islands. Blake had now to resolve whether to divide his fleet or to abandon the blockade and lead the bulk of his force to the Canaries. Ultimately he chose the latter course, and, leaving only a few frigates behind, sailed with his main fleet for Santa Cruz. Here the Spanish galleons lay under the protection of the shore batteries but were so disposed that they masked their fire, provided that the enemy had the daring to engage them closely. This Blake ordered, repeating on a larger scale his victory at Porto Farina. While Captain Stayner boarded the galleons, Blake himself engaged the shore batteries. All the Spanish ships were sunk except five that were captured and burnt. The treasure had already been removed from them, but earlier Stayner had taken a treasure fleet.

Blake's victory on April 19th, 1657, had brought the Spanish War to a close, just as his victories over Tromp and De With had ended the Dutch War. To Blake Cromwell owed Edmund Waller's tribute:

> The sea's our own; and now all nations greet
> With bending sails, each vessel of our fleet.

But Blake's course was run. As his flagship, the *George*, ploughed homewards across the Bay of Biscay in the summer of 1657 he was sinking fast. He had hoped to reach the shore of his homeland. But he died where he had earned his fame — at sea, as the *George* triumphantly entered Plymouth Sound.

In Blake Oliver Cromwell lost the greatest, and the most disinterested, of all his Generals. No one who reads Blake's surviving letters can doubt the intensity of his loyalty to the Lord Protector or the strength of his devotion to his country. Like Cromwell, Blake detected in the sudden storms of the seas and the occasional disappointments of a fighting life the determining finger of Providence. Like Cromwell, he harmonized his faith in the puritans' God with a patriotism free from blemish. The captain of the *George*, on board which

Blake died, spoke his epitaph: 'As he lived, so he continued to the end, faithful.'

BIBLIOGRAPHY TO CHAPTER VII

Lives of Robert Blake by C. D. Curtis and Roger Beadon appeared in 1934 and in 1935 respectively. John Oldmixon, *The History and Life of Admiral Blake* (1746), though unreliable, embodies authentic family traditions. *The Letters of Robert Blake* were edited for the Navy Records Society by J. R. Powell in 1937. Mr. Powell has also written a brief but useful biography of the Admiral and contributed important articles on Blake's career to *Mariner's Mirror*. For Edward Popham's correspondence see the Historical MSS Commission's report on the Leyborne Popham papers (1899). For the Anglo-Dutch War there is *Letters and Papers relating to the first Dutch war, 1652-1654*, edited by S. R. Gardiner and C. T. Atkinson and completed in 1930. For Penn there is G. Penn, *Life and Times of Sir William Penn* (1833) and for Venables C. H. Firth's introduction to *The Narrative of General Venables* (1900). The life of Penn, as of Deane, is necessarily out of date, but in 1926 Sir Charles Firth contributed a valuable article to vol. XII of *Mariner's Mirror* on 'Sailors of the Civil War, the Commonwealth and the Protectorate'. For the earlier period see C. D. Penn, *The Navy under the Earlier Stuarts* (1920). A. R. Bayley, *The Great Civil War in Dorset* (1910) contains details about the early careers of Blake and the Pophams.

CHAPTER VIII

THE VACILLATIONS OF MAJOR-GENERAL ROBERT OVERTON

Robert Overton was born in 1609 and died in 1668

WHILE Blake was winning victories at sea, Cromwell's other Generals had been trying to secure peace at home. On the whole, the middle classes were pleased with the Protectorate and the ordinary people had accepted it submissively. But, as John Buchan wrote, 'London was subdued, puzzled, and vaguely alarmed. There had been a succession of portents — the river flowing and ebbing hours before its time, part of St. Paul's tumbling down, a comet in the heavens, and the ghost of Charles walking in Whitehall.' Not only were Major-General Harrison and his Fifth Monarchist friends indignant, but other officers in England whose sympathies lay with the extreme puritan sects expressed their misgivings. Among them was one General: Robert Overton.

Overton is described by contemporaries as being a scholar as well as a soldier: 'a scholar, but a little pedantic', was the appraisal of the Royalist Sir James Turner. He was the son of John Overton of Easington near York where he was born about 1609. Presumably he was educated at one of the universities and afterwards is known to have studied at Gray's Inn. At first he served with credit under Lord Fairfax in Yorkshire, particularly in the defence of Hull when during a sally he 'carried himself with much honour and gallantry'. In 1647, through the influence of the Fairfaxes, he obtained command of a foot regiment, previously under a Presbyterian colonel, and in 1648 he was appointed acting Governor of Hull. While he was in Hull he was at one time accused of Royalism, at another, with more plausibility, of being in sympathy with the Levellers. In 1649 the officers of the Hull garrison thought it worth their while to publish a 'Humble Remonstrance' in which they vindicated both their colonel and themselves. In 1650 Overton sought and obtained employment under Cromwell in Scotland, after he had written to assure the new Commander-in-Chief that no one could more acceptably have succeeded Fairfax than he.

Overton was present at the battle of Dunbar and for a time was Governor of Edinburgh. In this capacity he ordered the soldiers not to throw squibs among the market people and the citizens not to empty chamber pots out of their windows. It was he who led the crossing of the Forth, the manœuvre which in the end compelled the Scots to march to their doom at Worcester. Subsequently Overton became a name in Scotland. At one time he was Governor of Perth, at another of Aberdeen. Awarded a foot regiment for his services in October 1651 (he had lost the command of his previous regiment in May 1649 — it is not clear why) he established a garrison in the Orkneys and was made Sheriff of Fife. In December 1652 before Major-General Deane left Scotland, he appointed Overton as Major-General to command all the forces in the west (where later he was succeeded by Alured), but in 1653 and 1654 he reverted to his duties at Hull, which became important on account of the Dutch War. Thus Overton was an influential and successful commander whose word carried weight both in Yorkshire and in Scotland. John Milton wrote a panegyric about him.

Nevertheless Overton was a somewhat unstable character, the sort of person who is inclined to accept the opinion of the last person to whom he has been talking. As a scholar he experienced scruples; as an individualist Christian he felt responsibilities; as a successful soldier he had ambitions. Indeed his Christian zeal and personal aspirations blended in his character to a point of overbearance. According to one of his friends, he possessed the spur of the discontented — an imperious wife and 'many pretty children'. He had approved of the dissolution of the Long Parliament and was an admirer of Cromwell, but now openly announced his doubts about the establishment of the Protectorate. Nevertheless in 1654 he travelled up to London from Hull in search of better paid employment. In an interview with Cromwell he informed him that if he 'did only design the setting up of himself, and not the good of these nations', he could not serve him. 'Thou wert a knave if thou wouldst', retorted Oliver with equal candour. Overton returned to Hull, but later took over the command of the north of Scotland under George Monk. In Overton therefore we have on the highest level of Cromwell's army a questioning figure, who (some thought) might become a storm centre and set the Commonwealth on fire. But it was typical of him that far from taking immediate action against Cromwell when he became Protector he nursed his ambitions and bided his time.

Before Overton returned there, rumblings had already been heard in Scotland when the Protectorate was set up, but the army of occupation had its hands full for the time being with the now resurgent Highlanders. In Ireland another of Cromwell's Generals had protested at once. Lieutenant-General Ludlow was the second in command to Cromwell's new son-in-law, Charles Fleetwood, who had been in Ireland since the autumn of 1652. Ludlow, whose republican faith was never stained, denounced the 'usurpation' of a 'false hypocrite'. He refused to sign the proclamation of the Protectorate in Dublin, informing his fellow Commissioners that he would rather 'cut off his hand'; and after Fleetwood ordered the artillery to fire a salute in honour of the new ruler 'the report', so Ludlow recorded, 'was very unwelcome music to me, who, desiring to be as far from this pageantry as I could, rode out of town that afternoon'. Though ceasing to function as Commissioner, Ludlow clung to his command on the ground that it had been conferred on him by Parliament and could not be taken away except by Parliament. In the following March, 1654, Cromwell's son, Henry, visited Ireland and Ludlow inveighed against his father's illegalities. Henry Cromwell answered: 'You that are here may think he has power, but they made a very kickshaw of him at London.' Fleetwood, a mild man, put up with his subordinate's obstructiveness for over a year, but eventually in January 1655 deprived him of his lucrative command.

In Wales also there had been some opposition to the new Government: Harrison's friend, Vavasour Powell, who had been the guiding star of the Assembly of Saints, after trying to rally his sympathizers in London against Cromwell, managed to escape to his native country where he continued to preach resistance with zest and impunity.

While these stirrings manifested themselves on the fringes of the now theoretically united Commonwealth (according to the Instrument of Government Scotland and Ireland were each to be represented by thirty members at Westminster) the Council of State in Whitehall was settling down to the business of governing. Besides Cromwell himself five of his Generals, Lambert, Fleetwood, Skippon, Desborough and Montagu, were appointed to the Council of State. Fleetwood was for some time absent in Ireland and John Lambert was inevitably a dominant personality. In the first month of its existence he attended fifteen out of seventeen of its meetings and in the first three months forty-four out of sixty-three. We know that within the Council he opposed Cromwell's foreign policy; a realist, he would have preferred to fight the French rather than the Spaniards. He had been against the West Indian expedition and would understandably have preferred to sell cloth of good Yorkshire wool to Spain rather than indulge in Elizabethan buccaneering in the name of Protestant Christianity. However, Cromwell overruled him, but often employed him as his diplomatic agent. Not only did Lambert work hard in the Council, but he became responsible for the military government of the north of England (where Robert Lilburne, after he had been replaced by Monk in Scotland, became his deputy at York), he was, with Robert Blake, joint Warden of the Cinque Ports, colonel of two regiments, and a Visitor to Cambridge University and Eton College. His duties also extended to caring for York Minster and considering a project for a university at Durham. The families of Lambert and Cromwell were on intimate terms during these months. Cromwell is said to have again visited Lambert's Yorkshire home and to have shown a liking for his wife. But the ladies of the two families were reported not to have hit it off: Oliver's youngest and fairest daughter, Elizabeth, did not care for Frances Lambert any more than did her sister, Bridget Fleetwood. During this period the young and successful couple were often referred to as Lord and Lady Lambert. A contemporary newsletter avers that the title was formally bestowed on

General John Lambert by the Lord Protector as 'the first Lord created by him'. If that is so, Lambert must have been singularly unpopular with the more austere Republicans. Free as he and his wife appear to have been from any fervent religious leanings, the Lord and Lady who dwelt stylishly in Wimbledon Palace may well have appeared incongruous characters in what was after all largely a puritan middle-class world. Would-be assassins paid Lambert the compliment of coupling him with the Lord Protector whenever they embroidered their plans.

The first Protectorate Parliament met on Sunday, September 3rd, 1654. Lambert and Henry Cromwell sat in the coach with the Protector when he drove up to the formal opening ceremony at the Abbey. In the procession Lambert followed his master carrying the sword of state. Lambert was M.P. for the West Riding of Yorkshire and the majority of Cromwell's other Generals, even including Fleetwood and Blake, who were absent on service oversea, were members. But Cromwell's supporters did not command a majority in the House. Parliament had been freely elected, except that the franchise was more restricted than before and representatives were required to take an oath to the new regime, and most of them were republicans or moderate Presbyterians. Consequently Lambert and his followers of the 'Court Party', many of whom had been elected for the 'pocket boroughs' provided by the new constituencies in Scotland and Ireland, fought a losing battle in the debates that followed.

But while the electors had not given a majority to the army party and the system propounded by Lambert in the 'Instrument of Government' they had also repudiated the eager revolutionaries who had composed the Assembly of Saints. Cromwell could therefore afford to try to reconcile himself with Major-General Thomas Harrison. On September 13th, the day after his cousin, Commissary-General Whalley, had closed the Chamber at Westminster thereby compelling the members to take an oath not to alter the Government 'as it was settled in a single person and parliament', the Protector sent for Harrison to dine with him in Whitehall. Rich wines and eight or ten good dishes of meat were provided. 'After dinner', so the story runs, 'the Protector came, and professed his great affection for him, and high esteem of his great worth, which alone moved him to send for him now, that he might discharge the office of a friend by admonishing him not to persist in those deceitful and slippery ways whose end is destruction.' Harrison, who had previously been under surveillance, was then set free. But his friends, the Fifth Monarchy preachers, later attacked Cromwell's conduct as being both treasonable and anti-Christian, and the fear that this sect was plotting insurrection led to the arrest of Harrison on Christmas Day, though he was at once released on a promise of good behaviour. But the imprisonment of some of the preachers in the sect induced Harrison, together with a deputation including Colonel Nathaniel Rich and Clement Ireton, one of the late Major-General's sons, to seek an interview with the Protector in February 1655, to ask that these 'prisoners of the Lord' should be released. Cromwell answered that 'if they were prisoners of the Lord, they should soon be set at liberty, but he was sure there was nobody in England in prison for the Lord's sake or the Gospel's sake'. Nevertheless he refused their petition, but said he would be willing to discuss the question with them again later.

Afterwards Cromwell twice sent for Harrison and twice Harrison failed to appear. Finally he was brought before the Lord Protector and the Council of State on February 16th. Here these ancient comrades-in-arms, Cromwell, Lambert and Harrison, confronted each other. One of the Fifth Monarchy preachers present accused the Protector of having taken the crown from the head of Christ and put it on his own. These acrimonies did not cut much ice, but Harrison and his friends would not promise to refrain from disturbing the peace. There was thus no alternative but to commit them to prison. Cromwell derived no pleasure from punishing one of his finest Generals. 'I know,' wrote his Secretary of State, John Thurloe, 'it is a trouble to my Lord Protector to have any one who is a saint in truth to be grieved or unsatisfied with him.' Harrison was dispatched to Portland and afterwards removed to Carisbrook Castle in the Isle of Wight, where Charles I had been imprisoned. Here he passed his time in pious communing with one of the Fifth Monarchy preachers, John Rogers, who denounced Cromwell as 'the seed of the Dragon' and 'the Bastard of Ashdod'. But Harrison himself was more acquiescent. Even when in 1658 he was released from Carisbrook and allowed to live, under surveillance, in his father-in-law's house in Highgate, where another of Cromwell's discontented Generals, Edmund Ludlow, visited him, he did not express animosity. He told Ludlow that he had joined Cromwell in the first instance 'because he pretended to own and favour a sort of men, who acted upon higher principles than those of civil liberty'. He had no sympathy for Ludlow's parliamentarianism and remained convinced that the prophet Daniel had been right when he said that 'the Saints shall take the kingdom and possess it' and he blamed those who had wasted the opportunity they had been given. As for himself, he knew his heart had been sincere and upright and he felt no regret for the part he had played in destroying the Long Parliament. But he had no wish for revenge on Cromwell. On July 12th, 1656, he had written: 'I can affirm I desire not a hair from any of their heads for any unkindness to me, I could bless them that curse and pray for my persecutors, as they are mine.'

When General Monk in Scotland heard from Thurloe what had happened to Harrison he replied that 'unless His Highness be very severe with those that are disturbers to the peace, we shall never have any certain settlement'. But it was in Scotland that the greatest danger was later to arise.

In England the first Protectorate Parliament devoted itself almost entirely to tearing the Instrument of Government to pieces, even after its members had been compelled to accept the fundamentals of the new Constitution. The majority, conscious of the proud heritage they enjoyed as belonging to the Parliament of the English Commonwealth, were determined to assert their rights and to pare the powers of the Protector and the Council of State. Lambert, Desborough and the rest of the Court Party in the House, which appears to have numbered about sixty, were, on the other hand, still conscious of the affronts offered to the army by the Rump both in 1647 and in 1652. Between October 16th and October 19th a four-day debate was held on the question whether the office of Lord

Protector should be hereditary. Lambert delivered a long speech in favour of the proposal, but it was decisively rejected. General John Desborough on November 10th discussed the subject of the Protector's right to veto legislation. (According to the original Instrument he had a suspensory veto for twenty days.) Desborough's speech was a masterpiece of tactlessness. He argued that

> Parliament had no cause to be jealous, to trust the Lord Protector with the half, that not long since had the whole, and might have kept it without any competitor. He had power to have done it, and yet he hath given us some part of it, and in truth, we have had an opportunity to do what we will; but to amend the Government only where (in effect) he would give us leave. . . .

Ultimately Cromwell himself brought to a close the interminable debates of this would-be constituent assembly.

Cromwell's biographers are not in agreement as to why he dissolved his first Parliament. Naturally he was irritated and disappointed with the inflexibility of the talking shop. The contemporary French ambassador in London alleged that he was annoyed because the Commons had rejected Lambert's proposal to make his office hereditary. But the chief reason appears to have been that the majority had tried to wrest the control of the army from him and at the same time to reduce the size of the existing forces as well as abstaining from providing their pay. It was the old story again. As at that very time Blake and Penn were at sea with large fleets, an insurrection was in progress in Scotland, and reports were coming in of incipient Royalist and Leveller risings, Cromwell and his Generals dared not let military control slip from them. Thus in the dissolution of January 20th, 1655, most of Cromwell's Generals stood by the Lord Protector.

In any case by this date Cromwell had taken care to purge the armed forces of their incendiary elements. In that Cromwell was supported by his invaluable Secretary of State, John Thurloe. Thurloe, a barrister of Lincoln's Inn, had originally proved his capacity in administration as secretary to the Council of State. On the formation of the Protectorate he had become Cromwell's sole Secretary of State and served him with devotion until the day of his death and after. Though some thought him 'too grave and wise for this mercurial, quick age', Cromwell's 'little secretary' was a counterpoise to his often fanatical and sometimes ambitious Generals, a modern Permanent Secretary in advance of his age, absorbed in his duties and his master's interests. Thurloe's intelligence service provided Cromwell with the means to strike against his political opponents before they were ready for him.

The Republicans in the House of Commons had not been without sympathizers among the officers of the army and the Levellers exerted influence over the navy. We have already recounted how Cromwell had sent his brother-in-law, that blunt, if occasionally inept officer, to satisfy grievances in General Penn's fleet. These grievances were, on the whole, not concerned with politics. But Vice-Admiral John Lawson was known to Thurloe to be actively sympathetic with the Levellers. Cromwell and Thurloe, however, gave Lawson plenty of rope and ultimately, sensing that he was suspected of disloyalty, he resigned.

In the army the discontented party centred on three colonels, John Okey, Matthew Alured and Robert Saunders. Okey had a distinguished career. A Londoner by birth, he had been selected to command the only regiment of dragoons in the New Model Army. He had been one of the King's judges and signed the death warrant. In the Scottish campaign of 1651 his regiment (converted from dragoons into cavalry) had fought under Lambert at Inverkeithing. He appears to have approved of Cromwell's dissolution of the Long Parliament. Matthew Alured had been the colonel of a foot regiment raised in 1650 for the Scottish war and in 1653 he was put in charge of the west of Scotland. Both he and Okey served under General Monk in the Highlands in the summer of 1654. Subsequently he was sent to Ireland by the Protector to raise a force to be landed in the western Highlands. Not much is known about Colonel Saunders but he had raised a regiment of foot for service in Ireland in 1650. These three colonels all found themselves in London at the time the first Protectorate Parliament was meeting. Alured had already been recalled from Ireland for insubordination: when he was there he had asked 'Was there ever any nation so cheated out of all their privileges?' No doubt he and Okey had together formulated their antagonism to the Protector while serving in Scotland. At any rate they afterwards entered into confabulations with Major John Wildman, the Leveller leader, better known for his oratory than his soldiering, who drew up on their behalf a manifesto which he hoped to induce other colonels to sign. In it the complaint was embodied that far too much power had been placed in Oliver Cromwell's hands. In October all three of the discontented colonels were arrested. Saunders at once submitted and was restored to his command. Okey, after being acquitted of treason by a court martial, was compelled to surrender his commission. But Alured, whose offence had been heightened by his previous behaviour in Ireland, was not only cashiered but imprisoned. It was in connection with this movement against the Protector that the name of Robert Overton reappears.

As we have seen, Overton had openly stated his misgivings about the Protectorate to Cromwell, though after seeing him he had returned to Hull and then taken a command under Monk in Scotland. But while he had been in London interviewing the Protector he had also, like Okey, Alured, Saunders and Lawson, visited Wildman's plotting centre. And after he returned to Scotland he had written letters to Wildman to let him know that there was a party there that 'would stand right for a Commonwealth'. Wildman and his fellow conspirators therefore naturally counted on Overton to head a movement against Cromwell in Scotland and to hand over Hull to their supporters. Yet Overton had told his Commander-in-Chief Monk (as Monk reported to Cromwell) that 'when he saw a settlement of government under your Highness, and could not with good conscience submit he would deliver up his commission, but till then he would serve your Highness faithfully'. This attempt to run with the hare and hunt with the hounds was asking for trouble. In spite of his promises both to Cromwell and Monk, Overton lent his patronage to a group of dissatisfied officers who were beginning to intrigue against the Government in the north of Scotland.

In December 1654 Overton and his group met in Aberdeen

and drew up a circular convening a meeting in Edinburgh on New Year's Day. How far they intended to go is not altogether clear. But they had already gone far enough for their own safety. General Monk was not the man to stand for such indiscipline. As soon as he learned of these plottings he asked the Protector if he should secure Overton. Finally — apparently on his own initiative — Monk sent for Overton and when he did not come as ordered, Monk put him under arrest and dispatched him to London. A letter of Overton's to a friend survives from this period and throws some light on his habit of mind; the following extract gives its full flavour:

> The Devil, like a swallow, may show himself a summer friend; but God is for winter storms of trial; and then He must assuredly make our utmost extremities His happiest and most helpful opportunities. I have in the late wars resisted the common enemy of my country (through the Almighty's mercy) to blood and frequent hazards of life; and since (blessed is His name) He hath carried me through reproaches, good and bad reports, loss of places, preferments and rewards: but now perhaps the Lord will a little more show his strength in my weakness and try me with the temptation of skin for skin . . . Oh that I could wrestle with Him in prayer, as some Jacobs do at this day . . . I trust I shall not need to fear what man can do unto me for anything I have done since my coming into Scotland. . . .

When Monk arrested him, Overton was searched and a copy of some verses was found in his pocket which ran:

> A Protector, what's that? 'Tis a stately thing
> That confesseth itself but the ape of a King;
> A tragical Caesar acted by a clown;
> Or a brass farthing stamped with a kind of a crown.

Monk forwarded these verses to Cromwell together with other information he had acquired about the movement against him in the north of Scotland. Both Cromwell and Monk were angry with Overton because they considered that he had broken his word not to enter into political intrigues if he received a command. Thurloe was of the opinion that Overton was a weakling who was being used by a more cunning man, such as Wildman. But he had dipped his feet into the waters of mutiny. On the day he arrived in the capital he was committed to the Tower and kept a prisoner there and elsewhere for the remainder of the Protectorate.

Overton's conduct had been vacillating, ineffective and fatalistic. Yet he had his consistencies. For after Cromwell's death, when he was restored to his Governorship of Hull, he again tried, though feebly, to maintain the Good Old Cause. But Monk, once bit, was twice shy. And for a second time in his life Overton failed in a time of crisis to prove that he possessed the mettle of martyrdom.

Most of the army extremists who were disappointed with Cromwell belonged to the left-wing sects, except Wildman, who was a sceptic. Colonel Nathaniel Rich, who, like Okey, lost his command in Scotland, was a Fifth Monarchy man. Overton was either a Fifth Monarchy man or a Baptist. Alured was a Baptist. Okey was possibly a Fifth Monarchy man. Monk had no sympathy for such views as being stumbling blocks to discipline. He had pressed for the arrest of Overton; he had asked Cromwell to send him reliable field officers to take over the command of the regiments of Harrison and Rich; and writing from Dalkeith he had told Thurloe that the news of Harrison's imprisonment 'gave a great deal of satisfaction to the officers here'. General Fleetwood in Ireland, who was reputed to have Baptist sympathies, was less sure. 'It is very sad,' he wrote to Thurloe on February 22nd, 1655, 'that there should be breaches among such as have gone together in this work. The cause is the same as it was....'

It has never been proved how far Wildman and his Leveller group had planned at this stage to form an alliance between Overton and the malcontent officers on one side and the Royalists on the other to destroy the Protectorate and set up some kind of constitutional monarchy under the paradoxical name of a Free Commonwealth. It is true that later Major Wildman, and his friend Colonel Edward Sexby, entered into direct communication with the exiled Court. They may well have turned over some such idea in their minds. But it is almost incredible that men like Overton or Ludlow can have been willing so to stultify everything for which they had fought in the civil wars. After all if the army in Scotland and Ireland and the navy under Lawson could have been incited to move together, they might have hoped to construct a Leveller republic without any help from the Royalists, who could scarcely have been attracted to such a cause. The truth seems to be that the movement against the Lord Protector in the House of Commons and the dissolution of January 1655 naturally conjured up hopes in the hearts of all Cromwell's enemies. A stronger leader than Overton might have done the Protectorate much damage. But owing to the promptness of General Monk he had still not decided on revolt when he was arrested. Three weeks later Wildman was also apprehended in a village near Marlborough while dictating a declaration inviting 'the people' to take up arms against Cromwell. Thus the Levellers had their plans discovered and their allies in the army rendered impotent before Royalist schemes awoke into the realm of action. That did not happen until March 1655, when it heralded the experiment of rule by Cromwell's Major-Generals.

BIBLIOGRAPHY TO CHAPTER VIII

There is an article by Firth on Overton in the *Dictionary of National Biography*. The evidence that Overton was moved by personal or family considerations as well as public motives is in the *English Historical Review*, XXII, 313. The quotation on page 147 is from *Thurloe State Papers*, III, 47, which contain a number of other letters of Overton. For John Wildman see Maurice Ashley, *John Wildman* (1947) and the authorities quoted there. There is a life of John Rogers, fellow prisoner of Harrison, by E. Rogers (1867). The religion of Cromwell's sectarian officers is discussed in the first chapter of L. F. Brown, *The Political Activities of the Baptists and Fifth Monarchy Men in England during the Interregnum* (1912).

CHAPTER IX

CROMWELL'S MAJOR-GENERALS

Cromwell's Major-Generals were John Barkstead, James Berry, William Boteler, John Desborough, Charles Fleetwood, William Goffe, Thomas Kelsey, John Lambert, Phillip Skippon, Edward Whalley and Charles Worsley

THE Royalist rising of 1655 was a damp squib. Only in Wiltshire did any movement of significance occur. There Colonel John Penruddock managed to collect 400 men, entered Salisbury, and captured two judges and the High Sheriff of the county in their beds. Then they marched away to Blandford and proclaimed Charles II King. As soon as he had heard the news, Cromwell appointed John Desborough Major-General of the West. Desborough acted promptly. The Royalists retreated into Devonshire where they were rounded up by a single troop of cavalry that happened to be stationed in Exeter. Penruddock was beheaded, ten others executed, and a number imprisoned, though some of them escaped. Such was the swift end of the Royalist plot against the Protector in the early months of 1655. It was followed by the establishment of the system of government by Major-Generals.

The Major-Generals were born of financial necessity. Once the civil wars were over and peace had been concluded with the Dutch the classes which had supported the Parliament against the King expected the armed forces to be diminished and taxes to be lowered. In the first Protectorate Parliament it had been proposed to halve the size of the army and thereby cut direct taxation by one-third. After the dissolution Cromwell tried to fulfill that policy by reducing the establishment of each regiment and the pay of his soldiers. But the plots of the Levellers and the rising of the Royalists, coming on top of the war against Spain, made it impossible to manage with so small an army. It was therefore decided to raise local militia for police purposes.

The new militia was to consist almost entirely of cavalry organized in troops commanded by captains. But unlike the old pre-Cromwellian militia, it was to be permanently embodied, was to be paid, and was to serve, if necessary, outside its own area. The project first put forward by a committee of officers to the Council of State in May 1655, was that the horse militia should be only a reserve force, undergoing training once every three months, being paid at the rate of £8 a year for each trooper, and being called out purely in emergencies. The more far-reaching scheme, which came into effect during the late summer, was estimated to cost £80,000 a year and, though less expensive than the regular army, since the men lived at home, was a burden on the straitened exchequer. To control the new militia the country was divided into large districts or Associations, each of which was put in charge of a Major-General. The Major-Generals, to whom were given extensive powers over local questions, were appointed in August 1655.

The Major-Generals had three main duties. First, they had to sustain law and order and prevent any tumults, plotting or insurrections; secondly, they were required to 'promote godliness and virtue' by enforcing the laws against drunkenness, blasphemy and immorality of every kind; thirdly, they were to impose a tax on all known Royalists to meet the upkeep of their troops and thus make the system self-supporting.

It has been pointed out that the employment of Major-Generals to fasten a code of puritan behaviour on the whole of England and Wales was Oliver Cromwell's own contribution to the scheme. General Lambert, as the leading figure in his Council and probably the inventor and perfector of the system, was responsible for all the administrative details, but neither his character nor record leads one to suppose that he had any enthusiasm for the extension of the Major-General's duties to carpeting the remotest villages with a moral pattern. 'Is it wandering too far into the regions of conjecture,' asked S. R. Gardiner, 'to suggest that the readiness to add to the burdens originally laid on the shoulders of the Major-Generals the enormous task of encouraging virtue and discouraging vice must surely have proceeded from the Protector himself? . . . Should this view of the case be accepted [Gardiner argues that there must have been some difference of opinion on the subject since the Major-Generals had been appointed in August, but did not receive their commissions until two months later] much that followed afterwards in the growing estrangement between Oliver and Lambert becomes easily intelligible without the necessity of having recourse to merely personal motives on one side or the other.' Thus, with the imprisonment of Harrison and Overton, the extreme puritan Generals had been cast aside and Cromwell had fallen into the hands of the realists like Lambert and Monk. But the Lord Protector himself still gave an uplifting twist to the maintenance of order.

Let us consider who these Major-Generals were. First came Cromwell's two most experienced and trusted commanders, Lieutenant-General Fleetwood and Major-General Lambert. Fleetwood, who had been promoted to be Lord Deputy of Ireland in August 1654 — a fact that can scarcely have pleased Lambert who had been promised and then deprived of this honourable post — returned to England in September 1655. In his absence Cromwell's second son, Henry, was left in command of Ireland as Major-General. Fleetwood became responsible for seven counties stretching from Oxfordshire to Norfolk. To Lambert was assigned his home county of Yorkshire and the whole of the north of England except Lancashire. These posts were of the first importance. Thurloe described them as 'the greatest creations of honours his Highness hath made since his access to government'. But Fleetwood and Lambert were too valuable to the Protector for him to allow them to leave Whitehall. Hence, on Lambert's suggestion, each of them was permitted to have two deputies: Fleetwood's deputies were Major Hezekiah Haynes (a major in Fleetwood's cavalry regiment since 1649) and Major William Packer (who had been a captain in Cromwell's own regiment in 1644); Lambert's deputies were Colonel Robert Lilburne, who stayed at his post in York, and Colonel Charles Howard, the Governor of Carlisle, a former captain in Cromwell's lifeguard.

The first of the Major-Generals to be appointed had been John Desborough (or Disbrowe, as he was more usually spelt). Desborough was born at Eltisley in Cambridgeshire in 1608. He was a qualified attorney but, like Cromwell, he practised farming and in June 1636 had married Cromwell's sister Jane. Quartermaster in Cromwell's own original troop of horse, he later became a captain in Cromwell's first cavalry regiment. Afterwards he was promoted a major in Fairfax's cavalry regiment and obtained his own regiment in 1649, which was handed over to him by Cromwell when he went to Ireland. Although therefore Desborough did not rise to the rank of colonel until after the King's death, he had been prominent before that. In May 1647 he had attacked two troops that sympathized with Parliament and a year later had suppressed a rising at Bury St. Edmunds. Thenceforward honours flowed upon him. He is said to have fought as a Major-General at Worcester and in August 1654 was appointed one of the Generals-at-sea. He had also been a member of the Council of State and a Commissioner of the Treasury under the Protectorate and had been in the running for the post of Commander-in-Chief in Scotland.

Desborough's rustic origin and manners were the constant subject of ridicule by the Cavaliers. But a fellow Member of Parliament, who knew him well, described him as being 'blunt and honest'. For that very reason perhaps, he was deficient as a statesman: at least he was tactless, as was shown by the way he offended General Venables. He was certainly the prototype and one of the chief advocates of the Major-Generals of 1655. Making Salisbury his headquarters, he was kept hard at work supervising a vast area and on one occasion, when he was in Somerset, observed with feeling that he wanted to return to his poor wife.

Cromwell's cousin, Commissary-General Edward Whalley, was put in command of Lincolnshire, Nottinghamshire, Derbyshire, Warwickshire and Leicestershire. Whalley was born in Nottinghamshire and his mother was the daughter of Sir Henry Cromwell of Hinchingbrooke, the uncle of the Lord Protector. He was, as we have already seen, one of Cromwell's best Generals and was a zealous supporter of the Protectorate. Of all the Major-Generals he was the most concerned to be fair, while doing his duty.

The Major-General in charge of Worcestershire, Herefordshire, Shropshire, Monmouthshire, and ultimately the whole of Wales was James Berry. Berry was born about 1610, probably in the west Midlands, where he was employed later at an iron foundry. He was a typical member of the puritan middle classes. His earliest extant letter, written when he was about twenty-eight, exhorted the Reverend Richard Baxter to 'keep in with God and walk comfortably'. At the beginning of the civil wars he appeared out of the blue as captain-lieutenant of Cromwell's own troop of horse in his own regiment, thus serving along with Desborough and Whalley. At the battle of Gainsborough he was commended by Cromwell for slaying a godson of King Charles I 'with a thrust under his short ribs'. Later his troop was transferred to Fairfax's regiment and in 1647 he was a major in Colonel Twistleton's cavalry regiment with which he fought in the battle of Preston. After the battle he carried Cromwell's dispatch to the House of Commons and was awarded £200. He obtained his own cavalry regiment (formerly Hazlerigg's) in June 1651, but after its return from Scotland in the autumn of 1653 Berry spent little time with it. Berry, whose religious sympathies lay with the Independents, had been active against the Presbyterian leaders in Parliament in 1647. His regiment had expressed its approval of the dissolution of the Long Parliament and, according to Baxter, Berry had been one of the 'two chief men' (that is, with Lambert) in drawing up the Instrument of Government. As Major-General his headquarters were at Shrewsbury; but as his was one of the most Royalist districts in the country he was occupied most of the time touring round it. On one occasion he wrote from Lincolnshire: 'Our ministers are bad, our magistrates idle, and the people all asleep; only these present actings have a little awakened them.' On another occasion he reported from Monmouth: 'I am much troubled with the market towns; everywhere vices abounding and magistrates fast asleep.' But even his exuberance was insufficient for Cromwell who reproved him when he ventured to return to Lincoln for a holiday. Berry enjoyed a sense of humour rare among puritans and dealt tactfully with General Harrison's friend, Vavasour Powell, the firebrand of Wales.

William Boteler, the Major-General for Bedfordshire, Northamptonshire, Rutlandshire and Huntingdonshire (one of the smaller Associations) was the son of Neville Boteler of Barnwell, Northamptonshire, was educated at Oundle, and a leading personage in his county. He was a J.P. and a member of the commission for ejecting scandalous ministers. At one time he is said to have had extreme views about the need for toleration. Boteler became the major in Berry's regiment and his troop was stationed in the west of England when the Royalist rising was being prepared in February 1655. He was particularly energetic in Bristol where the Mayor and Aldermen were said to have Royalist sympathies and he recommended their dismissal and the establishment of a garrison there. He reported himself as being 'diligent to discover Cavalier designs' and when the insurrection occurred at Salisbury he was among the first to join Desborough in pursuing Penruddock's force into Devonshire. On March 28th he reported to Thurloe from Marlborough (near where Wildman had been arrested): 'Everything is lovely in its season; the same justice upon these offenders [i.e. Penruddock and the Royalists] would lose much of its glory if its execution should be deferred.' Although Boteler did not obtain a regiment of his own until 1658, his appointment as Major-General was the reward of his industry in the early months of 1655. He reported from Northampton, his headquarters, that there were 'many malignants' and 'some . . . not very hearty in our work neither'. Boteler himself, however, was exceedingly hearty — for example he expelled the Mayor and five other officials from the Corporation of Bedford — and earned the reputation of being the least popular of all Cromwell's Major-Generals, at any rate among the Royalists.

Colonel William Goffe, the Major-General in charge of Sussex, Hampshire and Berkshire, was General Edward Whalley's son-in-law. Goffe was born in Haverfordwest and, having served as a quartermaster and afterwards captain in a foot regiment, became lieutenant-colonel in Colonel Harley's (later Pride's) regiment of foot with which he fought at Naseby, next transferring to General Fairfax's regiment of foot which was to become Cromwell's. This regiment he commanded at the battle of Dunbar and was awarded by Cromwell the colonelcy of his regiment for his services there. Goffe's regiment fought under Fleetwood at the battle of Worcester and helped to suppress Penruddock's rising. Goffe was a strong anti-royalist and a knowledgeable interpreter of the ways of the Almighty.

He was loquacious in the debates of the Army Council at Putney, using the name of God twenty-six times in one speech alone. He was one of the King's judges and signed the death warrant. His regiment afterwards furnished the guards which protected the Council of State in Whitehall. He was one of the officers who presented the army's petition in August 1652, and in December 1653, on Lambert's orders, although he himself had Fifth Monarchy sympathies, he turned the minority in the Assembly of Saints out of their House. A conscientious puritan soldier, he laboured hard as a Major-General, but constantly complained about his difficulties over money and the opposition he habitually encountered in his Association. In fact he was better liked than he imagined, so that when in the election of 1656 he was after all chosen M.P. for Hampshire he found it 'a special providence of God'.

Lieutenant-Colonel Thomas Kelsey, the Major-General in charge of Kent and Surrey, was said to have begun life as 'a mean trader in London . . . a godly button maker'. He first appears as a major in the foot regiment commanded by Colonel Richard Ingoldsby, who was Oliver Cromwell's cousin. Later he was promoted lieutenant-colonel in the same regiment. He was extremely critical of Parliament's proposals for disbanding the army in 1647 and in 1648 he was, like Goffe, prominent in the proceedings of the Council of the Army. His commanding officer, Ingoldsby, sat among the King's judges and signed the death warrant. For a time Kelsey was Deputy Governor of Oxford and for more than two years sustained the Visitation and Reformation of the University. He deposed the Vice-Chancellor and a number of heads of Colleges, using his soldiers to enforce his orders where necessary. In return the University gave him an honorary M.A. In the spring of 1650 he received orders to convert Oxford castle into a citadel, but soon afterwards he was appointed Governor of Dover. He married a sister of John Graunt, the earliest English statistician. As Major-General he established his headquarters at Maidstone. Like his neighbouring colleague, Goffe, he found the utmost difficulty in raising money to pay for his troops.

Under the original scheme Major-General Phillip Skippon was the officer responsible for the City of London. Skippon was an old soldier who, like Hopton, Goring, Monk, Fairfax and others, had learnt his trade on the Continent and was for many years in Dutch service. 'From a common soldier,' wrote Clarendon, 'he had raised himself to the degree of a captain and to the reputation of a good officer.' As soon as the civil war broke out the Common Council had put him in charge of the trained bands of London. He served as a Major-General both under Essex and under Fairfax and was highly commended by Cromwell who left him in military command of London when he marched north in 1650. At the time that the Major-Generals were appointed Skippon was about fifty-five and past his prime. Whether because of his health or for some other reason he did not in effect act as Major-General but left the responsibility for London to his deputy, Colonel John Barkstead, who was as well the Major-General for Middlesex and Lieutenant of the Tower of London. Skippon's sympathies lay towards the Presbyterians and he has left to posterity one or two religious pamphlets, including *A Salve for Every Sore* and *The Christian Centurion's Observations*, in which he expounds his own particular brand of religious musing and intolerance.

Barkstead, a Baptist by faith, was built of sterner stuff. Of German descent, his father, Michael Barkstead, was a London goldsmith. John began his military career as a captain in Colonel Venn's regiment of foot. For two-and-a-half years he was Governor of Reading and then in 1647 he succeeded to the colonelcy of one of the New Model regiments of foot after it had refused to go to Ireland under its old colonel. In 1648 he put down riots in the City of London and accompanied Fairfax in his campaign in Kent and Essex. He was then ordered to bring the King from Windsor to London for his trial, where he was one of the judges. He attended every session of the Court and signed the death warrant. In April 1650, the Council of State ordered that his regiment should guard Parliament and the City. In all this he was extremely forward: he trained and drilled recruits and provided drafts for Scotland. His appointment as Lieutenant of the Tower dated from August 1652. In 1654 he became M.P. for Colchester and was later knighted by Cromwell. When the Royalist rising broke out in March 1655, he received orders to collect all the horses he could and bring them to the Tower. As a Major-General he suppressed bear baiting, cock fighting, wrestling, vagrancy, and much of the crime in the City of London.

Finally we come to Lieutenant-Colonel Charles Worsley, the Major-General in charge of Lancashire, Cheshire and Staffordshire. He was the youngest of the Major-Generals, being born near Manchester in 1622. A captain in 1644, he sprang into prominence after the execution of the King when in 1650 he raised a foot regiment for Cromwell in Lancashire in which he served as the lieutenant-colonel throughout the Dunbar campaign. During the Worcester campaign he reinforced Lilburne at Manchester and took part in the interception of the Scots when they retired after their defeat. Afterwards he engaged in the operation to conquer the Isle of Man from the Royalists. In 1652 he went to London and assisted in the dissolution of the Rump. He was the first M.P. for Manchester in the Protectorate Parliament. An unswerving supporter of Cromwell and the Protectorate, he reckoned that his duties as Major-General were inspired from on high. 'I plainly discern the finger of God going along with it, which is indeed no small encouragement unto me,' he told Thurloe. Of all the Major-Generals none was more industrious in the duty of closing ale-houses which he regarded as 'the very womb, that brings forth all manner of wickedness'. Being in charge of the most Royalist district in England he succeeded in raising money from the beaten Cavaliers to pay for his troops and a bit over. But he toiled so unsparingly that he killed himself. He died in June 1656, and all the other Major-Generals attended his funeral. He was succeeded by Colonel Tobias Bridge.

The most striking thing about Cromwell's Major-Generals of 1655 was that they were such a close-knit group. Lambert had been Cromwell's most capable and trusted commander ever since Fairfax resigned. Fleetwood was his son-in-law; Desborough was his brother-in-law; Whalley was his cousin. So much for the family relationships. But in addition, James Berry, Whalley and Desborough had all been captains together in Cromwell's original Ironside regiment, and William Packer, one of Fleetwood's deputies, had been a captain in the same regiment from 1644, while Charles Howard, one of Lambert's deputies, had served in Cromwell's lifeguard. William Boteler had been the major in Berry's regiment and the young and unfortunate Charles Worsley had raised Cromwell's foot regiment for him in 1650. Kelsey had been the major in a regiment commanded by another of Cromwell's cousins. In fact with the exception of Skippon, who was *persona grata* in the City of London, and Barkstead, about whose early history we know little, every one of the Major-Generals was known personally to the Lord Protector as an officer on whom he could rely to do his duty in the teeth of every temptation.

In the second place, all the Major-Generals had long since burnt their boats politically. Three of them, Barkstead, Goffe and Whalley, had sat among the King's judges and signed the death warrant; they knew their lives were forfeit should the Stuarts return. Kelsey's senior officer had also signed the death warrant and plainly Kelsey would have done so too had he been asked. Though Lambert and Fleetwood were not technically 'regicides', they were too closely identified with Cromwell to hope for mercy in the event of a Restoration. Boteler, Berry and Worsley had not been among the King's judges merely because they were insufficiently important to have been asked. Each of them was a 'committed' man. So long as they survived they were dependent on the Protectorate, and indeed by their very acceptance of the post of Major-General, which required them to chastise the Royalists, they were sworn enemies to the exiled monarch. Not only that. They were also foes of the irreconcilable republican group. For they all of them, either overtly or by implication, approved of the dissolution of the Long Parliament and, except for Skippon, who had ceased to count or did not function, they had actively resisted the Presbyterian majority which had ruled the Commons until 1647. For good or ill, their fortunes were linked with Cromwell's.

A third consideration about these Major-Generals was that they all of them belonged to the rising middle classes which had brought about the revolution against the Stuarts. Not one of them was an offshoot of the traditionally governing aristocracy and most of them were self-made men of comparatively humble origins. The point was emphasized by their enemies. When disgruntled members of the Parliament of 1656 met in the Bull's Head or Half Moon in the City of London, they reminded each other how Barkstead was 'a thimble-maker', how Kelsey had 'sold leather-points' and continued to dilate with relish upon 'the mean extraction of many more Major-Generals'. In fact Lambert, Fleetwood and Desborough came from the same social stratum as Cromwell himself. But Phillip Skippon and Tobias Bridge, Worsley's successor, were self-made soldiers, and Kelsey, Berry, Barkstead and Whalley belonged to the trading class which was usually still looked down upon in the middle of the seventeenth century. But that any of them were 'on the make', as their critics asserted, is not susceptible of proof.

A final generalization that may be ventured upon this group of Major-Generals is that they were, on the whole, not religious fanatics. Indeed only Fleetwood and Goffe appear to have been in the line of inspired English Christian Generals who range from Cromwell himself to General Gordon and General Dobbie. On the one hand, they had few links with the Fifth Monarchists who had fallen into disrepute along with Harrison and Overton. On the other hand, they no sympathy for the Levellers' point of view. In Cromwell's own character two strands intertwined — that of the puritan enthusiast and the astute politician. But the Major-Generals, though ready and eager to impose the accepted puritan restrictions of their time on the districts under their charge did so in the name of discipline rather than of faith; they were far more empiricists than evangelists. It was because of their passion for order that they acted so firmly against the Quakers and other sectarian extremists who disturbed the placidity of the market towns.

In another way most of these Generals differed from their master. Few of them had succumbed to that parliamentary tradition which was holy to those who had struggled in the Long Parliament against the Stuart monarchy. All of them were to be M.P.s in the next House of Commons, but they understood little of the atmosphere of that self-conscious club. None of them would have said (like Cavour) that the worst of Chambers was better than the best of ante-chambers. In the last resort if they had been obliged to choose between order and liberty, they would have preferred order.

How did the Major-Generals carry out their duties? As usually happens when capable men undertake the same administrative task they experienced and recognized the same difficulties. According to their instructions they were required to levy a tax of ten per cent on land of rentable value of £100 a year or more or £10 on every £1500 of personal property belonging to Royalists. Almost all the Major-Generals came to agree that the limit of exemption was too high. For they argued that Royalists who owned land worth £50 a year in more than one district ought to pay the levy. Kelsey wanted the limit to be reduced to £50 a year; so did Desborough; Worsley advocated a limit of £40. They were also troubled about what they should do with regard to encumbrances upon the Cavaliers' estates. The original intention was that each group of counties should raise enough to pay for its own horse militia. But hardly any of the Major-Generals succeeded in collecting sufficient for the purpose, and Major-General Goffe suggested that they should all pay into and draw out of a common treasury. Both Desborough and Berry complained about lack of means to pay their militia and wrote to Thurloe that they would have to find some of the money out of their own pockets. Eventually instructions were received that six months' pay should be provided by the Major-Generals out of what they had managed to raise. But even that proved insufficient and in April 1656 it was decided that the establishment of the militia troops would have to be reduced in number from one hundred to eighty. That decision caused much dissatisfaction and Berry, rather than dismiss men after six months' service, paid them for the whole year, compassionately offering to meet the excess cost out of his own salary.

The second common difficulty that most of the Major-Generals discovered was in co-operating with the local government. Special commissions had been appointed to recruit the militia and also to eject or replace local clergy. The Major-Generals did not find it hard to work with these commissioners who were, like themselves, selected for their loyalty to the Protectorate. But the local Corporations, Assizes and J.P.s were not always so forthcoming. In some cases the very presence of the Major-Generals gingered them up; in other cases they were as unhelpful as they dared to be. Local friendships and patriotisms were invoked against the incoming high constables. And although the Major-Generals were invariably appointed to districts where they were known and where their homes were, the very presence of high-powered officers with orders from Whitehall created a spirit of antagonism they could not assuage. Sometimes the Major-Generals elected to sit alongside the Justices to ensure that the law was carried out or gave orders to the Corporations which they were compelled to obey. The atmosphere, however, was not everywhere the same. Whalley reported from Nottingham: 'the heart of the people is sound', while Desborough wrote from Launceston on almost the same date (in August 1656) 'designs are on foot to the subversion of what has been done for the nation's peace and safety'.

Some of the Major-Generals were stricter than others in promoting the virtue and morality deemed suitable in puritan England. For example, they had instructions to close down solitary ale houses, as they might become centres of conspiracy. But Worsley, Berry and Boteler positively delighted in shutting down as many ale houses as they could. Again, while Whalley was reluctant to forbid all horse races, informing the Earl of Exeter that 'it was not your Highness's intention in the suppressing of horse races to abridge gentlemen of that sport, but to prevent the great confluences of irreconcilable enemies', Worsley prohibited all racing in Cheshire. Barkstead gave orders that bears in their gardens and cocks in their pits should be put to death by soldiers of the Commonwealth. Boteler fined a man £6 for saying 'damn'. Finally in their religious duties some were severer than others. While Worsley and Haynes grumbled about the Quakers, Desborough and Berry had a reputation for tolerance towards the extremer sects.

But although a few of the Major-Generals might have been more easy-going and more tactful than the rest, by interfering with local government and customs, ejecting local preachers, closing down ale houses, banning horse races, and levying a discriminatory tax on one section of the community (which might otherwise have accepted as inevitable the change in government), they all of them courted, or at least were resigned to, unpopularity. However high-minded they were, they were imposing a scheme of centralized dictatorship which has only been seen in England in times of war or revolution. Whatever they did, they could scarcely hope to survive a counter-revolution should it come. Cromwell and Lambert had chosen them as men they could trust, and they in turn had to trust the Lord Protector to defend and uphold them and never to abandon them to the malice of their enemies. Though they were all too conscious of the suspicion, hatred and malignancy lapping round them as they rode out daily on their tours of duty, they felt proudly that they were the intimates of Oliver Cromwell, the instruments of his choice, as he was the instrument of the Almighty. They could not imagine for one moment that he would ever betray them.

BIBLIOGRAPHY TO CHAPTER IX

For the Major-Generals the standard works are Gardiner's *History of the Commonwealth and Protectorate* (edition of 1903 in four volumes) and the article by D. W. Rannie in the *English Historical Review* for 1895. In addition Sir James Berry and Stephen G. Lee, *A Cromwellian Major General: the career of Colonel James Berry* (1938) is valuable. Articles on all the Major-Generals, with useful additions from *Notes and Queries*, are in the *Dictionary of National Biography*, with one exception, William Boteler. For Boteler see 'William Boteler: A Cromwellian Oligarch' in *The Huntingdon Library Quarterly*, vol. XI (1948). This article seems to me incomplete and not entirely accurate: even the title is questionable, but it contains many useful references. For Boteler's behaviour at Bedford see also *The Minute Book of Bedford Corporation, 1647-1664*, ed. Guy Parsloe (1949) and for his activities in Northampton *Quarter Sessions Records of the County of Northampton* (ed. Joan Wake, 1924). Berry's letters are printed in full by Berry and Lee. There is a long chapter on Skippon in C. E. Lucas Phillips, *Cromwell's Captains* (1938). All the quotations from the letters of Major-Generals in the text are taken from *Thurloe State Papers*, vols. IV and V. The quotation about Desborough on page 154 is from Sir Francis Russell's letter to Henry Cromwell in Lansdowne MSS 822, f. 132.

CHAPTER X

CROMWELL'S GENERALS AND THE OFFER OF THE CROWN

Cromwell refused the title of King on May 8th, 1657
Lambert was dismissed on July 13th, 1657

In July 1656 the Lord Protector reluctantly agreed that another general election should be held. The Major-Generals had established order at home, but the war against Spain was proving costly. If the structure of constitutional government according to the terms of Lambert's 'Instrument' was to be maintained, only a parliament could provide the additional taxation necessary to meet the existing scale of national expenditure. 'The Major-Generals told Cromwell', wrote Sir Charles Firth, 'that they could secure the election of members favourable to the Government.' If that indeed were so, the Major-Generals were optimists of a high order. For their activities, whether as moral policemen, as tax collectors, as guardians of the puritan Church, as licensing authorities, or as defaulters on their obligations to pay the militia, had not endeared them to their fellow countrymen. They appear to have had a tip from Cromwell to do their best. 'I shall be careful to follow your instructions,' wrote Major-General James Berry to the Protector from Shropshire on August 12th, 'I hope things may succeed well'; but he went on to add that 'some dissatisfied persons attempt to be chosen' and to suggest that if Cromwell would make them Lords, 'they would give you leave to be King'. The suggestion can scarcely have been intended seriously because Berry was afterwards opposed to Cromwell's becoming King, but his letter reflected the difficulties with which the Major-Generals, for the most part, knew that they were confronted in their new role as election agents.

Soundings had already been going on in the constituencies for some weeks before the election campaign opened. On June 27th Hezekiah Haynes had written to the Secretary of State, Thurloe, from Bury St. Edmunds: 'I understand there is liberty now given to discourse and to try the tempers of many as to a parliament.' On August 8th Major-General Goffe noted from Winchester 'The unquiet spirit of discontented men doth begin to show itself, hoping to make their advantages out of the approaching assembly.' On August 23rd Goffe wrote that in Sussex it was the plan of the 'disaffected party' to 'have no soldier, decimator, or any man that hath salary'. One of Lambert's Deputies had the same kind of report to send from Northumberland and Durham and Major-General Kelsey stated that the Cavaliers in Kent 'give out that they will down with the Majors-General, the decimators and the new militia'.

Of course the Royalists did not have a vote, but the Major-Generals were aware that the delay in paying or the failure to pay the local horse militia at all had made the Protectorate unpopular with its own supporters. Haynes was particularly emphatic on that point. Only Whalley in the Midlands struck a note of optimism. After the election in Kent Kelsey asserted that 'there is such perverseness in those chosen that without resolution in you and the Council to maintain the interest of God's people, which is to be preferred before a thousand parliaments, against all opposition, we shall return to our Egyptian taskmasters'.

In spite of the forebodings of most of the Major-Generals, the Cromwellians were well represented in the new Parliament. With one exception all the Major-Generals themselves and their Deputies were elected members and all except two of the Council of State. The opposition was not united, for it consisted of various elements ranging from Presbyterians to concealed Royalists. Many precautions were taken by the Protector or his Council to insulate Parliament from outside pressure. But to make assurance doubly sure the Council of State, on the advice of at least some of the Major-Generals (Kelsey, for example), decided to exclude from the new House about a hundred of the 460 members elected. They did this by perverting two clauses in the 'Instrument of Government' which had laid it down that only persons of 'known integrity fearing God and of good conversation' might become M.P.s. Certificates were refused to members of whom the Council disapproved. This purging of Parliament took place on September 17th.

Cromwell afterwards asserted that the purge was forced upon him by the army. If that were so, the most powerful instigator of the purge was presumably Major-General Lambert, who had the reputation of still being the directing light among the soldiers in the Council of State. For some months the Royalists had been telling each other that it was in Lambert's power 'to raise Oliver higher or else to set him in his place' and there had been rumours in the early summer of a movement in the army to persuade Cromwell to detach the office of Commander-in-Chief from that of Protector and give it to Lambert. That was inviting Cromwell to cut his own throat: no ruler in his position could afford to let go his grip over the Armed Forces. But Lambert was certainly Cromwell's mouthpiece in conveying military orders to the army and when the Protector opened Parliament he again drove with him in his coach. At the same time Cromwell appears to have been in the closest touch with his other Generals in those autumn days. Eleven days before he met his new Parliament he had addressed a meeting of officers, in which each regiment was represented by a field officer, and had given them a dress rehearsal of the speech he was going to deliver to the new House. Thus, although Cromwell was absent from the meetings of the Council of State that examined the returns of the new M.P.s, it is hard to believe that it was without at least his knowledge and acquiescence that the Opposition members were excluded by the men of the sword, his trusted intimates, and his closest counsellors.

Before the purge actually took place Cromwell had addressed all the elected members of his second Parliament in the Painted Chamber. In his speech he went out of his way to defend and praise the Major-Generals:

> Truly (he said) if ever I think anything were honest, this was, as anything that ever I knew; and I could as soon venture my life with it as anything I ever undertook . . . And truly if any man be angry at it, I am plain and shall use a homely expression, let him turn the buckle of his girdle behind him.

Later in the speech he became even more animated: the institution of Major-Generals, he said, 'hath been more effectual towards the discountenancing of vice and settling religion than anything done this fifty years. I will abide it, notwithstanding the envy and slander of foolish men. . . .'

At first then in the autumn of 1656 everything seemed to roll forward harmoniously between Cromwell, his Generals and the new Parliament. In addition to the members refused admission by the Council of State other opponents of the Protectorate voluntarily withdrew by way of protest so that nearly all who remained were Cromwell's assured supporters. They proceeded to pass bills for renouncing and annulling the 'pretended title of Charles Stuart' and for the security of the Lord Protector's person. Yet while on the surface all was smooth and agreeable, divisions soon began to show. For it proved that the supporters of the Protectorate were split among themselves. On one side was the army party, led by the Major-Generals who, proud of what they had achieved in purifying and pacifying the counties, were willing to sustain their new method of local administration as a permanent feature of government. But on the other side, there was forming a new Court Party consisting of lawyers like Bulstrode Whitelocke and John Glyn, the Lord Chief Justice, officials like John Thurloe, the unique Secretary of State, and ex-Royalists like Roger Boyle, Lord Broghil, who wanted to put the Protectorate on a secure constitutional footing, to bring to an end the rule of the Major-Generals, and to prove themselves to be members of a real, effective and even traditional Parliament of England. These New Courtiers were sensitive to outside criticism. 'It is reported abroad,' said one of them, Denis Bond, 'that we are but the rag of a Parliament. They say that we are now made up of none but soldiers and courtiers, and I know not what friends to my Lord Protector. This is a scandal to us.' 'I hope no man thinks it a scandal,' retorted Major-General John Desborough, 'to be a soldier, or my Lord Protector's friend . . .' Nevertheless the division between the courtiers and the soldiers was plain and it shaped the whole history of the Parliament. And soon it became still plainer. In order to thwart the soldiers, the courtiers brought in a proposal to revise Lambert's 'Instrument of Government' by making Cromwell King.

Since 1653 people's opinions had altered about the wisdom of re-establishing the monarchy in the family of Cromwell. It appears that when Major-General John Lambert was consulting with his fellow officers at the time of the Assembly of Saints about a new form of government their original intention had been to offer the crown to Cromwell, and Cromwell had refused it. At any rate in his speech of January 22nd, 1655, Cromwell had protested against the suggestion that the new Government should be a 'patrimony' and had asserted that his judgment was against making the office of Protector hereditary. Whether Lambert himself had offered the Crown to Cromwell or the question had merely been explored is uncertain; but it is a fact that Lambert had been willing that the office of Protector should be hereditary. However, according to the actual 'Instrument', Cromwell did not even possess the right to nominate his successor; the choice was left to the Council of State. Since that time Lambert, Fleetwood and the rest of Cromwell's Generals had performed good services to the Protectorate; they had worked hard in the Council of State; they had equipped and dispatched the fleets of Blake and Penn; they had imposed peace and order in Scotland and Ireland as well as in England; they had crushed Royalist risings and eliminated centres of discontent; they had brought some semblance of uniformity into the affairs of the puritan churches. Hence they had reason to feel that if the existing regime, having proved itself, was to continue, one of them had the right to be considered as Cromwell's successor as Protector. Lambert, who was twenty years younger than Cromwell, was an obvious candidate. But Fleetwood, who was about the same age as Lambert and was Cromwell's son-in-law, was also in the running. On the other hand, the lawyers poured a flow of telling arguments into Cromwell's ears. A Protector was unknown to the English law, as a King was. After all, they argued, if his designation were changed, it would have little significance from the administrative point of view. The Council of State and Parliament would continue to exist. Other titles had been perpetuated; for example, as Lord Protector, Cromwell had conferred several knighthoods. The title of King would be a mere 'feather in his cap', but it would enable the law courts to function as of old. Finally a hereditary monarchy would guarantee the permanence of the puritan revolution and sanctify the changes in the distribution of property — such as the sale of crown and church lands — which accompanied it; while if there were no agreed successor, Cromwell's Generals would fight it out among themselves when he died and anarchy would follow.

The inspirer of the monarchical movement was the ex-Royalist and Irish peer, Lord Broghil. But when it came to the struggle over the question of the Crown it is not exact to say that it was a contest between Cromwell's Generals and the lawyers. For Broghil himself had served Cromwell as a General in Ireland and the first advocate of the idea of making Cromwell King in the Commons has been described as 'Major-General' William Jephson. General Edward Montagu also favoured making Cromwell King. But Broghil, Jephson and Montagu did not belong to Cromwell's once cherished military circle who had fought side by side with him in the civil wars; they were new men recently promoted. Incidentally there is no clear evidence that Jephson was a Major-General at that time. He was a colonel in command of an Irish regiment, who was M.P. for Youghal and one of Broghil's cronies.

Jephson's original proposal, introduced on October 28th, 1656, was to amend the thirty-second clause of the 'Instrument of Government' so as to make the Protectorate hereditary instead of elective. Lieutenant-General Ludlow has a story in his memoirs that Cromwell was secretly pleased and subsequently rewarded Jephson by giving him, among other things, a regiment. But Ludlow is an entirely unreliable authority and such other evidence as we have suggests that Cromwell's first reaction was unfavourable and that Jephson already had a regiment. Most of the English officers in and outside the House were definitely against the proposal. But on November 14th a deputation came to see Cromwell about the matter. Cromwell declined the honour, but not finally, for five days later it was again discussed between him and its advocates. Broghil and his friends were convinced that they could in the end persuade Cromwell to accept and were not going to give up trying. But the Major-Generals were equally vehemently opposed to it. On November 21st, for example, Major-General Berry and Major-General Desborough were engaged in argument in the

Speaker's Chamber and in the Smoking Room of the House of Commons with Colonel John Bridge, another Irish member who belonged to Broghil's group, on the subject of the succession. Desborough said that rather than make Cromwell King he would prefer to give him the right to name his successor as Protector, for that would be as good a guarantee against anarchy after his death and would not be offensive to the convinced republicans.

The question was left to simmer for three months. Meanwhile two events occurred which induced Cromwell himself to reconsider it and to look with more pleasure on the proposal of kingship while they tempted Lambert and the Major-Generals to resist it more violently. Early in November the Commons, whose activities, like those of the Council of State, ranged between matters of large public policy and minor details of local administration, began to debate the case of a Quaker, James Naylor. Naylor, under the influence of a number of women disciples, had suffered from the temporary aberration that he was either Christ returned to earth or a new Messiah. This blasphemy scandalized the M.P.s, who occupied many hours debating whether Naylor should be put to death or given some less severe punishment. Cromwell, a merciful man where matters of religion were concerned, could not understand why the question was considered one for Parliament and was inclined to ask himself whether, if he had been King, his right to intervene to save Naylor's life would more readily have been recognized. He saw the issue in its broadest light. As he said afterwards, every man's case might be Naylor's case. Most of the Major-Generals, however, regarded themselves as fully competent to cope with blasphemy; it was (like the closing of the ale houses) their acknowledged speciality. But not all were certain whether Naylor's crime was blasphemy in its most horrid sense. Desborough, Goffe and Whalley were willing to tread the path of mercy. But Skippon, Kelsey and Boteler were for the heaviest penalties. Lambert, as always, was on the side of clemency. In the end Naylor escaped death, but not before his crime had reminded Cromwell that even a Lord Protector was not in a position to protect 'liberty of conscience'.

The second political event in these winter months was the

proposal brought forward by Major-General Desborough when the House was half empty on Christmas Day to turn the decimation tax into a permanent imposition on all former Royalists. We must assume that Cromwell had approved of this proposal; at any rate it was supported not only by the Major-Generals but by John Thurloe and three other members of the Council of State. But Broghil, the ex-Royalist, and his group were against it and so were the lawyers who contended that it was contrary to the Act of Oblivion of 1651. When the bill was read a first time on January 7th, 1657, not only did Broghil and the lawyers speak against it but so did Cromwell's latest son-in-law, John Claypole, who was married to his youngest daughter, Elizabeth. Desborough and Lambert put their case skilfully. 'It was blows not fair words,' exclaimed Desborough, 'that settled, and must settle, the peace of England.' 'The quarrel,' observed Lambert, 'is now between light and darkness; not who shall rule, but whether we shall live, or be preserved, or no. Good words will not do with the Cavaliers.' But the majority was against them and finally on January 29th the bill was defeated by 124 votes to eighty-eight.

Where had Cromwell stood on this? As we have seen, four months earlier he had sworn that he would abide by the institution of Major-Generals 'notwithstanding the envy and slander of foolish men'. Now, however, the division between Lambert and the Major-Generals, on the one side, and Broghil and the New Courtiers, on the other, had defined itself. In the last stages of the debate on the Decimation Bill Major-General Desborough had 'high words' with James Ashe, M.P. for Bath, and Major-General Boteler and Harry Cromwell, the Protector's cousin, had nearly fought a duel. After their defeat some of the Major-Generals had gone in deputation to the Lord Protector and complained 'how much thereby the House reflected on him, and discouraged the godly'. But Cromwell had now changed his mind about their work and decided to throw in his lot with their rivals. He perceived that the reaction against military rule had strengthened the demand for constitutional government. He believed that as a reward for abandoning the Major-Generals the majority in the Commons would vote the taxes needed to continue the war against Spain. And while he expressed but little sympathy with the complaints of the Major-Generals, who had served him honourably, he sent for Broghil and was said to be so satisfied with his explanation of why he opposed the Decimation Bill that he began to distrust those who had advised him to institute the system in the first instance, that is to say he began to turn against Lambert.

A month after the defeat of the Major-Generals in the House of Commons, Broghil reverted to his scheme of making Cromwell King. On February 23rd a 'Remonstrance' was read to the House by Alderman Sir Christopher Pack proposing that Cromwell should take the title of King, that a House of Lords should be re-established, and that the excluded members should be re-admitted to the Commons. Pack, another figurehead, was put up by Broghil and the lawyers. Even before the terms of the 'Remonstrance' were explained, the military party, guessing what was in the wind, objected to its being read. However, they were beaten and afterwards Lambert led the resistance to the new proposals on the ground that they were contrary to the principles for which the army had fought. Earlier Lambert had said that the question now was whether they should go backwards to monarchy or forwards to a permanent republic. Desborough, who had likewise contended against an earlier motion in the Commons that Cromwell should be offered the Crown (on January 19th), also spoke against Pack's scheme. Lambert and Desborough were supported by all the other Major-Generals and their Deputies, except Colonel Charles Howard, and by Lambert's fellow Yorkshire M.P.s. Thurloe was disturbed at the virulence of Lambert's opposition: 'he will, if it can be done,' he wrote to Henry Cromwell, 'put the army in a ferment'. On the following evening

> Some of the Major-Generals were with his Highness, tarried a quarter of an hour in the room before one word passed from either. At length they began and complained of parliament. His Highness answered hastily: 'What would you have me do? Are not they of your own garbling? Did you not admit whom you pleased and keep out whom you pleased? And now do you complain to me?

> Did I meddle with it?' And so they withdrew without further declaring.

So the accents of Cromwell's anger ring down the centuries. While the debate continued in Parliament a deputation from the officers of the army interviewed the Major-Generals who were meeting in Desborough's lodgings to inform them of their objections to kingship. Lambert counselled moderation and advised them to see the Lord Protector.

On February 27th therefore a hundred officers visited Cromwell in Whitehall to protest against the terms of Pack's 'Remonstrance'. Once more Cromwell expressed his indignation and reminded them that there had been a time when they had not boggled at the word 'king' and that Lambert's original scheme for the 'Instrument of Government' had provided for a monarch. Then he launched an attack upon his Major-Generals. They had made him their 'drudge'; they had forced him to dissolve the Long Parliament; they had compelled him to summon an Assembly of Saints that had let fly at liberty and property. They had obliged him to summon the existing Parliament instead of maintaining their own system of government. They had failed to obtain a majority in the new Parliament who would confirm their system of local administration and had laid themselves open to a setback by the rejection of their own Decimation Bill. How could they complain of the members of the Commons who now remained after they themselves had 'purged' the House? In fact the remaining members were 'honest men' who had 'done good things'. Were they offended at the idea of having a House of Lords? 'I tell you that unless you have some such thing as a balance you cannot be safe', for either their civil or religious liberties would be subject to unrestrained attack: that was the lesson of the case of James Naylor.

Cromwell's frank speech profoundly impressed his audience. Thenceforward the army was to some extent divided over the new constitutional proposals, which were later renamed the 'Humble Petition and Advice'. Colonel Charles Howard and Colonel Richard Ingoldsby and the Irish officers organized counter-demonstrations in favour of kingship. Broghil was busy behind the scenes. Lambert and Desborough, though sullen, were temporarily abashed, and Cromwell's cousin, Edward Whalley, Whalley's son-in-law, Major-General Goffe, and William Boteler were reported to have become almost indifferent about the whole question.

For three weeks there was a lull as far as the problem of the Crown was concerned, during which the other clauses in the 'Remonstrance' were debated, but on March 25th the House voted by 123 to 62 that Cromwell should be invited to accept the title and office of King. Howard was one of the tellers for the Ayes, Boteler for the Noes. In the debate Lieutenant-General Charles Fleetwood delivered a long invective against monarchy and could not hold back his tears. Already he had written to his brother-in-law, Henry Cromwell, that the passing of the question in the affirmative 'will be a sad grief to the hearts of good people whose hopes are only in His Highness'. Major-General Desborough was passionate in his opposition. But with the vote it seemed as if they had to confess themselves beaten. A party of officers interviewed the Protector five days afterwards and assured him that they now accepted the inevitable as demonstrated by 'a series of providence in it'. Whalley, Goffe and Boteler gave up the fight. Fleetwood did not 'mutiny but lament'. Only Lambert, Sydenham and Desborough were reported to 'still stand out upon the sullen posture'. But neither Lambert nor Fleetwood had decided to abandon the struggle; and in fact they had an ally: that was Cromwell himself. For Cromwell, as in 1647 and again in 1653, could not make up his mind and failed to close at once with the offer of the Crown.

While during April 1657 Broghil and his supporters interviewed Cromwell again and again to try to persuade him to accept the Crown, an attempt was made to reach an agreement between the two Cromwellian parties. Fleetwood, after wavering, urged his father-in-law to reject the title and accept the rest of the clauses in the 'Humble Petition and Advice'. Whalley was also keen for a compromise. And in fact all the Generals were willing enough that Cromwell should be asked to nominate his successor, for then after all each of them would stand a chance. On April 21st, Thurloe wrote that Fleetwood and Desborough 'oppose them in all earnestness [to the offer of the Crown] but think other things in the "Petition and Advice" very honest. The other gentleman [Lambert] stands at a distance, hath given over his opposition, and lets things take their course'. But a fortnight later Thurloe added that Fleetwood and Desborough 'seem to be very much fixed against his being King and speak of nothing but giving over their commands and all employment if he doth accept that title'. So, he wrote a week later, would Lambert.

Thus came the crux. There was no doubt that Cromwell, who had an empirical approach to forms of government, had been persuaded by the arguments of the lawyers that he would be well advised to become a constitutional king. His own contributions to the discussions on the point, as even his nearest friends admitted, were vague and cloudy. But, though convinced as to the principle, could be break with his Generals, with the men who had fought with him at Marston Moor and Naseby, at Preston and Dunbar? Moreover he was aware that while some of the officers would acquiesce, others among the Independents would be bitterly offended by the destruction of the Commonwealth. Nevertheless on May 6th he determined to accept the Crown. That day he met Desborough in St. James's Park and told him of his resolution. Desborough answered that in that case he would resign his offices and, though he would not go into opposition, would cease to support him. Fleetwood and Lambert said the same. Desborough went home and spoke to his friend, Colonel Thomas Pride. Pride retorted that he would prevent Cromwell from becoming King. Thereupon the two of them, with the help of Dr. John Owen, an Independent minister and one of Cromwell's own chaplains, drew up a petition to Parliament and started collecting signatures from the army officers. When Fleetwood heard of the petition he informed Cromwell. 'I confess,' observed Fleetwood, 'I like not the army's interposings.' Cromwell begged his son-in-law to have the petition suppressed. But Fleetwood was a quarter of an hour too late for that. Hurrying down to the House he arrived on the scene just as the Commons were discussing whether or not the petition should be read. Fleetwood persuaded them to postpone the debate. This was on the morning of May 8th. Yet, after all, the Generals had won. That very day Cromwell finally refused the Crown.

The contest between Cromwell's Generals and the New Courtiers over the question of kingship was to result in a breach that was never to be completely healed in the last two years of Cromwell's life. The story is indeed a strange amalgam of human emotions and ambitions. In the case of Fleetwood there was unquestionably a deep religious antipathy to the very institution of kingship such as was felt by the Fifth Monarchists, for whom the only monarch was Christ. Had Harrison not been in prison, he would have acted much as Fleetwood did. Although we know painfully little about Desborough's personal history, we may assume that his passionate opposition was inspired by similar feelings. He was a Cambridgeshire man and intermarried with the Cromwells so that he is likely to have been a strong Independent — and it was among the Independents that the republican movement had sprung up in the late forties. Lambert, however, was not guided by any such religious convictions. His latest biographer suggests that he 'proceeded from disinterested concern to confirm the Protectorate as he had created it, and above all to maintain the full sovereignty of Parliament'. But this interpretation has to contend with the awkward fact that Lambert himself had proposed not so long before to make the office of Protector a hereditary one — and did not a Protector but 'ape the manners of a King'? — nor is there any proof that he denied the accusation which Cromwell hurled in his face that in the first draft of the 'Instrument of Government' he had provided for kingship, while Cromwell himself had rejected it. Moreover Lambert's anxiety to maintain the rule of the Major-Generals does not suggest any tenderness for the sovereignty of Parliament. It is possible (as has been argued) that Lambert once having been rebuffed on the question of monarchy, did not wish to divide the army, which was the ultimate guarantee of the existing regime. But if Lambert, the army's hero, had given a lead, how much would the army have been divided? It is hard therefore to avoid the conclusion that Lambert, who had been Cromwell's right-hand man now for three years in the government of the country, the sponsor alike of the 'Instrument' and of the institution of Major-

Generals, had hopes — hopes which he is said openly to have expressed — of the succession for himself. More than one consideration no doubt influenced his conduct, but his inconsistency stood out. The fact that from this time onwards Lambert began to lose much of his popularity in the army rather suggests that his contemporaries suspected the interested character of his motives, which to them at any rate cannot have been hard to fathom.

On May 25th Cromwell agreed to the 'Humble Petition and Advice' with its provision for a House of Lords and its clauses that enlarged the power of Parliament and reduced that of the Council of State, while conferring on the Protector the right to name his successor. On June 26th, clothed in purple and ermine, Cromwell was solemnly installed under the new constitution. The Speaker spoke, a chaplain prayed, and heralds blew their trumpets. But it was noticed that it was General Edward Montagu and not, as hitherto, General John Lambert who was carrying the sword of state.

The new constitution required that members of the Council of State (who had been reappointed with some additions) should take an oath to be faithful to the Lord Protector and contrive nothing against him. Desborough and Fleetwood at once took the oath. Lambert refused to appear, yet showed no intention of resigning. Cromwell's friends advised him to get rid of Lambert, and foreign diplomatists in London reported rumours that Lambert would try to raise the army against Cromwell. Eight days after the first meeting of the new Council of State Cromwell sent for Lambert. The interview took place on July 11th. We do not know what happened between these two men who had been so intimate. One story was that Lambert refused on principle to take the oath, but it is more likely that they agreed, after his open opposition to the new constitution, that it was impossible for him to remain in office. Two days later Cromwell sent one of the clerks of the Council to Lambert with a letter demanding all his commissions. Lambert did not resist; he surrendered his commissions 'very calmly protesting that he desired nothing more than a retired life in his own house'. Maybe he did; maybe he remembered the fate of Thomas Harrison. His foot regiment was given to Fleetwood and his cavalry regiment to another of Cromwell's sons-in-law, Lord Falconbridge. But Cromwell arranged through the Council to pay Lambert a pension, said to have amounted to £2000 a year. Such a dismissal with a handsome pension attached tickled the popular imagination: for a time the phrase 'to Lambertize' became a part of the English language. Lord Lambert and his attractive wife retired to their palace at Wimbledon, the General to engage in gardening and painting; but among his tulips he still nursed his ambitions, awaiting what should befall when the Lord Protector died.

BIBLIOGRAPHY TO CHAPTER X

For the offer of the Crown see besides Firth's *Last Years of the Protectorate* (1909) his two articles on 'Cromwell and the Crown' in *English Historical Review* for 1902 and 1903. The quotations from letters of the Major-Generals are taken from *Thurloe State Papers*, vol. V. The debates on the Major-Generals and the Crown are in *Diary of Thomas Burton, Esq.* (ed. Rutt), vol. I. For Broghil see *A Collection of the State Papers of Roger Boyle* (ed. Morrice, 1742) and for Montagu, F. R. Harris, *The Life of Edward Montagu, First Earl of Sandwich* (1912).

CHAPTER XI

LIEUTENANT-GENERAL CHARLES FLEETWOOD AND THE END OF THE PROTECTORATE

Charles Fleetwood was born about 1618 and died in 1692

WITH the dismissal of John Lambert, Charles Fleetwood became Cromwell's principal General.

In rank Fleetwood seems to have been Lambert's senior, but Lambert was the better soldier, the stronger character, the more enlightened statesman, and the abler administrator. Fleetwood was about the same age as Lambert. We do not know the exact date of his birth, but as he was admitted to Gray's Inn as a student in November 1638, he was probably born about 1618. He was the third son of Sir Miles Fleetwood of Aldwinkle, Northamptonshire, and of Anne Luke of Woodend, Bedfordshire. His eldest brother, William, who succeeded to the baronetcy in 1641, was a Royalist. Another brother, George, became a professional soldier and distinguished himself in the service of the King of Sweden. Charles, who was much younger, entered the lifeguard of the Earl of Essex at the beginning of the civil wars. In 1643 when he was a captain of horse, he was wounded at the battle of Newbury. In the following year he raised his own cavalry regiment in the army of the Earl of Manchester and later it was transferred to the New Model Army.

Fleetwood's regiment, enlisted in the midland and eastern counties, was fanatically puritanical, being full of Independents, Anabaptists, and Fifth Monarchists (Harrison being its first major). The Colonel himself was an Independent, although he was often referred to as an Anabaptist and felt a warm spot for members of that sect. His emphasis on 'dispensations' may have made him sympathetic to Cromwell. For Fleetwood it was a 'dispensation' when a little niece died, a 'dispensation' when his own daughter, Nancy, was perilously ill. After it had done its duty in the first civil war Fleetwood's regiment firmly resisted the order that it should either be disbanded or sent to Ireland in 1647. In fact it stirred up the rest of the New Model Army to fight the proposals of Parliament. But after that the regiment lost much of its character. Its old officers left it on promotion. During the second civil war it was dispersed to undertake duties in different parts of England. And after the death of the King, its colonel, who had been elected M.P. for Marlborough in May 1646, was moved into higher military or political posts. But the regiment fought again both at Dunbar and Worcester, at the latter battle forming part of the division under its colonel, who was now Lieutenant-General of Horse in succession to the new Commander-in-Chief, Oliver Cromwell. Fleetwood's first wife, Frances Smith of Norfolk, having died in November 1651, Fleetwood, as we have seen, married Cromwell's eldest daughter, Bridget, the widow of Henry Ireton, in June 1652, and on July 10th was appointed Commander-in-Chief in Ireland in place of the dead Ireton.

While we have no reason to suppose that Fleetwood was not an efficient soldier of the amateur kind, no such instances of strategical or tactical insight survive to his credit as they do to Lambert's. His regiment fought bravely enough at Naseby, but failed to stem the onslaught of Prince Rupert owing to Ireton's poor handling of the left wing. At the battle of Worcester where Fleetwood enjoyed an independent command, his attack might have been held up had it not been that Cromwell himself directed the outflanking of the Scots across the Severn. Fleetwood's genius, as we have already suggested, lay chiefly in military administration. During the later part of the Scottish campaign he had organized the reserve army in England with credit.

Fleetwood had the gift of being able to get along with all sorts of people. Affability, coated with an unpleasing veneer of piety, was his stock-in-trade. He was a gentleman who, had it not been for the spirit of the times that settled on the Inns of Court in the early forties, might, like his eldest brother, have been on the side of the King. It was significant that he had refused to take part in the trial of the King and thus evaded the opprobrium of being a 'regicide'. However, he absorbed the extreme puritan point of view with appetite, which made him congenial alike to Cromwell, Harrison and even the difficult Edmund Ludlow.

Such were his virtues. On the other hand, his character was a weak one. This fact was recognized by his father-in-law who wrote to him on his appointment to Ireland: 'Take heed of your natural inclination to compliance.' Fleetwood lacked the facility to make up his mind about anything; thus he became the tool in the hands of tougher and less scrupulous personalities. Rubbed the right way, he was like putty; rubbed the wrong way, he grew prickly. When faced with a delicate problem he tended to procrastinate or to give way to those nearest to him. We have observed how over the question of kingship he faced both ways: he did not wish to offend his powerful father-in-law, but at the same time he was unwilling to break with his colleagues in the army who were opposed to the restoration of a system of monarchy. Hence he burst into tears when speaking against the plan to make Cromwell King, but hastened to notify Cromwell when inferior officers in the army were drawing up their petition to parliament against kingship. Like many weak men, he was often blinded by a sense of his own importance and would become worked up and angry at the wrong times against the wrong persons. These defects make him an uncongenial character, except to other men who understand their own weaknesses, and readers of his correspondence with his brother-in-law, Henry Cromwell, cannot escape the feeling that these letters have a flavour of Uriah Heep about them. A puritan outlook and a propensity to intrigue seldom afford an agreeable mixture. Fleetwood was not without his convictions. Unlike Lambert, he was a consistent critic of the monarchical system of government and an intense believer in the value of the Protestant way of life. Both his qualities and his shortcomings disclosed themselves during his tenure of office first as Commander-in-Chief and afterwards as Lord Deputy of Ireland.

When Fleetwood arrived in Ireland in 1652 the war was virtually over. Lieutenant-General Ludlow, who had been Acting Commander-in-Chief since the death of Ireton, had obtained the capitulation of Galway in Connaught and all organized resistance had come to an end. Fleetwood's task therefore was to establish internal security and to assure the defence of the country with a minimum of English troops. He had also to fulfill the promises given by Parliament to investors or 'adventurers' in Irish lands and to the soldiers whose pay had been secured upon them. The policy of Fleetwood and the Irish Commissioners was to shift as many of the native Irish as would go to Connaught; to set up a new English 'Pale' occupied by former English soldiers between the Boyne and the Barrow; and to encourage the Irish fighting men to leave the country and take up service abroad. The second part of the policy succeeded better than the first. It is estimated that some 40,000 Irish soldiers left their homeland in this period to enlist in Spain or elsewhere, so that during the eighteenth century and later many of the finest Generals in Europe were Irishmen. But the policy of segregating the Irish in Connaught was unworkable. In the first place it is never easy to compel men and women to leave their own homes; secondly, the new English settlers discovered that it was impossible to cultivate the confiscated lands without the help of the natives.

Yet although Fleetwood and his Council were given power to dispense with the acts for the transplantation of the Irish, Fleetwood clung obstinately to the policy of segregation. When Vincent Gookin and William Petty, two Englishmen with considerable knowledge of Irish conditions, published an anonymous pamphlet attacking general transplantation, Fleetwood was extremely indignant. Unluckily for him, Gookin had Cromwell's ear. So Fleetwood had constantly to complain of 'obstructions' from England. At the same time he was much affected by the news of the persecution of the Waldensians, the Protestants in Savoy about whom Milton wrote his great sonnet and Cromwell a famous letter. All the English officers in Ireland contributed a fortnight's pay and the soldiers a week's pay for the relief of the unfortunate mountain dwellers. And since Fleetwood had heard (rightly or wrongly) that Irish Catholics had been concerned in the massacre of the Waldensians, he became harsher still in his treatment of the native Irish. He harried the priests, expelled the Jesuits, and set up courts to try for murder anyone suspected of having

LIEUTENANT-GENERAL CHARLES FLEETWOOD

taken part in the rebellion of 1641. Some 200 persons were put to death in Dublin, largely on hearsay evidence. Fleetwood's policy of repression and transplantation met with success of a kind. In June 1653 the war in Ireland was officially declared at an end. Exhausted by its blood bath, Ireland sank into a state of sullen acquiescence, punctuated by those occasional murderous outbursts of guerrilla warfare for which the nation later grew notorious.

On January 30th, 1654, Cromwell was proclaimed Lord Protector in Ireland. Up to this time Fleetwood's second in command, General Ludlow, had worked harmoniously enough with his new master. But when the report of Ludlow's demonstration against the proclamation and his refusal to lay down his commissions reached Whitehall, Cromwell's second surviving son, Henry, was sent over to investigate the situation there. Henry Cromwell, who had been born in Huntingdon on January 20th, 1628, had already shown a promise of ability, his only failure in life having been the rejection of his proposal of marriage by the charming Dorothy Osborne. In his portrait, now at Chequers, we can detect much of his father's strength of character without its fanaticism. Colonel Henry Cromwell already possessed some knowledge of Irish conditions when he came back in 1654, for he had served there for two years under his sister Bridget's first husband, Ireton. His secret report to Thurloe was blunt and to the point:

> I have taken the liberty [he wrote] to be very plain with my brother [in-law, Fleetwood] and have, as near as I could, acquainted him with what I had in trust, and do find his desire rather to return than to continue here: but [he] is willing to be at my father's dispose. But to deal faithfully, I do think he is a little too deeply engaged in a partial affection to the persons of the Anabaptists to answer your end; though I believe it rather to proceed from tenderness than love to their principles . . . To offer my poor thought, I would take advantage by Ludlow's frowardness to put him out of the army and put General Desborough in his place . . . especially if you think fit for some short time to command my brother over and in his absence to constitute General Desborough his deputy.

That was pretty astute advice for a man of twenty-six. However, the presence of the Lord Protector's son in Ireland naturally gave rise to rumours demoralizing to General Fleetwood. Cromwell hastened to assure him that it was untrue that he was to be recalled and Henry Cromwell put in his place. Such an idea, Oliver Cromwell wrote on June 22nd, 'truly never entered my heart'. And no doubt partly to assuage his feelings, Fleetwood was that August promoted to the rank of Lord Deputy, the high office that had been denied to General Lambert. But at the same time the Council of State, impressed by the reports of Colonel Henry Cromwell, recommended that he should be appointed as Fleetwood's second in command with the rank of Major-General. But it was not until December that Henry Cromwell was added to Fleetwood's Council and not until the summer of 1655 that he returned to Ireland to take up his post.

Nothing revealed Fleetwood's weakness of character more clearly that his conduct towards General Ludlow and later his behaviour to General Henry Cromwell.

After Ludlow had refused to acknowledge the Protectorate or to surrender his commissions, the normal procedure under any effective military government would have been to put him under arrest. But Fleetwood, after vainly trying to convince Ludlow by argument of the error of his ways, left him alone until he was provoked by the discovery that Ludlow had been distributing leaflets and pamphlets aimed against the Government. Not until then did Fleetwood put into effect orders that he had received earlier from London to demand the surrender of Ludlow's commissions. And even now the Commander-in-Chief did so not directly but through intermediaries. Ultimately Ludlow was placed on parole and later was offered leave to return to England without formally giving up his offices if he would make a promise not to act against the Government. Ludlow suggested a compromise, clearly because he was aware of Fleetwood's softness, namely that if he were allowed to go home, he would undertake not to oppose the Protectorate until after he had first 'surrendered himself' either to Fleetwood or to Cromwell. Fleetwood accepted this extraordinary bargain, but then on one excuse or another delayed Ludlow's departure.

That was the position when Fleetwood himself left for England in September 1655, and Henry Cromwell took over the command in Ireland. Major-General Cromwell at once showed how dissatisfied he was with Fleetwood's dithering. He had all along been against Ludlow's being allowed to sail for England on the ground that so important a General would have to be dealt with in the same way as Harrison, that is to say put under arrest or surveillance and thus be transformed into a republican martyr. Henry Cromwell therefore gave orders that Ludlow was to stay in Ireland and personally report to him. Ludlow found an excuse not to do so and took ship for Wales. Henry Cromwell then sent an officer after him to arrest him and it was not until he had signed a promise of good conduct that he was allowed to proceed to London. Fleetwood was greatly annoyed at what Henry Cromwell had done and protested that since he himself as Lord Deputy had already given Ludlow permission to return to England, he had been disobeyed. But it was the young Cromwell's action and not that of Fleetwood which found approval in Whitehall.

Oliver Cromwell had treated Charles Fleetwood with the utmost tact and consideration ever since he had become his son-in-law. But in confidential letters he had warned him not to be either bitter or compliant and his wife, Bridget, not to be fearful nor subservient. Cromwell confessed to Fleetwood, since he knew that his son-in-law sympathized with the Anabaptists and Fifth Monarchy men, how he would 'fain have had his service accepted of the Saints (if the Lord will)' and how even 'if the day of the Lord be so near (as some say)' his 'moderation' would appear. When Cromwell at length decided to recall Fleetwood from Ireland he did not dispossess him of his high office — on the contrary, he promoted him — but suggested that if he had 'a mind to come over with your dear wife, etc., take the best opportunity for the good of the republic and your own convenience'.

Fleetwood's reports home can scarcely have given Oliver Cromwell much confidence in 'dear Charles's' firmness of character any more than had his supine treatment of General Ludlow. With regard to reducing the English forces now that the war was officially over, for example, Fleetwood wrote:

'We are through mercy in quiet, but what the sending away so many forces will produce, I know not, but trust the gracious presence of the Lord will be with us.' On the dismissal of the first Protectorate Parliament he said (and we may contrast General Blake's masculine reaction): 'The Irish are very high, but much troubled at the dissolution of parliament.' He urged humility and patience: a typical letter was one which he wrote to Thurloe in March 1655:

> I understand [he said] that our old enemies are still at work. It the less troubles me because 'tis with them, for though the Lord reproving us by them should awaken everyone to see what there is in us that might be a provocation to Him, yet I am confident the Lord will witness against them, and not suffer His righteous cause, which he hath so significantly owned, to be subject to their malice.

This characteristic waffle was intermixed with plaintive inquiries about the distribution of troops and pleas for money.

After he had settled in England again, Fleetwood's letters, written as Lord Deputy and brother-in-law to Major-General Henry Cromwell, exhibited a blend of apology and jealousy. While some of the English officers in Ireland had welcomed the change in the actual command, others, particularly Fleetwood's friends, the Anabaptists, had taken offence at the stronger hand of the new young Commander-in-Chief, whom they insultingly nicknamed Absalom, and regretted the easy-going times under Fleetwood — easy-going for them, not for the Irish. One of these Anabaptist officers, Colonel John Hewson, organized a petition to the Protector begging for the return of Fleetwood and his 'sweet healing peaceable spirit'. Fleetwood hastened to dissociate himself from Hewson's agitation. 'I beg of you', he wrote to Henry Cromwell on January 31st, 1656, 'to take heed of jealousies, I cannot but be plain with you, I hope you shall not find me unfaithful to you upon any account.' He apologized at once when Henry protested because Fleetwood did not write to him in his own hand. On July 8th, 1656, he wrote again: 'I understand by Dr. Harrison that there is some disquiet upon your spirit. I can clear myself of giving any occasion . . . I hope I will be as faithful a friend to you as any you have, let men report and say what they will.' In the following month Fleetwood hotly denied that he was a person with 'underhand ways' and Oliver Cromwell himself at this time tried to pour oil on the troubled waters flowing between his son and his son-in-law.

Nevertheless Fleetwood was obviously much upset when it was eventually decided that he himself should not return to Ireland and that Major-General Henry Cromwell, having served his apprenticeship with high skill and some grasp of the Irish point of view, should be given the rank as well as the duties of Lord Deputy in his place. 'I shall continue,' he wrote on November 3rd, 1657, 'the freedom of that expression ['dearest brother'] notwithstanding what additional honours the providence of God hath cast upon you on your being made Deputy of Ireland.' Seven weeks later he added: 'I hope my affection towards your own person as well as the desire I have to serve the public will not suffer me to decline or neglect anything which may be in my power to serve you or your affairs.' Yet as late as July 1658, Fleetwood still found it necessary to assure Henry Cromwell that he was not putting his father against him, and, nine days before the death of the Lord Protector, he was asking his brother-in-law what he had done to cause him offence.

Oliver Cromwell had good reason not to want his son, Henry, and his son-in-law to fall out with each other. For in the last years of his life the circle of Generals on whom he could rely was narrowing, while he himself was becoming more dependent than hitherto on the counsel of others. It is true that the fall of Lambert had no serious repercussions on the loyalty of the army. 'Most of the officers of the army', noted Thurloe, 'and those most suspected show rather satisfaction than otherwise.' But in August 1657 General Blake had died and been replaced by the relatively inexperienced Edward Montagu. Cromwell's cousin, Whalley, was raised to the rank of Lieutenant-General to assist Fleetwood in the control of the army and the only other General in Cromwell's confidence was John Desborough; it had been rumoured, but incorrectly, that he was going to succeed either Lambert or Blake.

When Cromwell needed Generals to take command of the

expeditionary force that was being dispatched to Flanders to fight the Spaniards according to the terms of the offensive alliance with France concluded in March 1657, he had sent to Ireland and to Scotland. The selected Commander-in-Chief was Sir John Reynolds, a Cambridgeshire man who had served in Ireland since 1649. Since he had at one time been captain of a troop in one of Oliver's own regiments and since he was married to a sister-in-law of Henry Cromwell (who had married Elizabeth, daughter of Sir Francis Russell of Chippenham), Reynolds's relationship with the Cromwell family was a close one. He had been knighted by the Lord Protector in January 1657, but Henry Cromwell had been most reluctant to spare him from the Irish army and Reynolds had agreed to go only on the clear understanding that he was to be in full command of the expedition, which carried a rate of pay of £5 a day. The second in command was a Welsh professional soldier, named Thomas Morgan, who had been serving with Monk in Scotland. As a young man Morgan had fought under the great Protestant General, Bernard of Saxe-Weimar, and since 1652 he had been a Major-General and Colonel of Dragoons in the English army in Scotland. The organization of the expeditionary army fell largely on Morgan; on one excuse or another Reynolds kept coming to England, partly to see his young wife. Returning to England in December 1657, after the capture of Mardyke, on this or some other mission, his ship was wrecked on the Goodwin Sands and he was drowned. Cromwell could not find another friend of the family to replace him. Morgan was appointed Governor of Mardyke and a Scottish officer, who had formerly fought for King Charles I and had been knighted by him, Sir William Lockhart, was given command of the British army in Flanders, with which he helped Marshal Turenne to win the battle of the Dunes on June 4th, 1658. Lockhart was also Ambassador to the Court of King Louis XIV.

While the campaign was thus progressing in the Low Countries, the Lord Protector was choosing his new House of Lords in accordance with the terms of the 'Humble Petition and Advice'. He had much difficulty over this as those who wanted to be Lords were considered not to be good enough, and those who were considered good enough did not want to be Lords. Of sixty-three peers named by him (of whom thirty-seven were to appear when the new House met) the following were Generals: Fleetwood, Desborough, Whalley, Goffe, Barkstead, Berry and Skippon; all of them had been Major-Generals of the Militia; and Montagu, Monk and Henry Cromwell. Other soldiers lifted to the peerage were Broghil, Alexander Popham, Sydenham, Pride and Ingoldsby. William Boteler, over whose conduct as Major-General clouds hung, remained in the House of Commons.

The summoning of Parliament was a signal for disturbances. The republican and anti-Cromwellian members, who had been excluded at the behest of Cromwell's Generals in September 1656, came out of the shadows to resume their places: that was the price paid by the Lord Protector for his additional dignities — such as they were — and his useless Upper House. Since all these indignant, critical and noisy M.P.s were back at Westminster, whereas nearly all Cromwell's closest and ablest supporters, from the New Courtiers, like Broghil and Thurloe, to the Generals like Fleetwood and Desborough, had now been wafted up to the House of Lords, there was hardly anyone to contend with them on behalf of the Protectorate. And when they started questioning the credentials of the Other House, as they called it, thereby undermining the whole basis of the new Protectorate, their republican doctrines infected sections of the army. These internal disputings encouraged the hopes of the Royalists. But in any case Cromwell knew that his power rested on the army and he dared not risk its being tampered with. A fortnight after Parliament met he determined to strike again. He drove down to Westminster in a hired coach and while he was drinking a cup of ale and eating some toast was met by Fleetwood. Fleetwood was no Harrison or Lambert. When Cromwell told him that he intended to dissolve Parliament, the General said to him: 'I beseech your Highness consider first well of it; it is of great consequence', and tried to dissuade him. Cromwell clapped his hand upon his breast and replied: 'You are a milksop; by the living God, I will dissolve the House.' When Henry Cromwell, who loathed Fleetwood, heard of this, he wrote to Broghil: 'I believe the milk, wherein Fleetwood was sopped, had much water in it.'

However, whatever their private feelings might have been, Cromwell's Generals stood by him. Major-General Barkstead, one of the new peers, who was in charge of the Tower of London, was ordered to round up the Fifth Monarchy men; Harrison was again put under close arrest; and a week after the dissolution Cromwell addressed 200 officers, including his Generals, explaining that Parliament had unfortunately been called on the advice of his Council against his own wishes, but that it had only aroused the hopes of their old enemies. 'And he drank to them, and many bottles of wine were then drunk, but no reply made.' Nevertheless most of them expressed their resolution to 'stand and fall, live and die, with the Protector'. But not all. Major William Packer, who was the acting colonel of Cromwell's own cavalry regiment and had been Fleetwood's deputy as Major-General in the previous year, was there and then cashiered along with a number of other officers. William Boteler was given Packer's post at the head of Cromwell's regiment. That was on February 11th. On March 25th another meeting of the Generals and field officers was held in Whitehall. On this occasion Fleetwood was the principal speaker. He 'made a short speech', wrote one who was there, 'showing how necessary a thing it was for the army to unite themselves', and then produced an address of loyalty for them to sign: 'There was not a man made the least objection against it, but all signed it.'

So during the six months of Cromwell's life that remained Lieutenant-General Charles Fleetwood was his right-hand man. He attended conferences of foreign diplomatists along with him or as his representative; he made himself responsible for the loyalty of the army; and he drew up reports for the Protector on the strength and availability of the fleet. Together with Desborough, Whalley and Goffe, he was a member of an inner council of nine who advised the Protector on whether he should call another Parliament or try to raise money by some other means. Major-General Henry Cromwell let the cat out of the bag when he admitted privately to Thurloe his aversion to the adoption of extra-legal means to obtain money, as employed by the Major-Generals, because 'now Lambert is

MAJOR-GENERAL HENRY CROMWELL

removed, the odium . . . would now fall near His Highness'. Struggling with his own difficulties in Dublin, the new Lord Deputy of Ireland followed the drama in Whitehall with the closest attention. He was in touch with Lord Broghil, who was highly suspicious of the loyalty of his old antagonists, Fleetwood, Desborough and Lambert. Broghil, for instance, reported a rumour that these three Generals were again becoming intimate, and Henry Cromwell at once asked Thurloe if that were true and added: 'I hope His Highness will have an eye, etc.' Henry Cromwell had also heard that Desborough was indeed urging a return to the system of the Major-Generals. It is known that long discussions took place in the Council of State on the money question; but though Desborough may have wanted drastic measures, there is no evidence that there was any distinct line drawn between the Generals and the civilians in Cromwell's inner circle. After all, the Lord Protector had repudiated them once and put the blame on Lambert; Fleetwood was too cautious a man to fall into the same trap.

Thus in spite of the victory of the Dunes, which was followed on June 14th by the surrender of Dunkirk to British arms, the Protectoral system was running down when Oliver Cromwell died. Every constitutional scheme had failed; each time one had been tried Cromwell had been driven back on the support of the army. And yet the Protectorate was to cling to the tatters of parliamentary respectability. As Cromwell was sinking, the rumour spread in August 1658 that Fleetwood was to succeed him. But Sir Charles Firth long ago exposed this story, and added that 'Fleetwood's political incapacity had been shown in Ireland and the weakness of his character must have been well known to the Protector'. So, after all, it was not one of his Generals — not even his abler son Henry who succeeded to the Protectoral throne, but Richard, an idle country gentleman, nicknamed by the Royalists Tumbledown Dick, without either military or administrative experience. Whatever they might have taken from Richard's father while he lived, Charles Fleetwood and his friends were not going to stomach that now he lay in state. 'They would rule themselves', so Lord Falconbridge wrote to Henry Cromwell, 'or set all on fire.'

A fortnight after Oliver Cromwell's death Lieutenant-General Fleetwood presided over a meeting in Whitehall the purpose of which was to induce all the army officers to sign an address of loyalty to the new Protector. Yet at the same time it was persistently rumoured that Fleetwood himself would 'suddenly be appointed Generalissimo of the forces'. That was what Cromwell's old Generals who were still in position would have liked to happen. Fleetwood, they reckoned, was a figurehead, behind whom they could govern. And indeed in the first week of October Fleetwood had the impertinence himself to present a petition to his brother-in-law signed by 'some discontented officers of the army' asking that he himself should be made Commander-in-Chief throughout the three nations, that is be put over Monk and Henry Cromwell, that he should be given the power to confer commissions on all except field officers, and that no soldiers might be cashiered except by court martial. 'They are demanding things which no magistrate in the world can grant without divesting himself of all but the shadow', observed Falconbridge. Richard Cromwell, who had after all learned something from his father, had the spirit to refuse the demand and the Generals, at any rate those related to the Cromwell family, realizing that it would set their world about its ears to fight each other at this stage, quietened down the army. Nevertheless Fleetwood and his sponsors fully intended to renew their attack later.

In November 1658, the leading officers began to meet regularly for prayer and fasting. These meetings gave them the opportunity to pursue their ambitions in true puritan fashion. Desborough and Berry seem to have been among the most eager to wrest the control of the army out of the hands of the new Protector and, according to one account, during that month Desborough again presented the demand that Fleetwood should be put in supreme command of the army. The split that had opened between the New Courtiers and Cromwell's old Generals in the last years of Oliver's life swiftly revealed itself again. In December the French ambassador in London reported home that there was an open quarrel between John Desborough and Edward Montagu in the presence of Richard Cromwell. Montagu was accused of conspiring with

Lord Falconbridge to kidnap both Fleetwood and Desborough. That must have been an exaggerated story, but feelings were undoubtedly running high. Major-General Henry Cromwell, for example, had not hesitated to write from Ireland 'to discharge his conscience to his brother Fleetwood' for his 'lust and ambition'; 'I thought those,' he wrote, 'whom my father had raised from nothing would not so soon have forgot him, and endeavour to destroy his family, before he is in his grave.'

These quarrels were momentarily set aside when Richard Cromwell's first Parliament gathered in January 1659. So cleverly had Thurloe and his colleagues manipulated matters that the New Courtiers commanded a steady majority in the Lower House. But none the less the republican minority, which possessed the finest orators on their side, were soon absorbed in their customary pursuit of constitution-mongering and cocking snooks at the Upper House. All this irritated the army, which, as usual, was without regular pay or arrears. By the spring therefore the Council of the Army had started to meet again at Fleetwood's home, Wallingford House, that stood on the site of the present Admiralty. After a big meeting there on April 2nd a deputation went to Cromwell with a petition outlining the soldiers' grievances over pay and other questions, which the Protector promptly forwarded to Parliament. The House of Commons, noting that the petition had already found its way into print, read it but then ignored it. The House was in an anti-military mood and with difficulty had been dissuaded from cashiering Major-General Boteler for an offence alleged to have been committed by him three years before. Fleetwood was prepared to abide his time. He was a born procrastinator. Edward Hyde, future Earl of Clarendon, wrote of him about this date:

> The character which we have always received of the man is not such as makes him equal to any notable design, or to be much relied on tomorrow for what in truth he resolved to do yesterday; however as his wit is not so great as some of the rest, so his wickedness is much less apparent than theirs.

But a stronger man was waiting: for about this time Major-General Lambert began stirring in his retirement at Wimbledon and was soon to be attending the meetings of the Council of the Army. Moreover Desborough and Berry were pushing hard behind Fleetwood. Indeed all Oliver Cromwell's Generals were thrusting him forward.

On April 13th, noted a contemporary newsletter, the army spent the whole day 'in prayer and preaching' at Lord Fleetwood's house. The day afterwards the Council of the Army again assembled at Wallingford House and were urged — presumably by Fleetwood — to 'amity and unity and a strict walking before the Lord'. But these fresh meetings only provoked the House of Commons which four days later voted that the Council of the Army should stop its meetings altogether and that no officer should hold a command in the army or the navy if he failed to guarantee the free meeting of Parliament. Richard Cromwell tried to impose this vote on the officers. But Cromwell's Generals responded in their old way. Fleetwood refused to go to Whitehall when ordered to receive the vote. And after he and his colleagues, Desborough and Berry, had made it clear to the Protector that the army was behind them, they demanded that he should dissolve Parliament. Richard Cromwell, finding that he had no forces whatever at his disposal — not even his own lifeguards — yielded. General Fleetwood explained to General Monk, again as was customary on such occasions, that the *coup d'état* had been carried out because they had obtained 'very certain assurances' of a Royalist rising. The event in fact was simply a conspiracy, an alliance of most of Oliver Cromwell's Generals — Fleetwood, Lambert, Desborough, Berry, Whalley, Goffe, Kelsey, Boteler and others — with the malcontent minority in the Commons, for whom Lieutenant-General Ludlow was the intermediary. The officers that Oliver Cromwell had dismissed came out of the shadows, received back their regiments, and prepared for a millenium that never arrived.

After a brief and confused interlude — during which Lambert and Fleetwood intrigued against each other, Fleetwood being willing to retain the Protectorate, Lambert being against it — the Rump of the Long Parliament, half-forgotten men whom Lambert himself had helped to dispatch six years before, was recalled to Westminster, and Richard Cromwell submitted and resigned. On June 7th, 1659, Fleetwood at last gained his heart's desire, for which he had plotted and prayed so long, and was appointed Commander-in-Chief, though with many restrictions. But he did not retain that elegant post for more than a short space. While in Ireland, the Lord Lieutenant, Henry Cromwell (he had been promoted by his brother) also resigned and was replaced by the republican General Ludlow, in Scotland there was still one of Oliver Cromwell's Generals who had watched and waited but expressed no opinion as the kaleidoscope in London was shaken again and again: that General was a tougher character than the tearful Fleetwood, more popular with his men than Henry Cromwell, in a firmer tactical situation than the resurgent John Lambert: it was General George Monk.

BIBLIOGRAPHY TO CHAPTER XI

There is no life of Fleetwood except that by Sir Charles Firth in the *Dictionary of National Biography*, but there are many of his letters in the Rawlinson MSS in the Bodleian (printed in the *Thurloe State Papers*) and in the Lansdowne MSS in the British Museum. Some of the latter are printed in whole or part in R. W. Ramsey, *Henry Cromwell* (1949), but the quotations in the text are taken from the originals in the British Museum. Two other letters of Fleetwood in 1659 are in Add. MSS 15857, f. 150, and Egerton MSS 2618, f. 58. For Fleetwood's career in Ireland Ludlow's *Memoirs* and R. Bagwell, op. cit. should be consulted. Henry Cromwell's report on Fleetwood is from *Thurloe State Papers*, II, 149 and his comment on Fleetwood as a milksop is in ibid., VI, 811. Edward Hyde's character of Fleetwood is from *Clarendon State Papers*, III, 376.

CHAPTER XII

GENERAL GEORGE MONK AND THE RESTORATION

George Monk was born in 1608 and died in 1670

'THE Profession of a Souldier', wrote George Monk, 'is allowed to be lawful by the Word of God; and so Famous and Honourable amongst Men, that Emperours and Kings do account it a Great Honour to be of the Profession, and to have Experience in it . . .' Monk was before everything else a professional officer, proud of his calling. To him 'the greatest virtue which is required in a soldier is obedience', while a general should defer to the civil power. Yet, he added, 'it is most necessary for a general in the first place to approve his cause, and settle an opinion of right in the minds of his officers and soldiers. . . .'

Although his unique book, *Observations upon Military and Political Affairs*, was published posthumously in 1671, it was written during his imprisonment in the Tower of London when he was under forty, and besides its tactical lessons it embodied his approach to life. While he believed in rigidly accepting constituted authority, he first wished to be persuaded that the authority he served or the cause for which he fought was just. With a tidy soldierly outlook his preference was for unity in Church and State. Slow to make up his mind, when he gave his trust, he gave it wholly. Hence he was unshakably loyal to Oliver Cromwell until the great man died.

Born at Potheridge near Torrington in Devonshire on December 8th, 1608, George Monk belonged to a family whose ramifications reached out among many of the wealthiest households in the country and also stretched backwards to the Plantagenets. He was brought up by his grandfather and godfather, Sir George Smith of Exeter, but it was an incident connected with his father, Sir Thomas Monk, according to his earliest biographer, that propelled him at an early age into the service of arms. His father is said to have employed him, as a lad of sixteen, to bribe the under-sheriff not to arrest him for debt if he appeared in public when King Charles I was visiting Exeter in 1625. But the under-sheriff broke his bargain and George Monk started to thrash him until they were dragged apart. To escape the penalties of his passion Monk was shipped off under his kinsman, Sir Richard Greenville. But to go to sea and fight the foe was the natural destiny of a lusty young man in the county of Drake and Ralegh, and so, like Phillip Skippon, he acquired his military experience hardily in a 'Commonwealth where soldiers received and observed orders, but gave none.'

Through the influence of the Earl of Leicester, a connection of his family, Monk, on his return to England at the age of thirty, was given a lieutenant-colonelcy in a foot regiment which had a brief and unremarkable career in the so-called Bishops wars against the Scots in 1638 and 1639. Next, in 1642, he obtained, again through Leicester, the acting command of a foot regiment in Ireland. It was after he came back from Ireland to England and his capture at Nantwich by Lambert's men that he was lodged in the Tower and wrote his book.

No reader of Monk's book can fail to appreciate how absorbed he was in the art of war. It is a key to the understanding both of his character and his professional competence. Generalship, he reminds us, as indeed every great soldier has done, consists above all less in a mastery of strategy and tactics, than in the maintenance of supplies and morale. A general, he wrote, must ensure that his soldiers receive their pay punctually, are well fed and clothed, and know what they are fighting for. Discipline is essential, but a general needs 'to mingle love with the severity of his discipline'. It was not surprising that when the civil war was over Parliament was persuaded to employ a professional officer, so devoted and thoughtful, even with a dubious past, in the Irish campaign.

Probably the truth about what happened to him in Ireland will never be clear. For two years Monk skilfully carried out his duties as Major-General in Ulster, but after the execution of King Charles I the Ulster Scots turned against Parliament and a combination of Royalists, Irish nationalists, and Presbyterians threatened to expel the Parliamentary forces, commanded by Monk in the north and General Michael Jones in Dublin, before General Cromwell could relieve them. Under these circumstances Monk concluded in May 1649 a three-month armistice with Owen Roe O'Neill, a master of guerrilla warfare who led the native Irish in Ulster and with whom he had earlier been fighting. The armistice temporarily reduced the pressure on Monk's troops and prevented the King's Lord-Lieutenant, Ormonde, from overrunning the country. But Monk did not have the sanction of the English Council of State for the armistice, though he wrote to inform Cromwell: 'Since there was great necessity for me to do it,' he told him, 'I hope it will beget no ill construction.' He had gained time, though in the end he was compelled to surrender to the Royalists. Returning to England, he interviewed Cromwell as he was about to sail. What the two men said to each other is not known. But later the House of Commons voted that it 'utterly disapproved' of Monk's agreement with O'Neill because he thereby shook hands with the Popish monsters who had shed so much innocent Protestant blood. Nevertheless an amendment was carried excusing Monk's conduct on the ground of necessity. Thus he escaped punishment; but the motion was almost enough to ruin the career of a professional soldier. As it was, he lost his regiment and retired in dudgeon to his home in Devon.

It has been argued that Cromwell himself must have secretly encouraged and approved Monk's treaty with O'Neill. If that is true, he was in Monk's debt, for Monk took all the blame on himself. When Cromwell arrived back from his victories in Ireland, he formed a new regiment for Monk and soon afterwards conferred on him the post of Lieutenant-General of the Ordnance. Was that the price paid to Monk for keeping his mouth shut? But surely that is an over-simplification of the story. In the light of what we know about the characters of the two men, it is more likely that Cromwell was satisfied with the efficiency and loyalty of General Monk — who must have been tempted to desert the Parliamentary cause in Ulster — and had promised him that he should not suffer for what he had done. Nothing in Monk's subsequent correspondence or behaviour indicates that he felt any grievance against Cromwell.

After Cromwell departed from Scotland at the beginning of August 1651, he left Monk behind as Commander-in-Chief with an army of four cavalry and three foot regiments, together with dragoons, artillery and garrison troops totalling some 8000 men. The Highlands were still unsettled and much of the Western Lowlands unoccupied. On August 14th Monk completed the subjugation of Stirling and its castle; on September 1st he stormed Dundee and because it resisted his summons gave the town over to twenty-four hours' plunder by his soldiers. Some of the plunder was put aboard ships captured in the harbour which, being overloaded or scuttled, sank within sight of the town. There is no evidence, however, for the story that Monk allowed civilians to be massacred, and the plundering was stopped at the time limit. Colonel Alured at the same time captured the persons of the Scottish Committee of Estates, so that by the end of the year all organized resistance ceased. As soon as the battle of Worcester was won, Cromwell hurried reinforcements to Monk, who was able to dispatch Colonel Overton to capture the Orkneys. But that autumn Monk was taken ill: he reported 'lameness in my knees', presumably some form of rheumatism, and at his own request was relieved by Major-General Richard Deane and retired to Bath for a cure. But he remained, with Lambert and Deane, one of the Commissioners for Scotland, and was voted £500 out of the confiscated Scottish estates for his services.

Now a new phase in Monk's life opened. In November 1652 he was appointed General-at-sea, after having first been employed in converting Great Yarmouth into a naval port. It has been customary for Monk's biographers to treat his work as an admiral somewhat lightly. Even the late Sir Julian Corbett wrote that 'At the age of forty-four it is not easy suddenly to take up a new profession, and he made no pretence to seamanship. His complete ignorance of nautical matters became a standing joke.' The Reverend Thomas Gumble, who was afterwards Monk's chaplain, wrote that 'when the seamen, according to their terms of art, cried, "starboard and larboard", he [Monk] always cried, "Ay, Boys, let us board them".' But, as we have already shown in discussing the careers of Monk's fellow Generals-at-sea, Blake and Deane, there were few professional sailors at that time. It was normal to appoint an experienced artilleryman, like Monk, in a fighting role. It was also suggested by a contemporary that when Monk was given his post an English landing in Holland itself was contemplated. In any case Monk was not a mere administrator like General Desborough, who never put to sea. Whatever his deficiencies as a seaman may have been, he was able to apply both his knowledge of gunnery and also his mastery of strategy to the struggle against the Dutch. Furthermore he had at his disposal the advice of Vice-Admiral Penn, a professional sailor of competence.

Monk took up his command in December 1652, when Blake had not yet succeeded in winning any crushing victory over Tromp and when Blake himself was in poor health. Mr. C. T. Atkinson, who studied the history and authorities on the first Anglo-Dutch War more thoroughly than any historian, was of the opinion that 'to attribute to this professional soldier [Monk] the development in tactics which undoubtedly took place in the spring of 1653' — tactics which were pursued in the battles of the Gabbard and Scheveningen where he had the chief command — 'seems on the whole warranted'. 'Monk', he continued, 'seems equally with Tromp to have emphasized the importance of concentration and of bringing the enemy to battle.' Blake, Mr. Atkinson argued, learned from his failures; but for the change that came over the English war against the Dutch in 1653, following Blake's defeat at Dungeness, Monk was mainly responsible. Monk, he added, 'can stand comparison with Tromp as a strategist and tactician but not as navigator or seaman'. That is a notable tribute and ought to silence all future biographers who are tempted to be funny about Monk as an admiral.

The battle of the Gabbard, which was fought on June 2nd and 3rd, 1653, when Monk took control aboard the *Resolution* where Richard Deane was killed by his side, was, wrote Mr. Atkinson, 'in a sense the decisive encounter of the war' and marked 'a distinct epoch in the history of naval tactics'. At the battle of Scheveningen, also called the battle of the Texel, where again Monk was in sole command, a rudimentary example of the tactics of fighting in line ahead, as laid down in the fighting instructions written by Blake, Monk and Deane, is to be discerned. Monk and his fleet had been blockading the Dutch coasts when Tromp hove into sight with the aim of drawing him off to enable another Dutch admiral, De With, to come out. Monk has been criticized for falling into Tromp's trap. But the practice of concentrating his force and seeking battle with the enemy as soon as he could was good, far better than the traditional naval strategy of dispersing to destroy commerce and capture bullion. After a drawn battle the Dutch fleets joined and interposed between Monk and the Texel with the advantage of the weather gauge on their side, 'the Lord', as Monk wrote, 'seeming to encourage the enemy'. Despite this handicap Monk successfully manœuvred his ships so that they were able to charge through the Dutch and cut them in half. A flag officer who was present at the battle wrote:

> When all their fire-ships were spent, we rejoiced and fought them (as we thought) on equal terms, every commander observing their orders in a line to assist each other as much as could be. . . .

That was the contest at which, as one of Monk's contemporary biographers wrote, Tromp 'was killed by a small shot, and died like an admiral, with his sword in his hand, encouraging his men to the fight'. It was virtually the end of the war, and by the following April Monk was back in Scotland.

When Major-General Richard Deane gave up his command in Scotland at the end of 1652 in order to serve at sea it was reported that 'all things at present are at a strange kind of hush'. But it was the quiet before a storm. Lord Middleton, who had managed to escape from the Tower of London after being taken prisoner at the battle of Worcester, was nominated by King Charles II as his commander in the Highlands and pending his arrival there the Earl of Glencairne initiated a period of guerrilla warfare. Colonel Robert Lilburne, the Anabaptist officer who took over from Deane, though without the rank of Major-General, found his task too much for him. A rising began in the Highlands in July 1653 and Lilburne soon discovered that he had neither the strength nor the means to suppress it. Though the Marquis of Argyll remained cautiously neutral, his son, Lord Lorne, threw in his lot with the Royalists and Lilburne reported that without reinforcements of cavalry he was unable to cope with the outbreak. He was a sound officer, but he soon lost heart and was delighted when at the end of 1653 Monk was ordered to return to Scotland.

Monk did not assume his appointment until April 1654, when he was given extensive powers. Meanwhile Middleton had arrived and the fire of revolt spread. By February of that year Middleton had 8000 warriors at his command. It is a measure of Monk's personality and influence that while his demands on London were similar to those of Lilburne much more notice was taken of them. As soon as he reached Dalkeith, which he made his headquarters, and had grasped the situation, he asked Cromwell for reinforcements both of soldiers and of warships as well as for money — he had found only £500 in the Scottish Treasury. His needs having been met, he launched a campaign against Middleton's forces in the Highlands in June, as soon as the grass had grown enough to feed his horses. He divided his army into two columns, one led by himself, the other under the command of Major-General Thomas Morgan, and after a brilliant display of the art of manœuvre amid the lochs and hills, Monk drove his enemy back on to Loch Garry where Morgan awaited them. Mobility was the secret of Monk's success, for his men were provided with seven days' rations. Thenceforward Middleton was never able to collect a force of more than a few hundred men. Monk and Morgan systematically devastated the Highlands, imposing fines on fathers who let their sons fight and offering rewards for the capture of Royalist leaders. 'We have followed the enemy these five weeks,' reported Monk to Cromwell on July 17th, 'and have now dispersed them into many several parts, having marched them from 3000 to 1200 . . . We have burnt such parts of the Highlands where they were utterly engaged against us . . .' and since the Scottish Cavaliers, for their part, threatened to set on fire the estates of the neutral Marquis of Argyll, he thought 'that the whole of the Highlands will, in all probability, be laid waste'.

Afterwards Monk, who had established a first-class intelligence system, arranged for a policing of the Highlands that prevented his enemies from rallying or uniting. He also completed the building of fortresses at Inverlochy, Inverness, Ayr, Perth and Leith, which enabled him to maintain the peace and at the same time release troops for punitive expeditions. But the policy of allowing Scots to volunteer for military services overseas, which had been practised on the Irish by Fleetwood, did not work so well as it had done in Ireland, though Monk himself preferred it to the wholesale transportation of prisoners of war to the West Indies. By these means he was able to reduce the English garrison of Scotland from thirteen regiments of foot and seven of horse to eleven of foot and five of horse and also to lower the establishment of the regiments. Thus the burden upon the English Treasury was diminished, although Monk continued to complain to Whitehall that the pay of his men was nearly always in arrears. He also protested to Cromwell that the assessment of taxes on Scotland was higher than the country could bear and managed to persuade him to reduce it.

In 1655 the appointment of a Council for Scotland, in which Cromwell's new friend, Lord Broghil, was prominent, relieved Monk of some of his civil responsibilities. But it is noticeable that Monk, like Lilburne, thought that assemblies of Presbyterian ministers were a danger to order — 'trumpets of sedition' the Anabaptist commander had called them — and unlike Lilburne, Monk suspected the Marquis of Argyll of double-dealing. Monk was scrupulous in reporting his plans not only to the Protector but also to John Lambert, his old rival. He even gratified Lambert by asking Argyll to make him a present of hawks. And so long as Cromwell lived, Monk's loyalty to the Protectorate was absolute. It was on his initiative that Overton, who, under Lilburne, had performed useful services in the Highlands, had been arrested for conspiracy; he suppressed a petition which was circulated among his soldiers condemning the conferring of the title of King upon Cromwell; he kept under close surveillance the extremists, whether Anabaptists, Fifth Monarchy men, or Quakers; and during the Protector's last illness he published an order to his officers to maintain a sharp watch on 'discontented spirits'.

Because of the part he was to take in restoring King Charles II we are apt to forget that George Monk was one of the most loyal as well as one of the most expert of Cromwell's Generals. It is stated by Monk's early biographers that the Lord Protector had deliberately preferred him to his own brother-in-law, General John Desborough, for the highest post in Scotland, though Desborough was far from being an incompetent; and Clarendon remarked with justice that there was no man in any of his armies 'upon whose fidelity to him' Cromwell 'depended more'. When towards the end of Oliver Cromwell's life Monk informed him that he had received an approach from one of the supporters of King Charles II, Cromwell treated the matter as a joke.

Monk had his weaknesses upon which his enemies dilated. Clarendon, who did not care for him, noted that he was extremely fond of money and had the reputation of being close with it. He was certainly no gambler: 'he loved no manner of play,' wrote his chaplain, 'nor used any'. Undoubtedly he took advantage of his opportunities to acquire both Scottish and Irish estates, but he did nothing illegitimate according to the ideas of his times, and financial baits never tempted him from the line of duty. 'He had', Clarendon concluded in summing up Monk's character, 'no fancies of religion which turned his head, nor any credit with or dependence upon, any who were swayed by these tyrannies; only he was cursed after a long familiarity to marry a woman of the lowest extraction, the least wit and less beauty, who, taking no care for any part of herself, had deposited her soul with some Presbyterian ministers, who disposed her to that interest.' When Monk was in the Tower he had been tended by a laundress named Mrs. Ann or 'Nan' Ratsford; her husband had been a farrier in one of Monk's regiments, her mother was reputed to be one of the five women barbers of Drury Lane, and her father was a blacksmith. She and her husband were living in the Three Spanish Gypsies at the Exchange when she formed her liaison with Monk. She left her husband in 1649 and after his death was married to Monk at St. George's, Southwark, before he went to sea, on January 23rd, 1654. They had several children, one of them, George, dying of convulsive fits, another, Christopher, was to enjoy a dissipated career and perish of dropsy after becoming Governor of Jamaica. Though Ann Monk was always the subject of ribaldry, there must have been some quality about this woman who married into one of the best connected families in England and became a Duchess. Monk was alleged to have been 'more fearful of her than of an army'. He was over forty when he married. His chaplain averred that 'chastity was his second nature and I believe that after his marriage he never cast an amorous glance upon any other woman'.

Oliver Cromwell, remarked Dr. Gumble, 'died, as he lived, in a storm'. Monk, who for some years had lived 'very quietly, making no noise', accepted the succession of Richard Cromwell as Lord Protector without demur, although several of his junior officers openly said: 'Old George, for my money, is fitter for a Protector than Dick Cromwell.' Richard Cromwell is supposed to have offered Monk money to ensure his loyalty; that is most improbable if only because when Oliver died the State was in such debt that even the cost of the funeral was met with difficulty. However, the new Protector sent Monk's brother-in-law, Dr. Thomas Clarges, a physician, to Scotland in search of counsel, and Monk advised Richard Cromwell to be frugal, to be godly, and to rely on the New Courtiers, like Broghil and Thurloe, who had served his father so well. Suspecting that intrigues would soon begin among the Generals in London, Monk also suggested that he should amalgamate regiments and thus rid himself of any of the colonels who were 'insolent spirits'. But the new Protector did not heed the warning. 'Richard Cromwell forsook himself,' Monk observed afterwards, 'else I had never failed my promise to his father, or my regard to his memory.'

In the spring of 1659 neither Richard nor Henry Cromwell invoked Monk's help when Fleetwood and his friends were destroying the Protectorate, and Monk acquiesced in the recall of the Rump. 'The army here,' he told the new Committee of Safety, 'is very unanimous.' Taking advantage of the general confusion the Royalists planned a rising. Monk at once imposed on a number of noblemen and gentlemen who had already given sureties for their good behaviour an oath 'not to act or contrive anything for or in behalf of Charles Stuart' and imprisoned those who refused to accept the engagement. In England insurrections, directed chiefly by Presbyterian officers,

GENERAL GEORGE MONK

took place in various parts of the country, of which the most formidable were in Gloucestershire and Cheshire. Sir George Booth who, curiously, had earlier been recommended by Monk to Richard Cromwell, raised a banner at Chester in 'defence of the freedom of Parliament and the laws, liberty and property of the people'. Major-General John Lambert, who was now energetic in the Committee of Safety and the Council of State, and had received back his two regiments, marched north to deal with Booth, a gentleman of parts but no soldier. On August 23rd Lambert, advancing with all his old speed, encountered the Royalist party (some of Booth's adherents had been incautious enough to avow their true aim) and it soon fled in disorder: they 'retreated', Lambert caustically reported, 'without any loss other than that of reputation'. Booth himself dressed up in woman's clothes, but was ignominiously caught and sent to the Tower. Lambert then occupied Chester and after restoring order retired, mightily pleased with himself, to his home in the West Riding.

Delighted with these successes, the republican group that now ruled in the House of Commons became highly elated. 'Never,' wrote Guizot, 'had the position of the republican Parliament appeared more prosperous.' The parliamentary leaders tried, rightly from their point of view, to keep strict control over the Commonwealth armies. They had dispatched their trusted adherent, Lieutenant-General Ludlow, to replace Henry Cromwell in Ireland, who gave up his post without a fight; though they had appointed Lieutenant-General Fleetwood as Commander-in-Chief pending their sitting, the Speaker signed all commissions, the nomination of which was given to a committee of seven (including Fleetwood and Lambert) and had to be approved by Parliament. Oliver Cromwell's nearest friends, like his son-in-law, Falconbridge, were removed from their regiments; and when Monk, 'engaging for the fidelity' of his own officers, asked that no changes should be made in the army in Scotland, he received a rude answer. Though upset, Monk concealed his annoyance and took the rebuke with good grace: 'Obedience,' he wrote, 'is my great principle, and I have always, and ever shall, reverence the Parliament's resolutions in civil things as infallible and sacred.'

John Lambert, however, still flushed with his victory over Booth, refused to knuckle under. On September 20th, 1659, a number of his junior officers drew up a petition in Derby demanding that Fleetwood should be appointed Commander-in-Chief with full powers, Lambert Major-General, Desborough Lieutenant-General of Horse, and James Berry Commissary-General. Fleetwood, they fancied, 'was of an easy nature and would be contented with the name of General, allowing Lambert the power of it'. The Derby petition was circulated for signature in England, Scotland and Ireland, but Monk ordered his officers not to sign it, as some of the Anabaptists in particular wished to, as 'it hath always been against my way to sign petitions at all, either to the Parliament or General, from the forces here, and I am still of the same judgment'. That was consistent with Monk's attitude to politics as expressed ever since his younger days. And Parliament, which earlier had reproved him, was vastly encouraged by his behaviour, and the Speaker wrote on October 7th that his expressions of duty and faithfulness were 'very acceptable'.

Fleetwood had told Parliament that to the best of his knowledge General Lambert himself had not consented to the Derby petition. Thereupon Fleetwood was ordered to suppress it, and a meeting of officers was held at his house to receive the votes of Parliament. Lambert, back from his Yorkshire holiday, was present at the meeting, and after what must have been a hot discussion it was decided to set up a committee to frame modified demands. These demands included the requirement (of which Monk had expressed his approval) that no officer might be cashiered except by court martial or by order of his local commander. On October 10th the leaders in Parliament took these demands into consideration, but when an indiscreet letter signed by seven officers fell in their hands, they retorted by cashiering the signatories, who included Lambert himself, Desborough, Berry and Kelsey. Moreover Fleetwood's commission was declared void and two days later the powers of Commander-in-Chief were vested in a small committee which included both Fleetwood and Monk. Fleetwood, with typical pusillanimity, crumpled under the affront. But Lambert, who had been expelled the House and threatened with arrest, was built of sterner stuff. Hazlerigg, the leader of the republicans in the Commons and colonel of a regiment, vainly attempted to protect Parliament from Lambert's wrath. But with the aid of Desborough and Fleetwood, Lambert mustered enough troops to overwhelm the guard, and on October 14th, for the second time in its history, the Rump was dissolved by the army. Hazlerigg fled from London.

The news of the dissolution of Parliament reached Monk in Scotland on October 18th. True to his principles, Monk at once prepared to support the civil power against Lambert and his group of fellow Generals among whom Desborough and Berry were the most active. In fact Monk had already sent a secret message to London by his brother-in-law promising Hazlerigg that he would do so. Monk gave orders that any officers in the army in Scotland who were suspected of disloyalty to Parliament were to be dismissed, and on October 20th he sent letters to Fleetwood, Lambert and the Speaker notifying them of his point of view. 'I am engaged in conscience and honour', he declared, 'to see my country freed (as much as in me lies) from the intolerable slavery of a sword government and I know England cannot, nay, will not endure it.'

There followed during late October and November a period of declaration and counter-declaration between the two sides in the army and a brisk exchange of letters between Monk and Fleetwood. On October 25th Fleetwood dispatched a letter to Monk by the hand of Colonel Talbot whose regiment was posted in Edinburgh. Colonel Cobbett, who had brought the first news of the *coup d'état* to Scotland, had been put under arrest by Monk. In his letter Fleetwood wrote: 'I much wonder you should put yourself in a posture of opposition to your old friends upon a bare report.' Lambert, who wrote to Monk on the same date, referred to their old friendship and warned him that if the army were disunited now, only the Royalists would be the gainers. Generals Whalley and Goffe set off in haste to Scotland to try to effect a reconciliation. But on November 3rd Monk wrote firmly to Fleetwood from Edinburgh saying: 'let the Lord judge between you and me where the guilt will rest'. 'And when the Lord pleases to return the Parliament to their trust,' he added, 'I will submit my actings to their judgment.'

Cromwell's Generals were now at cross purposes with a vengeance. Fleetwood was willing to call a new Parliament; Lambert wanted things to remain as they were; Monk was loyal to the Rump. Yet none of them was anxious to fight the other. To avert such a disaster, Fleetwood proposed to Monk that a meeting should be held between commissioners representing the army in Scotland and the Council of Officers who were now virtually ruling in London.

Meanwhile the Royalists were rejoicing in their fresh opportunity. From July 1659, a daring group of young Cavaliers, headed by Lord John Mordaunt and his beautiful wife, had conspired to bring back their King and many pressures had been exerted upon General Monk to join their cause. His brother Nicholas, who was a clergyman in Devonshire, had been sent up to Dalkeith in the autumn on the pretext of discussing the marriage of his daughter, Monk's favourite niece, in order to convey an offer from King Charles II of £100,000 for his services. The General gave his brother no encouragement. His brother-in-law, Dr. Clarges, was more ingenious and more persuasive. He played upon Monk's respect for constituted authority. A messenger also arrived from Yorkshire with a communication from Lord Fairfax, now bestirring himself against anarchy, while Dr. Gumble, then the chaplain to the Scottish Commission, whom Monk liked and trusted, added his counsel that he ought to resist the machinations of the clique in Whitehall. Slowly but inexorably George Monk, who had always been antipathetic to Lambert, had come to the conclusion that if the Yorkshire General were to attack Parliament, he would go to its rescue. Thus even before the *coup d'état* of October 13th Monk had been making his preparations. But to ensure success his own army had first to be purged of extremists; Scotland needed to be held down before he dared move forward, and, even then, his problem was how to outmanœuvre Lambert who, with his henchman Robert Lilburne, barred Monk's way south.

Did Monk agree to negotiate with the army in London merely in order to buy time? It seems that he did; for the instructions he gave to his commissioners were that they should require the restoration of the Rump, which would have spelt ruin for

Lambert. At any rate neither Lambert nor Monk remained idle while their commissioners were meeting to talk peace. Monk's officers tried vainly to seize control of Carlisle and Newcastle, and Monk wrote letters to the Lord Mayor of London and to other English cities promising his support for the restoration of the Rump. Lambert, for his part, arrived with an army of some 7000 men in York on November 8th, and Lilburne laid hold of Newcastle. Although on November 15th Monk's commissioners signed a pact with the Council of Officers in London which would have healed the breach in the army, Monk himself refused to ratify it on the ground that his representatives had exceeded their instructions, and he wrote to Lambert on November 24th telling him to draw off his forces, offering at the same time to confer again at York or Newcastle. Instructions were actually drawn up for such a meeting; but Monk's commissioners were ordered to insist upon the restoration of the dismissed Parliament and to complain to Lambert because while the previous negotiations had been in progress, 'their army was recruited, the militia raised, and expresses stopped'. Monk's terms were virtually an ultimatum inviting John Lambert to cut his own throat. A battle between Cromwell's two ablest surviving Generals appeared unavoidable.

Not all of Monk's officers agreed with his policy of dividing the armies. Captain Robert Scrape, for example, wrote to his Commander-in-Chief from Dundee:

> My Lord, I have much considered, weighed, and pondered upon the late so great change in England, and upon the whole my spirit is drawn to conclude upon this: that though the army in England did attempt a matter of so high a nature, to interrupt and dissolve the late Parliament, from which we received our commissions, and though I cannot receive as yet full satisfaction as to their attempt in that nature, yet I cannot find it in my heart to be drawn out so far to engage against them as it hath been against those which they and we have been engaged together against, the great enemy of England's peace. Indeed, my Lord, it is so sad to me when I do think upon it that my heart is almost overwhelmed within me, that we which have prayed together, took counsel together, and rejoiced so often together . . . should be anywise provoked

> each against other so high to engage one another's head and hands for the fighting one against another to the destroying of each other. . . .

Monk had to get rid of men like Scrape and at the same time to rely on his former enemies, the Scottish Royalists, to keep the peace before he dared risk the crossing of the border.

In fact Monk dismissed at least three colonels of his regiments; from his own regiment, which contained many Anabaptists, over twenty officers and N.C.O.s were removed; and, according to Corbett, 'in his hour of need Monk had hardly a single field officer whom he could trust'. One outstanding officer, however, was at his service: that was another professional soldier, Sir Thomas Morgan, who had distinguished himself in the campaign under Turenne in Flanders, and now had returned home still holding his rank of Major-General on the Scottish establishment. Lambert had hoped to use Morgan as an instrument of conciliation, but Morgan sided with Monk. 'This little man,' wrote Dr. Gumble, 'was of more worth at that time than the seventeen score officers who had deserted the service.' Under Morgan the remodelling of the Scottish army went forward briskly, while Monk came to an agreement with leading Scotsmen that if he marched into England they would keep the peace, though he deemed it dangerous to leave arms in their hands. He also exacted a promise from the Scottish nobility 'to act nothing in favour of Charles Stuart's interests'. Even then he felt obliged to leave behind four foot regiments, and soon after entering Northumberland he sent Morgan back with one regiment of horse and one of foot.

On December 8th, 1659, Monk set up his headquarters in the village of Coldstream on the Scottish border. Since November 20th he had been at Berwick, but his men occupied all the passes between Kelso and Berwick and he picked this village in the centre as convenient for his purpose. Here he dwelt in a one-roomed cottage filled with smoke and slept in his clothes. The General pacified himself by chewing tobacco, but his companions reviled 'the poor town, and vowed it was justly called Coldstream, being a place for good Christians to perish in'. Monk's leisurely but effective plans were now at last completed. He had the advantages not only of an army so purged as to be devoted to him, but money to pay it — it is said that he possessed £70,000 and a good magazine. From Coldstream Monk continued to write to Fleetwood and Lambert expressing his willingness to negotiate with them if Lambert would draw off his forces from Northumberland and Cumberland. 'We were in no ways the beginners of the breach,' he told Lambert on December 14th. All was nevertheless procrastination. Lambert had a larger army than Monk and was a worthy foe. But Lambert dared not break off the pointless argument and try to thrust north over the border. For every day the discipline of his army was being weakened and undermined; he was given no money to pay his troops and was without the power to raise it; and if he advanced, he would have to requisition food and billets all the way, thus provoking the population against him and thereby helping Monk.

The detailed correspondence between Lambert and Monk during that critical December has survived the years; but it has little significance. Lambert was immobilized in his native Yorkshire by lack of means to move; Monk was playing for time. 'And this dallying it was,' wrote one of Monk's entourage, 'that proved the break-neck of Lambert, who accepted of this excuse at first, but afterwards found our delays.'

Meanwhile what was happening elsewhere? General Ludlow had hurried back to England on learning of the second breaking of the Rump, and in his absence the Irish garrison, headed by Sir Charles Coote and Sir Hardress Waller, had declared for Parliament. The navy, where Vice-Admiral Lawson, the erstwhile Leveller, had superseded Edward Montagu, who now secretly went over to the Royalists, had also come out for Parliament, and soldiers, dispatched by Fleetwood to besiege Portsmouth, which under Hazlerigg had revolted, deserted to their enemy. In London the little group who were trying to govern the country was harassed and perplexed. General Fleetwood, tossed up and down by contradictory advice, was told by Lord Whitelocke that he had only two practical alternatives: to seize the Tower of London and declare for a free Parliament or to restore King Charles II. Fleetwood, despairing, inclined to the second alternative. But he was resisted by General Desborough and General Berry. A quarter of an hour after he had informed Whitelocke that he was willing to restore the King, he went back to him and 'in much passion said . . . "I cannot do it, I cannot do it" '. Whitelocke asked him why not. Fleetwood answered that he had been reminded by his fellow Generals that he could not act without the consent of Lambert. Whitelocke replied that Lambert was too far away to be consulted. But Fleetwood repeated that he could not move without him. Then, retorted Whitelocke, 'You will ruin yourself and your friends.' Two days later, on Christmas Eve, there was a rising in London — Fleetwood, Desborough and Berry having thrown up the sponge — with the aim of reinstating the Rump. Colonel Sir Arthur Hazlerigg marched up in triumph with the garrison of Portsmouth. On the day after Christmas the Rump met once again in Westminster.

The sequence of events was reported to Monk on December 24th as follows:

> Lord Fleetwood sent to the Speaker yesternight that the Lord had blasted them and spit in their faces and witnessed against their perfidiousness and that he was freely willing to lie at their mercy.

The doors of Parliament were opened. The Grandees were 'in mourning' and thought it vain to flee. And on New Year's Day, as soon as he had digested the news, without orders from anybody, General Monk directed his army of six infantry and four cavalry regiments to cross the frontier from Coldstream.

These Coldstreamers, wrote Gumble, were 'like Sons of God in the Chronicles'. The roads were deep in snow or slippery with ice, but little or no opposition was met, for Lambert's men were fast deserting him. Lord Fairfax, Lambert's one-time patron, had sent his young cousin Brian disguised as a yokel across the lines to assure Monk that he himself would take the field from Nunappleton on his behalf against his fellow Yorkshireman. A previous attempt by Fairfax to occupy York had failed. But now the former Commander-in-Chief, though still racked with gout, set forth in his coach, put himself at the head of the Yorkshire militia, and, rallying his men on the battlefield of Marston Moor, helped to accelerate the breaking up of Lambert's forces. That was on January 3rd, 1660. Lambert's army had in fact melted as butter before the fire. He was left at Northallerton with only fifty troopers; he went into hiding, visited his birthplace for the last time, and then surrendered to the mercy of Parliament. He was deprived of his commands and later sent to the Tower. On January 11th General Monk entered York.

Had Monk when he left Scotland determined to restore the Stuarts? Did he, as a contemporary suggested, 'carry the King in his belly'? No one has known then or since. But at the end of November 1659, he had written to Dr. John Owen: 'as to the Cavaliers' interest, I think I may modestly aver it hath no greater enemy in the three nations than myself'. He had reproved one of his chaplains for his royalism, asking him: 'will you bring my neck to the block for the King?' And on January 16th, 1660, Mordaunt wrote: 'He is a black Monk and I cannot see through him.' As he marched south many reports came to Monk of demonstrations — in Durham, in Nottingham, in Bristol — on behalf of King Charles II. On February 3rd he arrived in London, was thanked by the Rump Parliament, who had awaited him nervously, and quartered his men in the City. Fleetwood's following, which had grown restive, was extruded. Monk was given the rank of full General. He did not hesitate to tell the Rump that they must fill up their vacancies and then dissolve. When the oath of abjuration was required of him by the Committee of Safety he refused to take it. 'The officers of my army,' he asserted, 'are very tender in taking oaths.' Had that significance or was it mere caution? The explanation of Monk's conduct would appear to be that as he moved across the face of England he had become convinced that the Restoration was the only alternative to anarchy.

Now the City of London entered the picture. The Common Council announced that it would pay no taxes until the House of Commons filled up its vacancies. The Council of State was livid and ordered Monk to place the leading citizens under arrest and to pull down the gates of the City. Monk obeyed, though he recommended leniency. Hazlerigg would not hear of it. 'Now George,' he is reported to have declared, 'we have thee for ever, body and soul.' That was the crux. Reports had continued to pour in to Monk since his arrival in the capital from throughout the country of demands for a 'free Parliament', which everyone knew in fact meant the return of the King. Now at last he moved slowly but remorselessly against the civil power. Like Harrison, Cromwell and Lambert before him, Monk raised his sword against Parliament, if in a politer way. Instead of marching a file of musketeers into the House, he withdrew the guards around it, and thus permitted the Presbyterian members, absent for over eleven years, to take their seats — but on his own conditions. He ordered the Commons to issue writs to fill their vacancies and told them that within eight weeks they must dissolve themselves and give place to a free Parliament. They acquiesced. And as the excluded members resumed their seats, Samuel Pepys noted on February 21st, 1660, 'it was a most pleasant sight to see the City from one end to another with a glory about it, so high was the light of the bonfires, and so thick round the City, and the bells rang everywhere'.

Thus it was not until General Monk had been provoked by the order to humiliate London that he finally broke the habit of a lifetime and coerced the civil power; and it was not until after the Long Parliament had been dissolved on March 17th that he sent for his cousin, Sir John Greenville, and himself entered into direct communication with King Charles II.

On April 9th Lambert, who had been sent to the Tower a month earlier, broke prison, escaped to Warwickshire, and rallied a handful of followers at Edgehill. Monk was alarmed and wanted to go himself in pursuit, but instead, dispatched, ironically enough, a regicide colonel, Richard Ingoldsby. At Daventry Lambert surrendered. He was virtually the only one of Cromwell's Generals to make so much of a gesture, and thus the Interregnum may be said to have ended where it began — on the field of Edgehill. Lambert went back to prison. On May 26th Monk embraced King Charles II after he had landed on the beach at Dover. Monk always denied that he had effected the Restoration, and of course this was true, but he had done his share. He was to disband his splendid army, save for the Coldstream Guards, and to fight again for his country at sea, but on that spring day in Dover the story of Cromwell's Generals, with its heroisms and tragedies, its fidelities and its intrigues, reached its end. The rest is epilogue and epitome.

BIBLIOGRAPHY TO CHAPTER XII

There are several popular biographies of Monk, e.g. by Oliver Warner and J. Griffith Davis (1936). Sir Julian Corbett's biography was published in 1889 and is now largely out of date. Valuable appreciations of Monk's capabilities as an admiral are in C. T. Atkinson's volumes on the Anglo-Dutch War published by the Navy Records Society and in David Ogg, *England in the Reign of Charles II* (1934), chaps. VIII and X where the authorities for the Restoration period are cited. The lives of Monk by his chaplain, T. Gumble (1671) and his physician, T. Skinner (1724) contain illuminating information. Many of Monk's letters have been printed in *Scotland and the Protectorate*, the *Clarke Papers*, *Thurloe State Papers*, *Letters and Papers Relating to the first Dutch War*, and *Historical Manuscripts Commission: Leyborne-Popham MSS*, but they have never been published together in one volume. Monk's *Observations upon Military and Political Affairs* (1671) was twice republished in the eighteenth century. For Monk's preparations and his march from Coldstream see especially vol. IV of the *Clarke Papers* and the Leyborne-Popham MSS (from which Captain Scrape's letter is quoted) and also G. Davies, *Early History of the Coldstream Guards* (1924). The best general account of the political history of England between the death of Cromwell and the Restoration is in the *Cambridge Modern History*, vol. IV; see also E. Phillips, *Continuation of Sir R. Baker, Chronicles of the Kings of England* (1665), which is based on papers of Thomas Clarges, Monk's brother-in-law, and Ludlow's *Memoirs*. For the events in Scotland before Monk took command in 1654 see *Scotland and the Commonwealth* (1895) and Firth's introduction to it. For Fairfax's part in the Restoration see C. R. Markham's biography.

CHAPTER XIII

THE FATE OF CROMWELL'S GENERALS

FIVE of Oliver Cromwell's Generals had predeceased him; these were Edward Popham, Robert Blake and Richard Deane, the first three Generals-at-sea of the Commonwealth; Henry Ireton, Cromwell's eldest son-in-law; and Charles Worsley, the youngest of the Major-Generals of the Horse Militia. Of the five, only Deane had been killed in battle. Nevertheless the hazards of sea warfare, then, as in more modern times, were bigger than those upon land. The foulness of the ships, the inadequacy of the diet, and the scarcity of fresh water during long voyages all contributed towards shortening a sailor's life, while the admiral's presence on the quarter deck of his flagship directing the battle marked him out as a conspicuous target for enemy gunners. In battles ashore the armour worn by a general, even though he was then expected to lead his men on the field, afforded a substantial measure of protection against the weapons of the seventeenth century; we have seen how General Lambert, possibly the most daring of all Cromwell's Generals, had escaped with his life, though often wounded, on one occasion having a bullet penetrate as far as his doublet. Ireton and Worsley did not die of wounds but through overwork and devotion to duty. One other General perished before the Restoration: that was Phillip Skippon who had performed little service during the Protectorate, as in its later stages he had left the management of London's military affairs mainly in the hands of the Lieutenant of the Tower, Sir John Barkstead. Skippon died of old age in March 1660.

Popham, Deane, Blake, Ireton and Worsley had all been buried with exceptional pomp in King Henry VII's Chapel in Westminster Abbey and their master had been placed alongside them after his lying in state and funeral in October 1658. On December 4th, 1660, King Charles II's first Parliament had voted that the bodies of Oliver Cromwell, Henry Ireton, John Bradshaw and Colonel Thomas Pride should be taken out of their graves in the Abbey, drawn to the gallows, and there hanged and buried underneath it, 'which (methinks),' noted Samuel Pepys apropos the Lord Protector, 'do trouble me that a man of so great courage as he was, should have that dishonour, though otherwise he might deserve it enough'. On January 30th, 1661, twelve years to the day since the execution of King Charles I, the order was carried out. John Evelyn, the other celebrated memorialist of the new reign, who, unlike Pepys, was an heir of the puritan spirit, recounted the proceedings in his own style:

> This day (O the stupendous and inscrutable Judgments of God!) were the carcasses of those arch-rebels, Cromwell, Bradshaw (the judge who condemned his Majesty) and Ireton (son-in-law to the Usurper) dragged out of their superb tombs in Westminster among the Kings to Tyburn and hanged on the gallows there from nine in the morning till six at night, and then buried under that fatal and ignominous monument in a deep pit. Look back at October 22nd, 1658 [the day of Cromwell's funeral] and be astonished! Fear God and honour the King; but meddle not with them who are given to change!

An eye-witness noted that whereas Cromwell's carcass was in 'a green-cere cloth very fresh embalmed', 'Ireton, having been buried long, hung like a dried rat, yet corrupted about the fundamental'. Before their trunks were buried the heads of Cromwell, Ireton and Bradshaw (but not of Pride) were set upon poles and placed on the top of Westminster Hall by the common hangman. Such was the fate of the last earthly remains of General Ireton. The skeletons of Blake and Deane were also removed from the Abbey and thrown into a pit. But the remains of Edward Popham were removed privately out of deference to his brother, Alexander, who was a member of King Charles II's Parliament, and buried in the chapel of St. John the Baptist. And the grave of Charles Worsley was forgotten or overlooked. Years afterwards, when a search was being undertaken for the corpse of King James I, the skeleton of a tall unknown man was discovered; and that was thought to be the last of Charles Worsley.

After long and complicated debates King Charles II gave his

assent to an Act of Indemnity (12 Carl. II, XI) on August 21st, 1660, from which all the surviving regicides, that is to say those who signed King Charles I's death warrant (forty-nine in number), were exempted. But nineteen regicides who had given themselves up, were by another clause in effect allowed to escape with their lives since there was a proviso that in the event of their being attainted for high treason, their fate should be suspended until the King, by advice and assent of both Houses, should order their execution. Among the other thirty completely exempted from the Act were Thomas Harrison, Edward Whalley, John Barkstead, Edmund Ludlow and William Goffe. Sir Hardress Waller, one of Cromwell's Generals in Ireland, and Colonel Robert Lilburne, the former acting Commander-in-Chief in Scotland, were among the nineteen.

On October 9th a special commission of Oyer and Terminer was opened at Hick's Hall to determine whether a bill of indictment should be returned by the Grand Jury against the accused regicides who had surrendered or been arrested. Two of Cromwell's Generals, George Monk, now Duke of Albemarle, and Edward Montagu, now Earl of Sandwich, were among the commissioners. Besides his titles Monk had been awarded £7000 a year out of the royal revenues and allowed to retain Irish lands worth £4000 a year. His brother, Nicholas Monk, was created Bishop of Hereford. 'It was a source of the greatest joy to Monk,' observes one of his biographers, 'to know that his dearest friends were to share in his good fortune.' But what, one wonders, were his thoughts when he saw General Harrison and other officers who had served with him under Cromwell standing before him in the dock?

The bill of indictment was duly returned by the Grand Jury, and on October 10th the new Lieutenant of the Tower delivered the prisoners to the Sheriff of the City who conducted them to Newgate prison and then brought them to Old Bailey on the morning of October 11th. Twenty-nine prisoners were on trial charged with high treason. The most important, as well as the most courageous, was Major-General Thomas Harrison.

Harrison had taken no part in the events that crowded the last years of the Interregnum. He had been arrested in April 1657, on suspicion of being concerned in a Fifth Monarchy plot, but was kept in prison for only a few weeks. Apparently he had been sounded by conspirators but had declined their invitation to join them on the ground that the Reign of the Beast had to last forty-two months and since Cromwell had become protector in December 1653, the date proposed for their rising was premature. In February 1658, he had again been taken in custody, because of fresh Fifth Monarchist stirrings and sent to the Tower, but by the time of Richard Cromwell's accession he was released and allowed to go to his home in Staffordshire. When the Rump was restored in May 1659, the members were still incensed against the General who had expelled them and later they deprived him of his seat and declared him for ever incapacitated from sitting in Parliament. On the whole, it seems that, like John Lilburne and some other extreme puritans of those days, Harrison in his middle age had turned to a quieter version of Christianity, the ardour of his youthful evangelism cooling into an acceptance of fate and the contemplation of an inner light. At any rate he awaited his arrest at Newcastle-under-Lyme with an unwonted placidity. Now, however, something of his old spirit returned and he breathed fire from the dock.

The first prisoner to be tried was Major-General Sir Hardress Waller. Waller had been Major-General of Foot in Ireland and senior officer there under Henry Cromwell. He had vainly tried to hold out for the Rump when Sir Charles Coote declared for the King. Waller gave himself up voluntarily and was virtually promised his life in the act of indemnity. The Court persuaded him to plead guilty. Harrison argued the toss. He pointed out that he had been kept a close prisoner for nearly three months, 'that nobody might have access to me'. 'Do you call me to give a legal answer', he asked, 'not knowing of my trial till nine of the clock last night, and brought away from the Tower, to this place, at six of the clock this morning?' But in the end he offered himself 'to be tried in your own way, by God and my Country'.

Harrison based his defence (he was allowed no counsel, it being a trial for treason) on two grounds: first, that the trial of King Charles I had been permitted and approved by a properly constituted Parliament; second, that he was obeying superior orders. To this it was answered that the Parliament was not properly constituted, it was only one House, and even that House had already been 'purged'. As to the question of superior orders the Court could not admit the right of any authority to order the trial of a king. Harrison did not deny the facts — 'the things that have been done,' he said, 'have been done upon the stage, in the sight of the Sun' and in particular he owned his signature on the death warrant. Nor was he prepared to confess any compunction. He had prayed to God and had examined his conscience. 'I have desired,' he said, 'as in the sight of Him that searcheth all hearts, while this hath been done, to wait, and receive from Him convictions upon my conscience ... and to this moment I have received rather assurance of it ...' He could expect no mercy. The Lord Chief Baron, who had been allowed to practise the law privately under Cromwell, treated Harrison with courtesy, but told the jury that the evidence was so clear and pregnant that there was no need for them to leave the box. Only the Earl of Manchester, who sat with the judges, had felt a qualm, 'I beseech you, my Lords,' he said, 'let us go some other way to work.' The prisoners were all found guilty, but only ten were executed. Sir Hardress Waller was to die a prisoner in Jersey; but for Harrison there was no reprieve.

Harrison had informed his wife when he was taken before the Grand Jury that the day was 'as his wedding day'. After returning from the trial to prison he told her: 'Not a tear, wife; what hurt have they done me, to send me so soon to Heaven?' From the moment of his condemnation he never ceased to give thanks — 'though men have judged, yet God had not condemned'. He was drawn from Newgate on a sledge or hurdle to Tyburn. As the rope was being tied round his neck, he repeated Isaac's words to Abraham: 'Father, here is the wood, but where is the sacrifice?' One of the spectators called out to him on the way: 'Where is your Good Old Cause?' He clapped his hand on his breast and cried: 'Here it is, and I am going to seal it with blood.' From the scaffold he addressed the bystanders: 'Gentlemen,' he said, 'by reason of some scoffing, that I do hear, I judge that some do think I am afraid to die ... I tell you no, but it is by reason of much blood I have lost in the wars, and many wounds I have received in my body which caused this shaking and weakness in my nerves . . . I speak this to the praise of God; he hath carried me above the fear of death.' It is said that his body was cut down before he was dead. His head, like Ireton's, was mounted on a pole and placed on the south-east end of Westminster Hall, looking towards the city of London. There is a tradition that his remains were finally buried by friends in St. Giles's churchyard, Newcastle-under-Lyme. The other regicides also died like men.

Four of Cromwell's Generals who were regicides escaped abroad: they were Major-General John Barkstead, Lieutenant-General Edward Whalley, Major-General William Goffe and Lieutenant-General Edmund Ludlow. The House of Commons had orginally voted that only seven regicides should be exempted from the bill of indemnity both as to life and estate, and Barkstead was the seventh to be named, being narrowly preferred to Ludlow. Barkstead, together with Colonel Okey and other Cromwellian officers managed to reach Germany where they obtained asylum at Hanau and were made burgesses. But in the spring of 1662 Barkstead came secretly to Delft to fetch his wife, and Sir George Downing, the British Minister in the United Netherlands, learned of his arrival. Downing himself had been a preacher in Colonel Okey's regiment and afterwards served as Scoutmaster-General (or chief intelligence officer) in Cromwell's army. Determined to buy his way back into favour, he had earlier persuaded the States General to grant him a blank warrant to arrest persons excepted from the act of indemnity, and if that warrant were not honoured, he was prepared to kidnap the fugitives. Barkstead, Okey and Miles Corbet, another regicide, were arrested by his minions as they were smoking a pipe of tobacco and drinking a cup of beer, and shipped back to England. Pepys deemed Downing 'a perfidious rogue', but Downing Street is named after him. Barkstead paid the supreme penalty in 1662, and 'performed that part with cheerfulness and courage, no way derogating from the character of a soldier and a true Englishman'. His last recorded words were to commend tolerance and Christian love.

Lieutenant-General Whalley and his son-in-law Major-General Goffe landed at Boston on July 27th, 1660, and were politely received by the Governor of Massachusetts. They took up residence at Cambridge (the site of Harvard University) and lived grave, serious and devout lives, attending lectures, fasts and thanksgivings. News of a royal mandate ordering their arrest reached Boston in the early spring of 1661 and they hastily left Cambridge for New Haven (the site of Yale). Two young Royalist merchants were appointed to search for them, but had no success, for Whalley and Goffe found many good friends among the Massachusetts puritans. They had, however, to remain in hiding, at one time concealing themselves in a cave. But they survived in retirement for some fifteen or sixteen years in the village of Hadley where they were much esteemed for their piety and grave behaviour. Some of Goffe's correspondence has survived. Mrs. Goffe wrote to her husband in 1664: 'To you it is given not only to believe but to suffer . . . My dear, my aunt and many others are very kind to me, so that through mercy I have no want of food and raiment, though in a mean way . . . Thou art as dear to me as a husband can be to a wife.' He replied in conspiratorial language, referring to his wife as his 'mother' and his daughter as his 'sister'; for example he wrote: 'My poor sister begins her housekeeping at a time when trading is low and all provisions dear, and I cannot but pity her in that respect.' On one occasion a fencing master, who gave exhibitions and prided himself on his prowess, had a bout with one of the strangers in Hadley. After admitting defeat he observed to his conqueror: 'You are either Goffe, Whalley or the devil, for there was no other man in England that could beat me.' Although commissioners arrived from England in 1665 and asked the Massachusetts Assembly what had been done about Whalley and Goffe, almost the whole Colony seems to have connived in protecting the two regicides. Indeed the Governor reported home that they had escaped to a Dutch Colony and thence taken ship for Holland. So they ended their lives unmolested. Whalley died in 1673 or 1674, Goffe about 1680. Their bones, one supposes, are in the soil of the New World.

Lieutenant-General Ludlow, though at first spared as to life by the House of Commons, did not give himself up, but hid in London to watch events. His caution was merited. After the House of Lords turned against him, he rode into Sussex and from Lewes took a small boat into France. Travelling by way of Rouen and Paris, where he thought the Louvre 'rather like a garrison than a court, being very full of soldiers and dirt', he arrived in Geneva and later settled with other English exiles in Vevey, the scene of Rousseau's *Nouvelle Heloïse*, where he stayed for many years.

None of Cromwell's Generals who did not sign the death warrant of King Charles I had to go into exile or was executed. Lieutenant-General Charles Fleetwood was among twenty named in the act of indemnity as incapacitated for ever from holding public employment. His wife Bridget, Oliver's daughter, died in July 1662, and was buried at St. Anne's, Blackfriars, but Fleetwood found a third wife, Dame Mary Hart, daughter of Sir John Coke of Derbyshire, who owned a house at Stoke Newington, where he passed his later days. Here he became a member of the congregation of his old friend, Oliver Cromwell's chaplain, Dr. John Owen. Fleetwood outlived his third wife, who died in December 1684, dying himself on October 4th, 1692, about the age of seventy-four. He was buried in Bunhill Fields cemetery, and his male line is extinct.

Another of Cromwell's Major-Generals, James Berry, appears to have borne Fleetwood company in his later years. Berry, who had refused to sign a parole not to act against the Convention, was arrested on the eve of the Restoration. He escaped, but was again imprisoned first in the Tower and then at Scarborough, whither he was brought by sea in August 1662. There he became the fellow prisoner of George Fox the Quaker and in spite of the unremitting efforts of his wife, Mary, was not released until 1672, after he had been taken back to London. It was then that he settled in Stoke Newington, where Fleetwood was Lord of the Manor. According to the Reverend Richard Baxter, 'he became a gardener and lived in a safer state than all his greatness'. He died at about the age of eighty on May 9th, 1691.

We may picture these two old Cromwellian Generals, whatever their past differences might have been, taking tobacco together in Stoke Newington, fighting the old campaigns over again, and no doubt rejoicing in the fate of King James II, whose removal from the throne was the belated postscript to the execution of King Charles I. Another of Cromwell's Generals who must have joined these gatherings in the sixteen-seventies was Major-General John Desborough. Desborough had made himself more obnoxious to the authorities than had Fleetwood and had an adventurous career. He was first arrested in 1660 by the Sheriff of Essex near the coast, evidently trying to flee the country. Like Fleetwood he had been declared in the act of indemnity merely incapacitated from public office. But he was imprisoned, on the suspicion of plotting, in the Tower of London whence he managed to escape and reach Holland. In April 1666 the Government ordered him to return to England on penalty of being proclaimed a traitor. He obeyed the order, came back, was arrested and sent to Dover Castle, and thence transferred to the Tower again, but was released early in the following year. He settled in Hackney with a second wife, whom he had married in 1658, his first wife, Cromwell's sister Jane, having been buried in Westminster Abbey in 1657 whence her remains were exhumed at the Restoration. In his will Desborough bequeathed to James Berry a mourning ring of the value of twenty shillings.

Three of Cromwell's other Generals appear to have ended their lives less comfortably than Fleetwood, Berry or Desborough; they were Kelsey, Venables and Overton. Major-General Thomas Kelsey had also fled to Holland at the Restoration where he lived in Arnheim and Rotterdam. But in April 1666 he returned, like Desborough, on the orders of the Government to England. He is said to have afterwards taken up brewing in the City of London, and to have died about 1680 'in a mean condition'. General Robert Venables, who had been released from prison in the Tower on October 30th, 1655, had been appointed Governor of Chester by Monk in February 1660. But when Monk helped to restore the King he did not approve and vanished into oblivion to die in July 1687, at the age of over seventy. Major-General Robert Overton, after his feeble plotting in Scotland against the Protectorate, had been imprisoned in Jersey and elsewhere until March 1659.

The Rump restored him to command of a regiment and to his Governorship of Hull. In October 1659 he was one of the seven commissioners in whom Parliament vested the administration of the army after Fleetwood had been demoted. Overton was energetic at Hull in arresting suspected Royalists and strengthening the fortifications. But with typical vacillation he blamed all sides for the woes of the anarchy. The counsel he distributed in a pamphlet called *Humble and Healing Advice* was 'You are brethren, why should you disagree?' When Monk marched on England, he could not divine Overton's intentions. After some correspondence Monk superseded him in favour of Colonel Charles Fairfax. Thus Overton's military career petered out in March 1660. Overton was not excepted from the act of indemnity, but in December 1660 he was arrested on suspicion of being concerned in the plotting of the Fifth Monarchists. He was sent to the Tower and in November 1661 imprisoned at Chepstow Castle. Freed for a time, he was again arrested on suspicion and in January 1664 taken to Jersey where, ironically enough, he had been held on Cromwell's orders ten years earlier. It was indeed appropriate that the General who could never make up his mind where he stood should have been the prisoner both of Cromwell and of Charles II in that self-same Channel Island. He died in Jersey about 1668.

A certain amount of obscurity surrounds the fate of one of Cromwell's Major-Generals, William Boteler. After the Restoration he set up in practice as an attorney or solicitor. But he was arrested in the summer of 1665 when the Government was becoming nervous on account of the Dutch War (that was why Desborough and Kelsey were ordered back from Holland). He complained from his prison in the Tower that no charge had been preferred against him, that he was exposed to the Great Plague, that he was losing all his business because his clients were not allowed to visit him, and that his wife and five children were on the verge of starvation. He claimed that he would do his duty according to the terms of the act of indemnity and that he had confessed all he knew 'about the company frequenting Gray's Inn Lane', but he refused to conform to the Church of England. All he asked was to be allowed to practise the law in peace. It seems likely that he was released at the same time as Desborough in 1667, but in 1670 he was again arrested on account of his puritan assiduity. It is not known where or when he died.

Three of Cromwell's Generals besides George Monk benefited from the Restoration: these were Edward Montagu, William Penn and Thomas Morgan.

Montagu had brought over the navy as Monk had the army, and received the Garter as well as the Earldom of Sandwich. In 1665 he was appointed Admiral of the Red, but met with a fiasco and temporary disgrace when, counting on Danish connivance, he launched an attack on Dutch East Indian merchant ships in the neutral harbour of Bergen. He failed completely in his aims, for the shore guns compelled his fleet to retire and his own son was killed in the action. In 1672 he was appointed Admiral of the Blue and although opposed to the third Dutch War, he fought magnificently at Sole Bay, the first battle of the campaign. His flagship, the *Royal James*, was set on fire and blew up, and Sandwich was drowned when the boat in which he rowed away from the sinking warship capsized. His body was rescued and he was buried in Westminster Abbey. Thus another of Cromwell's Generals perished at sea in the service of his country.

General Penn had helped Montagu in restoring the King and received a knighthood and other modest rewards. After the campaign of 1665 he was not again employed at sea, but was given work in the Navy Office where Samuel Pepys was also employed. Pepys recorded in his diary the opinion that Penn was a hypocritical rogue who was often befuddled. After being threatened with impeachment for peculation, he died in September 1670. Sir Thomas Morgan became Governor of Jersey in 1665, where Overton was a prisoner, and died in 1679.

As Duke of Albermarle, General George Monk himself performed many services for his new master. And, wrote Sir Julian Corbett, 'as the country recovered from its fever of royalism, and began to look back first without disgust, then with regret, to the days of Oliver, it saw in the Protector's old general the personification of all the glories of the Commonwealth'. When the plague of 1665 drove the Court to Oxford, Albemarle, now in his sixty-sixth year, stayed in Whitehall to assuage the panic in the capital. Later in the second Dutch War he was persuaded to take command of the fleet jointly with Prince Rupert; he directed the battle of the Four Days with all his customary art and defeated the Dutch at St. James's Fight on July 25th, 1666. But the careless policy of Charles II in the following year enabled the Dutch to surprise the great naval base of Chatham and only the hurried intervention of Monk saved the English navy from extinction. It may be doubted if he ever recovered from the dishonour. Smitten by the disgrace of the ultimate Dutch triumph in the war and by a disease that developed into dropsy, Monk clung to his manifold duties and possessions as long as he could. He gave to Charles II, as he had given to Oliver Cromwell, all the selfless loyalty of a superb professional officer. He saw his son married at the end of 1669, but on January 2nd, 1670, as the sun rose over Whitehall, the Coldstreamers who were keeping watch upon his chamber heard a 'single small groan' before the old warrior's spirit left him.

The fate of General John Lambert was unique. Though he had not signed the death warrant of Charles I and though he averred that he was opposed to his execution, the Restoration Government was doubtful about the wisdom of letting Cromwell's best general live on. The King had advised Parliament 'to have a care of any persons so ever who were dangerous to the State'. The King's principal Minister, the Earl of Clarendon, was in favour of Lambert's execution. After many delays Lambert was put on trial in June 1662 along with Sir Henry Vane before the Court of King's Bench on the charge of 'compassing, imagining, and intending to levy and stir up war, rebellion, and insurrection against the King within this kingdom of England'. Vane was defiant and invoked the authority of Parliament for his public conduct. He 'made a great noise, and gave the Court a great deal of trouble', and was put to death. Lambert assumed a more tactful demeanour. He waived any formal defence and 'showed a submissive and handsome deportment'. He also had friends working for him behind the scenes, including Lord Fairfax. So although the jury found him guilty and he was sentenced to death he at once received a reprieve on the recommendation of the Lord Chief Justice. But he spent the rest of his days in prison or under restraint. He was sent to Guernsey in 1662, where his wife was allowed to join him, and resumed his hobby of botany, specializing, it seems, in the Guernsey lily. While he was there his daughter, Mary, married the son of the Governor of Guernsey, Lord Hatton, who afterwards became Governor himself; so Lambert's position can scarcely have been intolerable. But in 1670 he was removed to St. Nicholas Island in Plymouth Sound. It was in this island that Lambert's one-time deputy, Robert Lilburne, had died a prisoner in 1665 after he too had been condemned to be executed as a regicide, though later reprieved. Here Lambert's devoted and once lovely wife died in December 1676. His own death followed in March 1684. In his last years he is said to have lost his memory. According to a contemporary who visited St. Nicholas in 1684, one day while John Lambert was working in his little garden some gentlemen came in a boat to inspect the island, and the Major-General had decided to change his clothes 'that he might wait on the company in more decent dress, and catched a cold that brought him to his grave'.

Throughout the whole of the reign of King Charles II the authorities were nervous about the possibility of a republican or Cromwellian rising in the name of the Good Old Cause. The names of several of Cromwell's Generals, such as Lambert, Desborough and Ludlow, were frequently mentioned in the State papers as likely leaders of plots. But in fact few of them appear to have conspired, the reason being no doubt that the more dangerous ones, like Lambert, were in prison or abroad, and the others were kept under surveillance by spies, of whom there were many eager to earn a few pounds for supplying information to an ever nervous administration. The link between the anti-Stuart movement in 1649 and that of 1688 was a handful of junior officers and former Levellers like Major John Wildman and not the retired Generals. Cromwell's old Generals, we may speculate, had the wisdom to see that a rising against a tolerably constitutional Protestant King was not practical politics. Major-General Henry Cromwell, who might have been an obvious rallying point, like the third Napoleon, was treated with a remarkable tenderness, mainly through the influence of his Royalist relations by marriage. He was actually allowed to retain some of his Irish lands. He farmed at Spinney Abbey in Cambridgeshire until he died there on March 23rd, 1674, at the early age of forty-six.

Possibly the General who was most feared by the Government of King Charles II was Edmund Ludlow. For alone of Cromwell's Generals he had been a consistent and incorruptible republican. He had signed the death warrant of King Charles I, had plotted against Oliver Cromwell, after the Protectorate had been set up, accusing him to his face of betraying the republican cause; he had helped to overthrow Richard Cromwell and done what he could to prevent the Restoration. Royalist fanatics attempted to assassinate him in his hide-out in Vevey. When the Glorious Revolution of 1688 occurred, Ludlow at once prepared to return to England. 'Though Mr. Ludlow is very old [he was seventy-one]', noted a contemporary journalist, 'he is still lusty and vigorous, and may be useful both in council and action'. He arrived in London in the early autumn of 1689, but a deputation from the House of Commons, which had just deposed King James II, expressed horror at the return of the elderly Cromwellian General, and asked King William III to order his arrest. The veteran republican was still nimble enough to avoid the indignity and find his way back to Vevey, where he died in 1693. He had caught a glimpse of a new world that did not wish to recognize that the 'liberty of conscience' it had attained and the constitutional monarchy it had framed owed anything at all to Cromwell's Generals.

BIBLIOGRAPHY TO CHAPTER XIII

Details of the exhumation of the bodies of Cromwell's Generals will be found in Karl Pearson and G. M. Morant, *The Portraiture of Oliver Cromwell* (1935), pp. 39 seqq. and the authorities there quoted. The trials of Waller, Harrison, Vane and Lambert are in *State Trials* (1810), vols. V and VI. For George Downing and the regicides see John Beresford, *The Father of Downing Street* (1925), chap. VIII. For Whalley and

Goffe in America see Ezra Styles, *A History of Three Judges of King Charles I* (1839). For Berry, Fleetwood and Desborough in their last years see Berry and Lee, op. cit., chap. XII. William Boteler's letters from prison are in S.P. 29/134, f. 16, S.P. 29/135, f. 99, S.P. 29/158, f. 110, and S.P. 29/211, f. 43 in the Public Record Office. Details of the last days of Cromwell's other Generals are given in the biographies referred to in the bibliographies to earlier chapters.

CHAPTER XIV

EPITOME: CROMWELL AND HIS GENERALS

THE ghosts of Cromwell's Generals have been on parade: they cast more than shadows on the wall of the past. Each is seen with his own characters and beliefs: Thomas Harrison, who gave up his command when he found that Cromwell was not a second St. John the Baptist, and perished on the scaffold, convinced that he had earned his passage to Heaven; Henry Ireton, designer of a blue print for a perfect republic, who killed himself by devotion to duty in Ireland; John Lambert, a natural genius among soldiers, as brave as he was bold, who never became the more worldly Oliver he aspired to be; Charles Fleetwood, the weeping General, whose capacities as an administrator and conciliator were palsied by his unwillingness either to offend the Saints or submerge his own love of position; George Monk, the complete professional, who in middle age proved himself as skilful an admiral as he was a general and after helping to restore the Stuarts, survived as the sunset of the Cromwellian age in the less glorious reign of King Charles II. If the others cannot be so sharply etched, most of them were men of parts from Richard Deane, the artilleryman whose body was cut in two by the guns of Tromp, to Charles Worsley, the young Major-General who found his joy and his death in imposing the puritan pattern on the north-west of England, a pattern it has largely sustained ever since.

What strikes us first in the story of these men is that they most of them formed a closely related group. Ireton and Fleetwood were both Cromwell's sons-in-law; Desborough was his brother-in-law; Whalley was his cousin; Deane was related to him by marriage; and his son, Henry, was the last and not the least able of his Major-Generals. Beyond that, Berry, Whalley, Desborough and Ireton had all commanded troops in Cromwell's original Ironside regiment. Harrison was the protégé of Fleetwood, Boteler of Berry, Kelsey of Colonel Richard Ingoldsby, another of Cromwell's cousins. Worsley had raised a regiment for Cromwell in Lancashire in 1650. Sir John Reynolds was linked by marriage to Henry Cromwell.

Apart from John Lambert, the chief of Cromwell's Generals who remained outside the intimate circle were professional soldiers like Monk, Skippon and Penn.

Here then we perceive one of the foibles of the great — the belief that men who have been near to them in their early struggles or have married into their families will be loyal to them always. For that reason high office is conferred not simply on grounds of merit. Such a method of choice must be a gamble. When Cromwell insisted that Ireton should command on the left wing at Naseby he did not find the best officer for the post; and when he appointed Fleetwood as Commander-in-Chief in Ireland he put a weak man where he needed a strong one, through preferring personal ties to the needs of the service.

It has sometimes been argued that favouritism is as sound a system of promotion as most. But it does not necessarily hold good that a man whose company one enjoys at dinner will be cool on the field of battle or wise in the Cabinet nor is sympathy of outlook always conducive to administrative efficiency. It is obvious that Cromwell was attracted by the religious feelings both of Harrison and Fleetwood. But before he died he found to his cost that each possessed his defects as a statesman. Even less reliable than a common faith, however, as a test of loyalty is relationship by marriage. The first Napoleon thought that he could bind Marshals or Kings to him by intermarriage and learned his mistake. Count Ciano, the son-in-law of Mussolini, was neither particularly loyal nor clever. Cromwell was fortunate in his son-in-law, Ireton, who was lost to him too soon. But Fleetwood was a failure both in Ireland and in England. Moreover it was Cromwell's brother-in-law, Desborough, more than any other of his Generals, who deprived him of the chance he was prepared to take of becoming King.

As it happened, most of Cromwell's Generals who were neither related to him nor intimately connected with him trusted him and served him faithfully so long as they held his commission. George Monk, for example, is known to posterity as the General who restored King Charles II to his throne and was buried in Westminster Abbey as the Duke of Albemarle. Yet in fact if we look at his life as a whole, we can see that he stands out as one of the most devoted, able and versatile of all Cromwell's Generals. Had Monk died when he was fifty-two, one would have speculated that by doing so he had escaped imprisonment or even execution for being too good a Cromwellian. Since the day he rode with him to Dunbar Monk had been trusted absolutely by Cromwell and he in turn served not only Oliver but his son, Richard, with unflinching obedience. Cromwell for once deliberately preferred Monk to his own brother-in-law Desborough as military governor of Scotland, and Monk's genius prevented the Highlands from becoming a running sore during the Protectorate. If Richard Cromwell had been a statesman, he would have brought back Monk from Scotland and put him in the place of Fleetwood, and the Stuarts might never have returned. As things were, even when Monk left Coldstream, he had not made up his mind to restore the Stuarts and he never claimed credit for doing so. It was the anarchy into which the nation fell when the hand of Oliver Cromwell fell limp that compelled the recall of the Stuarts by the growing articulate demand of ordinary people for a capable government, a demand which Monk felt himself in the end obliged to fulfil.

Or take the case of John Lambert. Lambert owed little to Cromwell. He had been the friend of the first Commonwealth Commander-in-Chief, Thomas Fairfax. His talents had helped Cromwell to win the battles of Preston, Dunbar and Worcester — some writers have argued that Cromwell could not have won them without him — and his services in the north of England had given security to the Protectorate. By destroying the Assembly of Saints and making Cromwell Lord Protector by means of the Instrument of Government he had, on the contrary, placed Cromwell in his debt. It was natural that he should be ambitious to succeed him. Yet when after the interval of rule by the Major-Generals Cromwell broke with Lambert, Lambert never attempted to conspire or raise the army against him, as some of Cromwell's officials thought that he would. It is ridiculous to suppose that a bribe of £2000 a year purchased the acquiescence of a man of Lambert's spirit. The explanation is surely that he, like Monk, was loyal, after his own fashion, to the Protector as long as he lived.

Three others of Cromwell's Generals disagreed with his form of government: they were Harrison, Ludlow and Overton. What stands out in their dealings with him? Is it not this? Each of them was willing to see him and talk to him to try to persuade him into their way of thinking, and all of them gave their promise that they would not engineer a revolt until they had argued with him face to face. After Harrison had been cashiered, he felt sufficient confidence in Cromwell's fairness to intervene with him on behalf of his friends, the Fifth Monarchist preachers. When Ludlow disapproved of the establishment of the Protectorate, he asked permission to go to London from Ireland to tell Cromwell to his face that he had betrayed the Good Old Cause. Likewise Overton had not hesitated to inform Cromwell that his conduct was on trial, but even after an almost insulting interview Cromwell had retained Overton in his command. It is certainly notable that these three Generals with their rigid and indeed fanatical approach to life should all have been so hopeful of convincing Cromwell that he had erred in his judgment that they preferred to take the risk of putting themselves in his power rather than exerting their considerable influence in the army against him.

Finally in this connection we may emphasize the position of Robert Blake. The tale that he was a critic of the Lord Protector has found its way into several modern history books, though there is no serious evidence to sustain it. The fact is that Blake, like Monk, was a patriotic officer who believed that things would not go much amiss for England so long as Cromwell ruled in Whitehall.

Thus because he trusted them and they trusted him there was never any open conflict between Cromwell and his Generals until the last two years of his life.

Cromwell, for his part, was influenced by the thoughts and opinions of his Generals. His own character was a blend of the patriot, the realist and the puritan Don Quixote. After the close of the first civil war he was unquestionably impressed by the fine intellect of Henry Ireton. Like Ireton, he hoped to frame a constitution or 'settlement' in which the stable elements in the community would be balanced, arbitrariness guarded against, and liberty of conscience guaranteed. After his return from Ireland in 1650 and Ireton's death in 1651, however, Cromwell was gradually drawn into the orbit of Harrison's hot evangelism. Many of the leading puritans of these years from Gerrard Winstanley the Digger to Robert Overton the soldier-scholar, were torn and even tortured by millenarian creeds, that is to say, they felt that with the destruction of the old monarchy and Church a new era was dawning that might presage the Second Coming of Christ. Cromwell convinced himself, wrongly, it seems, that many of the members of the Rump Parliament were sinners ill suited to rule England at a time of such high significance in the history of Christian men. The letters written by Cromwell and Harrison after the battle of Worcester show how their minds were then moving in the same direction — towards a reign of carefully chosen upright men with a definite programme of reforms. It was Harrison who was ordered by Cromwell to eject the Rump Parliament and it was Harrison's ideas that were embodied in the Assembly of Saints. But the evangelical or millenarian strain in Cromwell's thought began to evaporate when confronted with the boundless exuberance of the Chosen People. The practical side of his nature was affronted by the fantastic unworldliness of the Fifth Monarchy preachers who guided their deliberations and now he turned from Harrison to Lambert as his principal adviser. Lambert was no 'enthusiast' but a hard-headed Yorkshireman who inherited some of Ireton's qualities as a thinker if with more of an eye to the main chance. But when Lambert's 'Instrument of Government' also failed to produce a parliament willing to co-operate with the leaders of the army and the rule of the eleven Major-Generals was introduced instead, Lambert and Cromwell fell out. Cromwell in fact swung back from political realism towards high puritanism: in the instructions to the Major-Generals to purify and purge their Associations we may trace a measure of Harrison's old spirit, though Harrison himself was now a prisoner of state.

The last two years of Cromwell's life saw a contest for his

soul between his once harmonious group of Generals on the one side, and the New Courtiers on the other. Whatever his occasional divagations may have been, Cromwell had always yearned for a constitutional settlement. As a parliamentarian born and bred he had been seeking to reconcile liberty and order ever since those exciting days in 1647 when after the first civil war had ended, he had taken the chair at the acrimonious but thought-provoking debates in the Army Council. Experiment after experiment had followed: the oligarchical rule of the Rump with Cromwell as its Commander-in-Chief; Harrison's Assembly of Saints, an institution in tune with much of the political philosophy of the age; Lambert's 'Instrument of Government', too neat to work; the emergency institution of the Major-Generals. Now in 1657 the New Courtiers tried to persuade Cromwell that the only feasible solution was a constitutional monarchy with himself as King. Here came the biggest breach within his entourage.

The New Courtiers were either men with a Royalist past or lawyers steeped in the traditional *mystique* of the courts, and all of them guiltless of the killing of King Charles I. Their conservative aim was to restore the monarchy at all costs. Hence they pressed Cromwell to take the sceptre and revive the House of Lords; after his death they sustained his son as Protector as best they could; and finally they helped to bring back King Charles II. Indeed Lord Broghil and General Montagu were, in the long run, far more the architects of the Restoration of 1660 than was George Monk. Against them were ranged all of Cromwell's Generals with influence in the army. These, for their part, felt a conviction transcending personal ambitions that the soldiers who had fought to overthrow the Stuarts, to defend and justify the execution of a king, and to fashion a Free Commonwealth would not be ready to stultify their past by building a new monarchical system. Cromwell himself in his younger days had argued that the Army was no mere collection of mercenaries such as habitually formed the fighting forces of the European mainland, but the cream of the English puritans who risked their lives and gave their loyalties for a cause in which they passionately believed. He had indeed asked himself whether the army was not more truly representative of the best people in the country than ever the Rump Parliament had been. Thus on the one hand in 1657 Cromwell was assailed by the argument that the only effective way in which to marry order and liberty was for him to return to the old, tried institutions, cleansed and reformed but fundamentally unaltered; on the other, he was begged not to betray the trust of the Generals, officers and men who had fought with him and served under him for fifteen years. His answer was to compromise. What else could he do? His mistake did not even lie there. Where he erred irretrievably was in naming Richard Cromwell as his successor. In fact Oliver Cromwell's tragedy was that of Everyman. The progressiveness of youth had turned into the conservatism of middle age, and on his death bed he was blinded by the deceptive light of dynasty.

Could any of Cromwell's Generals have hoped to follow him as Lord Protector with any expectation of making the Commonwealth a permanent form of government in these islands? The only candidates mentioned by contemporaries were Lambert and Fleetwood. Lambert had burnt his boats by refusing of his own volition to take an oath of loyalty to the new Protectorate, though in fact he never opposed it nor, so far as we know, conspired against Richard Cromwell. Fleetwood was too feeble a statesman to survive any longer than Richard had done. Monk was not a politician; Desborough lacked the capacity. But in any case the Protectorate accorded too little with the ideas of the century to hold together after Oliver Cromwell died. Ultimately — and this is plain — the Protectorate rested on the strength of the army. And only Oliver himself inspired a sufficient degree of confidence among its officers and obedience among its men to keep the army united. Though Fleetwood, Lambert and Monk each had a following, nothing could have prevented the army from disintegrating, and, whatever political superstructure was erected — and dozens of constitutional schemes were conceived in the dying months of the Interregnum — it was bound to collapse as soon as the Generals fell out among themselves.

To say all this is not to affirm that Cromwell was a mere military dictator and his Generals a group of intriguing sycophants. In the past 300 years every generation has had its own conception of Cromwell's character and achievement. Thomas Carlyle invited his readers to study Cromwell's own letters and speeches and to forget the abusive tittle-tattle of the men who wrote before him. The later Victorian historians succeeded in rooting out many of the warts that had fastened themselves on the face of Cromwell's biography and showed unchallengeably how deep was the Protector's belief in liberty of conscience. In the twentieth century we have had more than our fill of dictators, and it has not been difficult for historians to draw upon 'hitherto unpublished materials' — the arcanum of their craft — to prove that Cromwell was after all little more than a puritan despot. The dispatches of the Italian, French and Dutch representatives in London (hardly any of whom could speak English and were purveyors of every kind of worthless gossip) and the letters of Royalist agents reporting wishfully to the Court in exile are favourite sources for a more cynical attitude to Cromwell's career. But one suggests that, whatever his faults as a historian may have been, Carlyle was right: that Cromwell's speeches, letters and conversations are a sounder means of probing his outlook and purposes than any amount of contemporary rumour fished up from the archives.

There is, however, another way of seeing Cromwell, and that is through the men who served him. The more one studies the lives of Cromwell's Generals, of men like Ireton and Harrison, Lambert and Fleetwood, Blake and Monk, the more convinced one becomes of Cromwell's essential humanity, tolerance and anxiety to do right by the English people according to the light of Providence that always beckoned him on. His Generals were assuredly no pygmies; they had their own faiths, hopes and skills. But he towered above them by reason of a genius, not of course free from many a blemish, which, for good or ill, has shaped our history right down to our own times.

APPENDIX

NOTE ON THE APPOINTMENT, POWERS AND PAY OF CROMWELL'S GENERALS

When the New Model Army was formed at the beginning of 1645 Parliament appointed Sir Thomas Fairfax as Captain-General and Commander-in-Chief and Phillip Skippon as Sergeant-Major-General. By an 'ordinance for additional Power to Sir T. Fairfax' of April 1st he was given 'Power to assign and grant Commissions to all such Commanders and Officers as shall be thought necessary and requisite for the Government and Command of the said Army'. These powers were automatically widened when from July 1647 Fairfax became Commander-in-Chief of all the Commonwealth armies in England and Wales. By implication these powers were transferred to Oliver Cromwell in the Act of June 26th, 1650, constituting him Captain-General and Commander-in-Chief in place of Fairfax. When on June 7th, 1659, an Act was passed by the restored Rump making Charles Fleetwood Lieutenant-General and Commander-in-Chief the phrase about granting commissions was omitted, but the Act of February 25th, 1660, appointing George Monk as Captain-General and Commander-in-Chief restored the power of granting commissions.[1]

It thus follows that during the Interregnum, except for a period of eight months, the power of appointing Generals lay with the Commander-in-Chief unless he delegated it. We know that in at least two instances this power was so delegated. For when on July 10th, 1652, Cromwell appointed Fleetwood 'Commander-in-Chief under myself of the Army and Forces within the Dominion of Ireland' he gave him 'full power and authority to assign and grant commissions to all such commanders, officers and governors of the same army, etc.'

[1] *Acts and Ordinances* (ed. Firth and Rait), I, 614, 661, II, 393, 1283; *Journals of the House of Commons*, VII, 852.

Similar power was granted by Cromwell to General Robert Venables when he set out on the West Indian expedition, but, on the other hand, it was not granted to General Monk when he was made Commander-in-Chief in Scotland on April 8th, 1654.[1] That no doubt is why officers like Lilburne, Overton and Morgan who, since they commanded large forces and were responsible for wide areas in Scotland, were in effect acting generals, did not necessarily assume the rank of Major-General.

Although therefore the appointment of Generals must have rested primarily with the Commander-in-Chief, there appears to have been cases, at any rate before the establishment of the Protectorate, when appointments were made and orders given directly by Parliament. For example, in June 1650 the Council of State wrote to Cromwell asking him 'to send the commission to Major-General Harrison, according to the order of Parliament . . .' and in April of the following year it also appears from the records of the Council of State as if Harrison's appointment as Commander-in-Chief in the north was decided upon in London. When in May 1651 Lambert as acting Commander-in-Chief in Scotland asked that Lieutenant-General Fleetwood should be sent back to his command in Scotland, the Council of State informed Lambert that 'considering that the charge of all the forces in these parts is upon him, he cannot be spared with safety'.[2] It seems therefore as if before the Protectorate, while the issuing of commissions was always the function of the Commander-in-Chief, nomination and the assignment of duties might lie with Parliament, though no doubt as a rule the Commander-in-Chief either inspired them (as in the case of Ludlow)[3] or was consulted.

The powers granted to Generals in their commissions took a more or less set form: they included the right to hold courts-martial, to commandeer carriages, horses and boats, and to invoke the assistance of local authorities.

In his introduction to Godfrey Davies's *Early History of the Coldstream Guards* (page xx) Sir John Fortescue wrote that up till 1814 'even general officers received no salary as such unless

[1] *Thurloe State Papers*, I, 212, II, 222, III, 16.
[2] *Calendar of State Papers* (*Domestic*), *1650*, p. 222, ibid., *1651*, pp. 156, 228.
[3] *Ludlow's Memoirs* (ed. Firth), I, 247-9; see page 25 above.

specially employed'. Presumably he meant that if they were on a peace-time establishment they received only their pay as colonels of regiments. But during the Interregnum there was virtually no peace and, as far as I have been able to trace the records, it seems that all Cromwell's Generals were paid a salary over and above their pay as colonels. The following are rates I have found, with the names of recipients in brackets:[1]

Rank	*Rate of pay per day*
Commander-in-Chief of all the Commonwealth armies and full General (Fairfax)	£10
Commander-in-Chief, Scotland (Monk)	£6
Lieutenant-General of Horse and Foot, i.e. second in command (Cromwell)	£5
Commander-in-Chief, expeditionary force overseas (Reynolds)	£5
General-at-sea (Blake)	£3
Major-General in England (Cromwell)	£2 10s.
Major-General in Scotland (Morgan)	10s.
Major-General of the Horse Militia (Berry)	£666 13s. 4d. a year

All Generals were also colonels of regiments and received their pay in that capacity, usually at a rate of about 26s. a day in the cavalry and 20s. a day in the infantry, even though they in fact deputed the actual command to their lieutenant-colonels. Some Generals — Lambert is the best known case — were colonels of more than one regiment. Furthermore Parliament voted large sums, usually out of confiscated Royalist estates, to the Generals who served it well. Fairfax and Cromwell as Commanders-in-Chief received lands worth £4000 a year; Fleetwood as Commander-in-Chief, Ireland, received £1500 a year; Lambert received £1000 a year; Whalley and Monk received £500 a year.[2] We may also note that the holder of the office of Lieutenant of the Ordnance,

[1] Fairfax MSS 32, f. 173 (in the Bodleian); *Scotland and the Protectorate*, 373; *Transactions of the Royal Historical Society*, XIII, 52-3; *Thurloe State Papers*, VI, 366; ROGER BEADON, *Robert Blake*, p. 69; BERRY and LEE, *A Cromwellian Major-General*, p. 290.

[2] *Journals of the House of Commons*, VII, 14, etc.; C. H. FIRTH, *Cromwell's Army* (1912), p. 190.

who at one time was Major-General Harrison, received traditional fees. Harrison obtained 6d. in the £ on the moneys he disbursed (at one time £3430 was owing to him) and £1500 a year for expenses.[1] Finally there is some evidence that general officers obtained their pay more punctually than the rank-and-file.[2] If we assume that the value of money then was at least ten times what it is today, Cromwell's Generals were very well paid indeed.

We may conclude that the appointments, status and pay of Generals were somewhat ill defined, as was understandable in time of civil war. Also the ranks did not necessarily bear any clear relation to responsibilities. During the Dunbar campaign Lambert as Major-General appears to have ranked before Fleetwood as Lieutenant-General; when Monk was put in command of the ordnance in Scotland in 1651 he assumed the title of Lieutenant-General but was junior to Deane as Major-General; Ireton as Lord Deputy in Ireland was still referred to as Major-General, though his second in command, Ludlow, held the rank of Lieutenant-General.[3] When Robert Lilburne succeeded Monk as Commander-in-Chief in Scotland he only used the title of colonel, though he assumed and assigned powers customarily wielded by Generals.

[1] *C.S.P. (Dom.) 1651*, p. 222, *C.S.P. (Dom.) 1652*, pp. 211-12.

[2] Fairfax MSS 32, f. 173 shows that Fairfax was paid nearly in full up till the time of his resignation in June 1650.

[3] For the theoretical hierarchy of generalship see *Cromwell's Army*, 60-7. Firth there stated that the rank of lieutenant-general of the ordnance, the rank long held by Monk, was junior to that of major-general of the foot.

INDEX

INDEX

INDEX

INDEX

INDEX